YOUTH QUESTIONS

Series Editors: PHILIP COHEN AND ANG

This series sets out to question the ways in which youth has traditionally been defined by social scientists and policy-makers, by the caring professions and the mass media, as well as in 'common-sense' ideology. It explores some of the new directions in research and practice which are beginning to challenge existing patterns of knowledge and provision. Each book examines a particular aspect of the youth question in depth. All of them seek to connect their concerns to the major political and intellectual debates that are now taking place about the present crisis and future shape of our society. The series will be of interest to those who deal professionally with young people, especially those concerned with the development of socialist, feminist and anti-racist perspectives. But it is also aimed at students and general readers who want a lively and accessible introduction to some of the most awkward but important issues of our time.

Published

Inge Bates, John Clarke, Philip Cohen, Dan Finn, Robert Moore and Paul Willis
SCHOOLING FOR THE DOLE?
The New Vocationalism

Cynthia Cockburn
TWO-TRACK TRAINING
Sex Inequalities and the YTS

Philip Cohen and Harwant S. Bains (eds)
MULTI-RACIST BRITAIN

Andrew Dewdney and Martin Lister
YOUTH, CULTURE AND PHOTOGRAPHY

Dan Finn
TRAINING WITHOUT JOBS: NEW DEALS AND BROKEN PROMISES
From Raising the School-Leaving Age to the Youth Training Scheme

Angela McRobbie (ed.)
ZOOT SUITS AND SECOND-HAND DRESSES
An Anthology of Fashion and Music

Angela McRobbie and Mica Nava (eds)
GENDER AND GENERATION

Forthcoming

Desmond Bell
ACTS OF UNION
Youth Culture and Sectarianism in Northern Ireland

Philip Cohen and Graham Murdock (eds)
THE MAKING OF THE YOUTH QUESTION

Robert G. Hollands
THE LONG TRANSITION
Class, Culture and Youth Training

Angela McRobbie
FEMINISM AND YOUTH CULTURE

Series Standing Order

If you would like to receive future titles in this series as they are published, you can make use of our standing order facility. To place a standing order please contact your bookseller or, in case of difficulty, write to us at the address below with your name and address and the name of the series. Please state with which title you wish to begin your standing order. (If you live outside the United Kingdom we may not have the rights for your area, in which case we will forward your order to the publisher concerned.)

Customer Services Department, Macmillan Distribution Ltd
Houndmills, Basingstoke, Hampshire, RG21 2XS, England.

Zoot Suits and Second-Hand Dresses

An Anthology of Fashion and Music

Edited by
Angela McRobbie

Selection and editorial matter © Angela McRobbie 1989
Individual chapters (in order) © Stuart Cosgrove 1984; Angela McRobbie 1989;
Kobena Mercer 1986; Dave Laing 1986; Ian Penman 1989; Jon Savage 1982;
Simon Frith 1983; Marek Kohn 1981; Martin Chalmers 1983; Atlanta and
Alexander 1981; Jon Savage 1983; Rosetta Brooks 1982; Kathy Myers 1983;
Richard Dyer 1983; Juliet Ash 1989; Janet Lee 1989; Dirk Scheuring 1985; Gina
Rumsey and Hilary Little 1985; Simon Reynolds 1986; Paul Oldfield 1989; David
Stubbs 1989; Greil Marcus and Artforum 1985

All rights reserved. No reproduction, copy or transmission
of this publication may be made without written permission.

No paragraph of this publication may be reproduced, copied
or transmitted save with written permission or in accordance
with the provisions of the Copyright Act 1956 (as amended),
or under the terms of any licence permitting limited copying
issued by the Copyright Licensing Agency, 33–4 Alfred Place,
London WC1E 7DP.

Any person who does any unauthorised act in relation to
this publication may be liable to criminal prosecution and
civil claims for damages.

First published 1989

Published by
MACMILLAN EDUCATION LTD
Houndmills, Basingstoke, Hampshire RG21 2XS
and London
Companies and representatives
throughout the world

Typeset by Wessex Typesetters
(Division of The Eastern Press Ltd)
Frome, Somerset

Printed in the People's Republic of China

British Library Cataloguing in Publication Data
Zoot suits and second-hand dresses: an
anthology of fashion and music.
1. Popular culture
I. McRobbie, Angela
306'.1   NX458
ISBN 0–333–39651–0 (hardcover)
ISBN 0–333–39652–9 (paperback)

Contents

	Acknowledgements	vii
	Contributors	viii
	Introduction	xi

PART I FRONTIERS

1	**The Zoot Suit and Style Warfare** Stuart Cosgrove	3
2	**Second-Hand Dresses and the Role of the Ragmarket** Angela McRobbie	23
3	**Monster Metaphors: Notes on Michael Jackson's 'Thriller'** Kobena Mercer	50
4	**The Grain of Punk: An Analysis of the Lyrics** Dave Laing	74
5	**The Shattered Glass: Notes on Bryan Ferry** Ian Penman	103

PART II TRANSGRESSIONS

6	**'Do You Know How to Pony?': The Messianic Intensity of the Sixties** Jon Savage	121
7	**Only Dancing: David Bowie Flirts with the Issues** Simon Frith	132
8	**The Best Uniforms** Marek Kohn	141
9	**Heroin, the Needle and the Politics of the Body** Martin Chalmers	150
10	**Wild Style: Graffiti Painting** Atlanta and Alexander	156

11	**The Age of Plunder** Jon Savage	169

PART III INTERIORS

12	**Sighs and Whispers in Bloomingdales: A Review of a Bloomingdale Mail-Order Catalogue for Their Lingerie Department** Rosetta Brooks	183
13	**Fashion 'n' Passion: A Working Paper** Kathy Myers	189
14	**Don't Look Now** Richard Dyer	198
15	**The Business of Couture** Juliet Ash	208
16	**From the Inside: An Interview with Three Women Fashion Designers** Janet Lee	215
17	**Heavy Duty Denim: 'Quality Never Dates'** Dirk Scheuring	225

PART IV MUSIC NOW

18	**Women and Pop: A Series of Lost Encounters** Gina Rumsey and Hilary Little	239
19	**Against Health and Efficiency: Independent Music in the 1980s** Simon Reynolds	245
20	**After Subversion: Pop Culture and Power** Paul Oldfield	256
21	**Fear of the Future** David Stubbs	267
22	**We Are the World?** Greil Marcus	276

Index — 283

Acknowledgements

The editor and publishers wish to acknowledge, with thanks, the following for permission to use copyright and other material: Apple, Artforum, Ally Capellino, Conde Nast Publications, E. G. Records, E.M.I. Records, Shelley Gurney, Celia Hall, History Workshop Journal, Pam Hogg, Levi Strauss & Co., Ray Lowry, Zadoc Nava, the Open University Press, Zimena Percival, Revlon, Rondor Music, Screen (Society for Education in Film and Television), Tseng Kwong Chi. The publishers have made every effort to trace all the copyright-holders, but if any have been inadvertently overlooked they will be pleased to make the necessary arrangement at the first opportunity.

Contributors

Juliet Ash teaches Fashion, Design History and Theory at Ravensbourne College of Design and Communication and is co-author with Lee Wright of *Components of Dress*.

Atlanta and Alexander were members of the *ZG* editorial board.

Rosetta Brooks is a writer and art critic living in New York. She created and edited *ZG* magazine.

Martin Chalmers is a journalist and translator living in London.

Stuart Cosgrove has been a Lecturer in Drama at West London Institute of Higher Education, and media editor at the *New Musical Express*. He is at present co-producer of a TV series for Channel 4.

Richard Dyer teaches Film Studies at Warwick University, is the author of *Stars* and *Heavenly Bodies* and is currently writing a book on independent lesbian and gay film.

Simon Frith is Director of the John Logie Baird Centre in Glasgow and writes about music in the *Observer* and *Village Voice*.

Marek Kohn is a freelance journalist and author of *Narcomania: On Heroin*.

Dave Laing wrote *The Sound of Our Times* in 1969. Since then he has published and edited several books on pop including *One Chord Wonders*. He is at present features editor of *Music Week*.

Contributors ix

Janet Lee is a research student at Middlesex Polytechnic, London, working on a study of the interrelationship between post-modernist and feminist theories. She is also a part-time lecturer at St Martin's School of Art, London.

Hilary Little is a freelance journalist and regular contributor to the *New Statesman*.

Angela McRobbie lectures in Sociology at Ealing College of Higher Education. She co-edited *Feminism for Girls* and *Gender and Generation* and is author of *Teenage Girls: Subcultures, Pop Culture and Femininity*.

Greil Marcus is the author of *Mystery Train: Images of America in Rock 'n' Roll Music* and a columnist for the *Village Voice*.

Kobena Mercer teaches Cultural Studies at the Centre for Caribbean Studies, Goldsmiths' College. He graduated from St Martin's School of Art and is currently completing a PhD thesis in sociology at Goldsmiths' College.

Kathy Myers is the author of *Understains: The Sense and Seduction of Advertising*. She was co-producer of *The Media Show* (Channel 4) and now works for the BBC.

Paul Oldfield is a freelance contributor to *Melody Maker* and *New Statesman* and was a co-founder of *Monitor*.

Ian Penman is a freelance journalist and regular contributor to the *New Statesman*, *Arena* and *The Face*.

Simon Reynolds is a staff feature writer on *Melody Maker* and pop columnist for the *New Statesman*, and was a co-founder of *Monitor*.

Gina Rumsey is a freelance journalist currently working in London.

Jon Savage is a regular contributor to the *Observer* and the *New Statesman*, and is a consultant to Channel 4's *The Media Show*. He is currently writing *England's Dreaming: Sex Pistols and Punk*

Rock, 1975–79 and is researching another book, *Teenage: A History of Postwar English Youth Culture*, with Peter York.

Dirk Scheuring is a music journalist working and living in West Germany.

David Stubbs is a staff feature writer on *Melody Maker*, and has written for *Monitor*.

Introduction

Two kinds of writing now feed into the study of youth and popular culture. These are the more conventional academic mode, and what might be called a new form of cultural journalism. Each is marked by its own history, its debates and disputes. *Zoot Suits and Second-Hand Dresses* attempts to bring these two together. In doing so, it is also concerned to highlight and explain the diverse ways in which popular culture shapes and influences everyday life around us. It is no longer accurate to pose media forms, images and representations as being on one side of an imaginary line, and lived reality on the other. The key question is how these interact, how reality is perceived through the many lenses and screens of the media. There is also the crucial question of consumerism. We don't just absorb the media, or let it determine our desires and personal fantasies, we also consume it. Buying need not necessarily follow looking or viewing. It might well be possible to read *Just Seventeen* for years and never step foot inside Miss Selfridges, or Top Shop, or the local Chelsea Girl . . . but it is unlikely.

Analytically we have got to retain the space between these various actions, but we also have to be able to perceive the connections. The systems of meaning within which these practices of looking, buying and even just day-dreaming take place, are constantly regenerating themselves. What we buy and consequently wear or display in some public fashion, in turn creates new images, new, sometimes unintended, constellations of meaning. In a sense we become media forms ourselves, the physical body is transformed into a compact portable 'walkman'.

Zoot Suits and Second-Hand Dresses falls into four sections. In the first longer section titled *Frontiers*, there are five articles each of which attempts to chart new ground in the study of fashion, style or music. This is followed by *Transgressions*, where a number of authors explore deviant styles, practices and their wider cultural meanings. *Interiors* considers fashion, fashion photography and images of the male body. Finally, in *Music Now* a number of young journalists upset the conventions of rock criticism and Greil Marcus adds a dissident voice to the populist clamour of Band Aid.

Many of the articles included here have already appeared in a number of journals and magazines. In the past few years these have often proved difficult to track down. Some have gone out of print altogether. A strong reason for putting a collection like this together is to make available to teachers and others as wide a range of teaching material as possible. The book was conceived, therefore, with Cultural Studies, Media Studies and the Sociology of Youth in mind. The idea was to combine a number of longer and more substantial pieces with a whole range of shorter articles which covered areas as diverse as the male pin-up, women and pop, and the Band Aid event of 1985.

This teaching function should not, however, blind us to other significant political and intellectual shifts which make it more possible now than it was ten years ago to place such diverse and eclectic material alongside each other. Serious pop journalism, for a start, has changed dramatically. Under the influence of Tom Wolfe, the best pop writing was found in the early 1970s in the *New Musical Express*. Wolfe had been given vast amounts of space in the influential American magazine *Rolling Stone*, and young British journalists followed suit by pushing for as much word-space as they could. The British music press has stood alone in this respect. There is no other media form which has allowed writers, fresh out of school or college, anything like the same freedom to develop a distinctive style or a particular set of interests. There are many reasons why this has been the case. It wasn't just the influence of *Rolling Stone*. Music itself, from the early 1970s, had become more self-consciously serious. Politics had also found its way into pop, and the music press was forced to recognise the influential way these had come together in the underground press. It was simply no longer feasible to attach a brief and breezy three-line review to albums and singles which cried out for something more substantial.

Tom Wolfe of course remains, even now, an important figure: not just for his breakneck fast prose style, and his often quoted maxim about 'getting it right', but because he wrote with conviction on objects, artefacts and events which were elsewhere considered trivial.

There were a number of other additional forces which encouraged young journalists working in this field to explore popular culture as a more general form: a recognition, for example, that pop music along with reggae, soul, rock, and everything else, could no longer be considered in isolation. These musics permeated a vast range of other media forms, as soundtrack, performance spectacle or simply as accompaniment to an endless flow of images. The star system, too, which continues to be a crucial ingredient in the day-to-day workings of the music industry, plays a much more prominent role, particularly in the tabloid newspapers. Pop stars rank alongside the Royal Family and the stars of soap as an unfailing source of gossip and news. There is more pop coverage in the quality dailies, pop is increasingly used to advertise everything from jeans to tights and office equipment, and it plays a central role both in girls' comics and on children's television. This makes it a form so deeply intertwined with other systems of meaning and communication as to be virtually inseparable from them.

Independent of where precisely the taste or preferences of the journalists fell, this continuing penetration of pop into the global media market made it difficult for them to perceive it any longer as a pure form. While the standard format of the review, interview or comment remained, many journalists none the less wanted to write about the cultural phenomena which came with the music. They were interested in the clothes, style and distinctiveness of the fans who congregated ritualistically at gigs and concerts. They wanted to know more about where these subcultural impulses came from, how they fed into the market for new consumer goods, and how they related to the world of politics. Indeed the journalists often felt better equipped to deal with these questions than the academics, who from the mid-1970s were publishing extensively on the same subject. By the late 1970s the relations between the music press and the record industry had short-circuited. The journalists were recruited, or else came forward themselves, from the sub-cultures, first from punk but then later, in the 1980s, from the various soul club scenes. It's well documented how the vituperative writing style of Julie Burchill, Tony Parsons, Paul Morley and Ian Penman brought them as much notoriety as the bands they were writing about.

It was this connection which allowed these young writers to claim that theirs was the authentic voice of youth. While the sociologists were destined to hover nervously on the margins, they could report direct from the pubs, clubs and dressing rooms. In their weekly chunks of prose they would frequently challenge the sociological fragments which, against a backdrop of unemployment and crime, were finding their way into popular discourse. Julie Burchill was the most prominent anti-sociologist around. Writing for *New Society* she provided its readers with a kind of in-house critique, a punk-influenced sneer and opinionated anti-intellectualism which allowed her to bring together a set of views which defied rational questioning.

Back inside the music press another set of changes could be detected. Writing about the culture which surrounded the music was beginning to give way to writing about both pop and culture as consumerism. Working for magazines like *The Face* or *Blitz*, young freelance journalists suddenly found themselves arbiters of taste, lifestyle, and even home decoration. This consumerism was accompanied by a set of gestures towards aestheticism. In the 1960s, pop art had brought painting, cinema, and visual imagery to pop in a generous act of validation. Andy Warhol and Richard Hamilton both courted and honoured Elvis, Jagger and others.

Twenty years later it is the musicians who are so anxious to display their artistic credentials. Even in *Smash Hits* interviews (a magazine whose average readers are 11-year-old girls) it is not unusual to come across Simon Le Bon of Duran Duran trying to impress a bookish and intellectual image on his fans, by referring to 'montage' or to the 'lingering influence of surrealism'. For the more upmarket style glossies this produces a real dilemma. The aestheticisation of culture means that they can fill their pages with images of art-deco sofas, classic 1950s tableware and kitchen furniture, and endless video installations, but ultimately their 'light' journalistic format confines them to the epithet or descriptive comment. The enormous space in magazines like *The Face*, *Elle* and *Blitz* given over to images and illustrations means that the printed word is pushed into the sidelines. There are few sustained reviews or critiques, though whether this is based on an assumption about what readers are looking for, or expect, is uncertain. A grounded analysis of art and design objects is abandoned in favour of a celebration of them in terms of lifestyle and consumerism. As Dick Hebdige has commented in his recent and influential article on *The Face* magazine,[1] this allows all sorts of cultural objects to be placed together on a shared, flat, postmodern surface. Ironically the outcome is a much more conventional and conservative unity, one which depends upon the reader being exhorted to display his or her taste and knowledge through old-fashioned consumption. You are what you buy, or what you aspire to buy.

The shortage of space in the style magazines for extended written articles was in part what prompted pop culture journalists back towards the more serious weekly and monthly magazines. Here it was possible to develop a more openly political profile, tackling questions like race, unemployment, sexual politics, and drug abuse, as well as issues around art and culture. Since a number of academic writers were also contributing to the same journals, much of the old antagonism began to fade. A strong overlap of interest surfaced, and this was compounded with the increasing popularisation, outside higher education, of semiology and structuralism which followed the publication of Barthes's *Image, Music, Text*,[2] and Hebdige's *Subculture: The Meaning of Style*.[3] Of course Peter York had already developed his own brand of instant semiology which he applied with wit and humour to London life around him. York was, and remains, primarily interested in how people carve out identities for themselves through what they consume. From this he has constructed numerous immediately recognisable social types which in turn have done away with the advertising agencies' old reliance on the drearier typologies of the Registrar General. The old As, Bs, CIs, and so on, have been replaced by any number of irritatingly zappy titled types.

Several of the contributors to this volume have followed a freelance route through the music press, the style glossies and the Sunday newspapers to the *New Statesman*, *ZG* and *Marxism Today*. Jon Savage's two pieces appeared in *The Face* ('The Age of Plunder' – one of the few depth pieces published there) and *ZG* ('Do You Know How to Pony?'). Jon Savage writes for almost all the magazines mentioned above as well as *The Observer*. He is currently writing a book on the Sex Pistols and Britain in the 1970s. Ian Penman was one of the most admired *NME* writers in the mid to late 1970s, where he wrote at length on, among other things, torch songs, Grace Jones, Paul Schrader and Fassbinder. Here, in 'The Shattered Glass', he unpicks the fine web of postures and gestures which made Roxy Music what they were. Like Penman, Marek Kohn is a regular contributor to *The Face* and to the *New Statesman*. His piece here first appeared in *ZG* in 1983. More recently he has published a book on heroin imagery, entitled *Narcomania*. Part IV, 'Music Now', includes work by Greil Marcus (author of the seminal 'The Mystery Train', and regular contributor to *Artforum*), and that of relative newcomers like Simon Reynolds (now of the *Melody Maker*), David Stubbs (likewise) and Paul Oldfield (freelance music writer).

Of the women contributors, only Kathy Myers, Gina Rumsey and Hilary Little work in the world of media journalism. Kathy Myers is now – following an academic career and two years as *City Limits*' television editor – an assistant producer at the BBC. Gina Rumsey and Hilary Little contribute one of the most telling and poignant pieces in the book. 'Women and Pop: A Series of Lost Encounters' offers an account of the other side of pop – not just the obvious sexism and macho posturing, but the whole network of social relations which make music a different experience altogether for women.

The question for women and girls entering the music press is still whether to become one of the boys (an early 1970s proposition), or whether to proceed as a woman, with all that entails. Even at her most anti-feminist it was on these latter grounds that Julie Burchill gained her reputation. Sitting at home churning out her scathing prose, she presumably saw no reason to endear herself to the boys. It was on the gruesome pretensions of music-business masculinity that she poured her greatest scorn.

Black journalists are equally under-represented in pop culture journalism. A similar web of exclusion prevents them from knowing who is who, and who wants to commission what. The substantial number of male and female black musicians in this country is not matched in the world of journalism. Like the majority of women contributors in this volume, Kobena Mercer writes about pop culture (the Michael Jackson *Thriller* video) from within academic media studies. The other side of media expansion, particularly in journalism, may well be that outside the feminist press or the ethnic press, 'equal opportunities' remains something generally applauded but only weakly applied.

* * *

Music journalism has evolved into a much broader kind of writing. It has explored the crossover and inter-penetration which now exists between all media forms. But where does this leave the more academic study of youth and popular culture? Have wider social changes also made their mark in this field? The answer to this is yes, for reasons we shall see in a moment. It might be said in the first instance, that while pop journalism has moved towards a more serious mode, academic writing has, to some extent, shifted towards a lighter, more essayistic, style. There are some very pragmatic reasons why this should be so. Cutbacks, under-funding and a more general hostility to the social sciences, have produced a climate hardly conducive to full-scale research, solitary study, or to the traditional pursuit of knowledge. The running-down of both the social sciences and the humanities in higher education, and the now likely overhaul of the whole system, have not, however, created only despair and inactivity. Many of those employed in the polytechnic sector have looked towards new forms of scholarship, in particular a more popular kind of *journal-ism*. The burden of heavy teaching timetables and the lack of resources for substantial research projects have undoubtedly played some role in precipitating this shift. It is one which is, more optimistically, reflected in the increasing number of journals and magazines which have grown up around Cultural Studies. Most are run on a shoestring; sometimes they have difficulty maintaining a momentum for more than five years. But this detracts neither from their importance nor from their influence. When one goes under it is usually replaced by another, springing up from some different source or institution.

At their best, journals like *Theory, Culture and Society, Ten 8, Screen, Formations, Block, Camerawork,* and *Feminist Review* (in the USA, *October, Social Text, Signs* and *Substance* have played a similar role) have provided a forum for work-in-progress and for short pieces ranging from replies and reviews to commentaries and critiques. This has made for interesting and stimulating reading. Some debates have spanned different journals, starting off in one and being picked up and developed in another, a feature contributing directly to the radical intellectual culture which, despite everything, continues into the late 1980s. In this collection, for example, we reprint Rosetta Brooks's article on fashion photography, 'Sighs and Whispers in Bloomingdales'. It originally appeared in the magazine she herself edited, *ZG*. Some months later Kathy Myers replied to this in *Screen*, and indeed extended her argument into the wider feminist discussion around pornography and erotica. This also appears here. In each case the authors are writing in a kind of dialogue with a set of chosen images. This too is a mark of the new scholarship, an active engagement with the fleeting-but-lasting effect of the images around us. The result of these visual conversations is a looser, more open-ended, style of academic writing. Richard Dyer's 'Don't Look Now', also first published in *Screen*, follows a similar format. Using this more imaginative mode, it explores how men look and how they are looked at.

A number of other articles in this volume blur the line between the academic and the journalistic. These include Martin Chalmers's piece on heroin and the body, Juliet Ash's views on the Paris fashion shows, Janet Lee's interviews with three women fashion designers and Dirk Scheuring's account of the never-ending popularity of denim.

The success of academic journalism has effects beyond the publishing of radical ideas and critiques. It allows those only recently embarked on postgraduate study to think out loud and speculate in print. It also demystifies the more traditional academic 'publication', and encourages collaborative work which in turn goes some way to ending the notion of intellectual work as a painful and solitary activity. All of these were practices championed from the early 1970s, by the Birmingham Centre for Contemporary Cultural Studies, in their influential Working Papers in Cultural Studies.

Standing a bit further back from the actual business of writing and publishing, two other distinct shifts in intellectual thinking can be detected. First, the lasting impact of French structuralism. It was not until the publication in English of Barthes's short essay, *The Grain of the Voice*,[4] that the analysis of music was able to move beyond a kind of weak and unconvincing literary criticism.

Dave Laing's detailed examination of Johnny Rotten's vocal delivery draws usefully on this text. In doing so it also contributes a new dimension to the study of subcultural forms. Where in the past much has been said about the meaning of style, only very little has emerged on the meaning of the musical text itself. The contributions from both Simon Frith and Greil Marcus also add to the subcultural repertoire. Marcus chooses one spectacular pop moment to produce a subtle reading of its theme tune, 'We Are The World', and Frith produces a detailed profile of David Bowie's fleeting identities. This too marks a point of departure from the established conventions of youth culture analysis. Previously there was very little emphasis on the stars themselves, since it was assumed that they were most often self-seeking individuals and otherwise mere commodities, iconic representations of the success of capitalism. From this viewpoint great attention was paid only to the collective actions and ritualistic behaviour of working-class youth, thereby losing much of the impact of pop culture and pop stars on youth. All three of these pop pieces are evidence therefore of the kind of loosening-up and broadening out of forms mentioned earlier. Gone, thankfully, is the need to establish a theoretical purity before proceeding to say anything more. Gone too is the need to be seen to be attempting to solve some theoretical problem in the course of a short piece of writing. This has been replaced by a more exploratory mode where theoretical questions inform a piece of work without necessarily overwhelming it. Alongside this is a wariness about the dangers of seeking too-easy answers. Overarching theories of class identity or ideological positioning have in the last few years been shown to be oblivious to other crucial and equally determining factors.

What is found, hopefully, in *Zoot Suits* is a greater openness, a more speculative quality of writing, and a lingering presence of some of the best insights from the field of subcultural analysis. The opening piece by Stuart Cosgrove certainly expresses this widening-out process. It is a history of events still relatively undocumented: the experience of urban blacks and hispanics in the years running up to and including America's involvement in the Second World War. Cosgrove shows how the fine details of black style, the adoption of the bright and brassy zoot suit, prefigured a later more political consciousness of race and social difference.

What of the other, second, shift in the study of youth and culture reflected here? This can be best expressed by the developing interest in the physical body (rather than the collective political body), and on how it registers social resistance. Kobena Mercer's reading of the *Thriller* video traces the fragmentation of identity, which is part of the black experience, back to its transposition on the body. In *Thriller*, Mercer sees Jackson's monster transformation as a metaphoric re-working of this theme, suggesting an instability which is defiantly asserted, and then celebrated, as the bodies – and particularly Michael Jackson's – break into dance. The body also figures strongly in Atlanta and Alexander's 'Wild Style'. Here the body in question is that of the black urban graffiti artist who dodges danger and prosecution in order to leave a trace, a signature, or simply a sign on the unwelcoming urban environment. In Martin Chalmers's piece, the body of the addict is the site for despair and a repository of power. In my own analysis of second-hand clothes, the body is the object upon which huge baggy shapes are draped as though to protect it from the world of well-fitting adult values.

ANGELA MCROBBIE

Notes

1. D. Hebdige, 'The Bottom Line on Planet One', *Ten 8*, No. 19, 1985.
2. R. Barthes, *Image–Music–Text*, London, Fontana, 1977.
3. D. Hebdige, Subculture: The Meaning of Style, London, Methuen, 1978.
4. R. Barthes (1977).

Part I

Frontiers

1
The Zoot Suit and Style Warfare*

Stuart Cosgrove

Introduction: the silent noise of sinister clowns

> What about those fellows waiting still and silent there on the platform, so still and silent they clash with the crowd in their very immobility, standing noisy in their very silence; harsh as a cry of terror in their quietness? What about these three boys, coming now along the platform, tall and slender, walking with swinging shoulders in their well-pressed, too-hot-for-summer suits, their collars high and tight about their necks, their identical hats of black cheap felt set upon the crowns of their heads with a severe formality above their conked hair? It was as though I'd never seen their like before: walking slowly, their shoulders swaying, their legs swinging from their hips in trousers that ballooned upward from cuffs fitting snug about their ankles; their coats long and hip-tight with shoulders far too broad to be those of natural western men. These fellows whose bodies seemed – what had one of my teachers said of me? – 'You're like one of those African sculptures, distorted in the interest of design.' Well, what design and whose?[1]

The zoot suit is more than an exaggerated costume, more than a sartorial statement: it is the bearer of a complex and contradictory history. When the nameless narrator of Ellison's *Invisible Man* confronted the subversive sight of three young and extravagantly dressed blacks, his reaction was one of fascination not of fear. These youths were not simply grotesque dandies parading the city's secret underworld, they were 'the stewards of something uncomfortable',[2] a spectacular reminder that the social order had

---

* This article was originally published in the *History Workshop Journal*, 1984.

4 The Zoot Suit and Style Warfare

failed to contain their energy and difference. The zoot suit was more than the drape-shape of 1940s fashion, more than a colourful stage-prop hanging from the shoulders of Cab Calloway; it was, in the most direct and obvious ways, an emblem of ethnicity and a way of negotiating an identity. The zoot suit was a refusal: a subcultural gesture that refused to concede to the manners of subservience. By the late 1930s, the term 'zoot' was in common

Boys in zoot suits, Harlem, 1943

circulation within urban jazz culture. Zoot meant something worn or performed in an extravagant style, and since many young blacks wore suits with outrageously padded shoulders and trousers that were fiercely tapered at the ankles, the term 'zoot suit' passed into everyday usage. In the sub-cultural world of Harlem's nightlife, the language of rhyming slang succinctly described the zoot suit's unmistakable style: 'a killer-diller coat with a drape-shape, reat-pleats and shoulders padded like a lunatic's cell'. The study of the relationships between fashion and social action is notoriously underdeveloped, but there is every indication that the zoot-suit riots that erupted in the United States in the summer of 1943 had a profound effect on a whole generation of socially disadvantaged youths. It was during his period as a young zoot-suiter that the Chicano union activist Cesar Chavez first came into contact with community politics, and it was through the experiences of participating in zoot-suit riots in Harlem that the young pimp 'Detroit Red' began a political education that transformed him into the Black radical leader Malcolm X. Although the zoot suit occupies an almost mythical place within the history of jazz music, its social and political importance has been virtually ignored. There can be no certainty about when, where or why the zoot suit came into existence, but what is certain is that during the summer months of 1943 'the killer-diller coat' was the uniform of young rioters and the symbol of a moral panic about juvenile delinquency that was to intensify in the post-war period.

At the height of the Los Angeles riots of June 1943, the *New York Times* carried a front-page article which claimed without reservation that the first zoot suit had been purchased by a black bus worker, Clyde Duncan, from a tailor's shop in Gainesville, Georgia.[3] Allegedly, Duncan had been inspired by the film *Gone with the Wind*, and had set out to look like Rhett Butler. This explanation clearly found favour throughout the USA. The national press forwarded countless others. Some reports claimed that the zoot suit was an invention of Harlem night-life; others suggested it grew out of jazz culture and the exhibitionist stage-costumes of the band leaders; and some argued that the zoot suit was derived from military uniforms and imported from Britain. The alternative and independent press, particularly *Crisis* and *Negro Quarterly*, more convincingly argued that the zoot suit was the product of a particular social context.[4] They emphasised the importance of Mexican-American youths, or *pachucos*, in the emergence of zoot-suit style and, in tentative ways, tried to relate their appearance on the streets to the concept of *pachuquismo*.

In his pioneering book, *The Labyrinth of Solitude*, the Mexican poet and social commentator Octavio Paz throws imaginative light on *pachuco* style and indirectly establishes a framework within

6 The Zoot Suit and Style Warfare

which the zoot suit can be understood. Paz's study of the Mexican national consciousness examines the changes brought about by the movement of labour, particularly the generations of Mexicans who migrated northwards to the USA. This movement, and the new economic and social patterns it implies, has, according to Paz, forced young Mexican-Americans into an ambivalent experience between two cultures:

Clyde Duncan, a bus-boy from Gainesville, Georgia, appeared on the front page of the *New York Times* at the height of the zoot-suit riots

> What distinguishes them, I think, is their furtive, restless air: they act like persons who are wearing disguises, who are afraid of a stranger's look because it could strip them and leave them stark naked.... This spiritual condition, or lack of a spirit, has given birth to a type known as the pachuco. The pachucos are youths, for the most part of Mexican origin, who form gangs in southern cities; they can be identified by their language and behaviour as well as by the clothing they affect. They are instinctive rebels, and North American racism has vented its wrath on them more than once. But the pachucos do not attempt to vindicate their race or the nationality of their forebears. Their attitude

reveals an obstinate, almost fanatical will-to-be, but this will affirms nothing specific except their determination . . . not to be like those around them.⁵

Pachuco youth embodied all the characteristics of second-generation working-class immigrants. In the most obvious ways they had been stripped of their customs, beliefs and language. The *pachucos* were a disinherited generation within a disadvantaged sector of North American society; and predictably their experiences in education, welfare and employment alienated them from the aspirations of their parents and the dominant assumptions of the society in which they lived. The *pachuco* subculture was defined not only by ostentatious fashion, but by petty crime, delinquency and drug-taking. Rather than disguise their alienation or efface their hostility to the dominant society, the *pachucos* adopted an arrogant posture. They flaunted their difference, and the zoot suit became the means by which that difference was announced. Those 'impassive and sinister clowns' whose purpose was 'to cause terror instead of laughter',⁶ invited the kind of attention that led to both prestige and persecution. For Octavio Paz the *pachuco*'s appropriation of the zoot suit was an admission of the ambivalent place he occupied. 'It is the only way he can establish a more vital relationship with the society he is antagonising. As a victim he can occupy a place in the world that previously ignored him: as a delinquent, he can become one of its wicked heroes.'⁷ The zoot-suit riots of 1943 encapsulated this paradox. They emerged out of the dialectics of delinquency and persecution, during a period in which American society was undergoing profound structural change.

The major social change brought about by the United States' involvement in the war was the recruitment to the armed forces of over four million civilians and the entrance of over five million women into the wartime labour force. The rapid increase in military recruitment and the radical shift in the composition of the labour force led in turn to changes in family life, particularly the erosion of parental control and authority. The large-scale and prolonged separation of millions of families precipitated an unprecedented increase in the rate of juvenile crime and delinquency. By the summer of 1943 it was commonplace for teenagers to be left to their own initiatives whilst their parents were either on active military service or involved in war work. The increase in night work compounded the problem. With their parents or guardians working unsocial hours, it became possible for many more young people to gather late into the night at major urban centres or simply on the street corners.

The rate of social mobility intensified during the period of the zoot-suit riots. With over 15 million civilians and 12 million military personnel on the move throughout the country, there was a corresponding increase in vagrancy. Petty crimes became more difficult to detect and control; itinerants became increasingly common, and social transience put unforeseen pressure on housing and welfare. The new patterns of social mobility also led to congestion in military and industrial areas. Significantly, it was the overcrowded military towns along the Pacific coast and the industrial conurbations of Detroit, Pittsburgh and Los Angeles that witnessed the most violent outbreaks of zoot-suit rioting.[8]

'Delinquency' emerged from the dictionary of new sociology to become an everyday term, as wartime statistics revealed these new patterns of adolescent behaviour. The *pachucos* of the Los Angeles area were particularly vulnerable to the effects of war. Being neither Mexican nor American, the *pachucos*, like the black youths with whom they shared the zoot-suit style, simply did not fit. In their own terms they were '24-hour orphans', having rejected the ideologies of their migrant parents. As the war furthered the dislocation of family relationships, the *pachucos* gravitated away from the home to the only place where their status was visible: the streets and bars of the towns and cities. But if the *pachucos* laid themselves open to a life of delinquency and detention, they also asserted their distinct identity, with their own style of dress, their own way of life and a shared set of experiences.

The zoot-suit riots: liberty, disorder and the forbidden

The zoot-suit riots sharply revealed a polarization between two youth groups within wartime society: the gangs of predominantly black and Mexican youths who were at the forefront of the zoot-suit subculture, and the predominantly white American servicemen stationed along the Pacific coast. The riots invariably had racial and social resonances, but the primary issue seems to have been patriotism and attitudes to the war. With the entry of the United States into the war in December 1941, the nation had to come to terms with the restrictions of rationing and the prospects of conscription. In March 1942, the War Production Board's first rationing act had a direct effect on the manufacture of suits and all clothing containing wool. In an attempt to institute a 26 per cent cut-back in the use of fabrics, the War Production Board drew up regulations for the wartime manufacture of what *Esquire* magazine called 'streamlined suits by Uncle Sam'.[9] The regulations effectively forbade the manufacture of zoot suits, and most legitimate tailoring companies ceased to manufacture or advertise any suits that fell outside the War Production Board's guidelines. However, the demand for zoot suits did not decline, and a network of bootleg tailors based in Los Angeles and New York continued to manufacture the garments. Thus the polarization between servicemen and *pachucos* was immediately visible: the chino shirt and battledress were evidently uniforms of patriotism, whereas wearing a zoot suit was a deliberate and public way of flouting the regulations of rationing. The zoot suit was a moral and social scandal in the eyes of the authorities, not simply because it was associated with petty crime and violence, but because it openly snubbed the laws of rationing. In the fragile harmony of wartime society, the zoot-suiters were, according to Octavio Paz, 'a symbol of love and joy or of horror and loathing, an embodiment of liberty, of disorder, of the forbidden'.[10]

The zoot-suit riots, which were initially confined to Los Angeles, began in the first few days of June 1943. During the first weekend of the month, over 60 zoot-suiters were arrested and charged at Los Angeles County jail, after violent and well-publicized fights between servicemen on shore leave and gangs of Mexican-American youths. In order to prevent further outbreaks of fighting, the police patrolled the eastern sections of the city, as rumours spread from the military bases that servicemen were intending to form vigilante groups. The *Washington Post*'s report of the incidents, on the morning of Wednesday 9 June 1943, clearly saw the events from the point of view of the servicemen:

> Disgusted with being robbed and beaten with tire irons, weighted ropes, belts and fists employed by overwhelming numbers of the youthful hoodlums, the uniformed men passed the word

quietly among themselves and opened their campaign in force on Friday night.

At central jail, where spectators jammed the sidewalks and police made no efforts to halt auto loads of servicemen openly cruising in search of zoot-suiters, the youths streamed gladly into the sanctity of the cells after being snatched from bar rooms, pool halls and theaters and stripped of their attire.[11]

During the ensuing weeks of rioting, the ritualistic stripping of zoot-suiters became the major means by which the servicemen re-established their status over the *pachucos*. It became commonplace for gangs of marines to ambush zoot-suiters, strip them down to their underwear and leave them helpless in the streets. In one particularly vicious incident, a gang of drunken sailors rampaged through a cinema after discovering two zoot-suiters. They dragged the *pachucos* on to the stage as the film was being screened, stripped them in front of the audience and, as a final insult, urinated on the suits.

The press coverage of these incidents ranged from the careful and cautionary liberalism of The *Los Angeles Times* to the more hysterical hate-mongering of William Randolph Hearst's west-coast papers. Although the practice of stripping and publicly humiliating the zoot-suiters was not prompted by the press, several reports did little to discourage the attacks:

> zoot-suits smouldered in the ashes of street bonfires where they had been tossed by grimly methodical tank forces of service men. . . . The zooters, who earlier in the day had spread boasts that they were organized to 'kill every cop' they could find, showed no inclination to try to make good their boasts. . . . Searching parties of soldiers, sailors and Marines hunted them out and drove them out into the open like bird dogs flushing quail. Procedure was standard: grab a zooter. Take off his pants and frock coat and tear them up or burn them. Trim the 'Argentine Ducktail' haircut that goes with the screwy costume.[12]

The second week of June witnessed the worst incidents of rioting and public disorder. A sailor was slashed and disfigured by a *pachuco* gang; a policeman was run down when he tried to question a car-load of zoot-suiters; a young Mexican was stabbed at a party

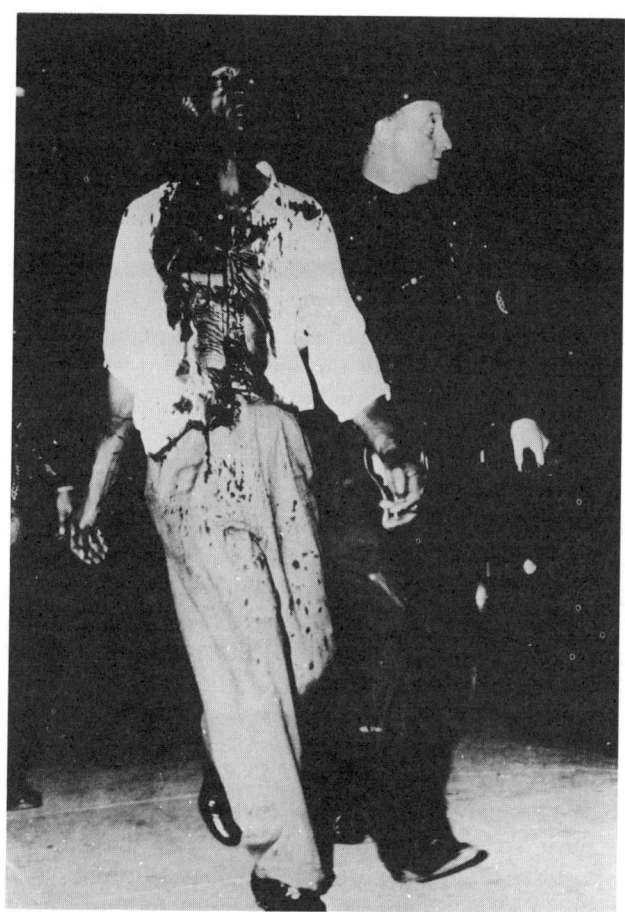

Zoot-suit riots in Harlem, 1943

by drunken Marines; a trainload of sailors were stoned by *pachucos* as their train approached Long Beach; streetfights broke out daily in San Bernardino; over 400 vigilantes toured the streets of San Diego looking for zoot-suiters, and many individuals from both factions were arrested.[13] On 9 June, the *Los Angeles Times* published the first in a series of editorials designed to reduce the level of violence, but which also tried to allay the growing concern about the racial character of the riots:

To preserve the peace and good name of the Los Angeles area, the strongest measures must be taken jointly by the police, the Sheriff's office and Army and Navy authorities, to prevent any further outbreaks of 'zoot suit' rioting. While members of the armed forces received considerable provocation at the hands of the unidentified miscreants, such a situation cannot be cured by indiscriminate assault on every youth wearing a particular type of costume.

It would not do, for a large number of reasons, to let the impression circulate in South America that persons of Spanish-American ancestry were being singled out for mistreatment in Southern California. And the incidents here were capable of being exaggerated to give that impression.[14]

The Chief, the Black Widows and the Tomahawk Kid

The pleas for tolerance from civic authorities and representatives of the church and state had no immediate effect, and the riots became more frequent and more violent. A zoot-suited youth was shot by a special police officer in Azusa; a gang of *pachucos* were arrested for rioting and carrying weapons in the Lincoln Heights area; 25 black zoot-suiters were arrested for wrecking an electric railway train in Watts; and 1000 additional police were drafted into East Los Angeles. The press coverage increasingly focused on the most 'spectacular' incidents and began to identify leaders of zoot-suit style. On the morning of Thursday 10 June 1943, most newspapers carried photographs and reports on three 'notorious' zoot-suit gang leaders. Of the thousands of *pachucos* that allegedly belonged to the hundreds of zoot-gangs in Los Angeles, the press singled out the arrests of Lewis D. English, a 23-year-old black, charged with felony and carrying a '16-inch razor sharp butcher knife'; Frank H. Tellez, a 22-year-old Mexican held on vagrancy charges; and another Mexican, Luis 'The Chief' Verdusco (27 years of age), allegedly the leader of the Los Angeles *pachucos*.[15]

The arrests of English, Tellez and Verdusco seemed to confirm popular perceptions of the zoot-suiters widely expressed for weeks prior to the riots. Firstly, that the zoot-suit gangs were predominantly, but not exclusively, comprised of black and Mexican youths. Secondly, that many of the zoot-suiters were old enough to be in the armed forces but were either avoiding conscription or had been exempted on medical grounds. Finally, in the case of Frank Tellez, who was photographed wearing a pancake hat with a rear feather, that zoot-suit style was an expensive fashion often funded by theft and petty extortion. Tellez allegedly wore a colourful long drape coat that was 'part of a $75 suit' and a pair of pegged trousers 'very full at the knees and narrow at the cuffs' which were allegedly part of another suit. The caption of the Associated Press photograph indignantly added that 'Tellez holds a medical discharge from the Army'.[16] What newspaper reports tended to suppress was information on the Marines who were arrested for inciting riots, the existence of gangs of white American zoot-suiters, and the opinions of Mexican-American servicemen stationed in California, who were part of the war-effort but who refused to take part in vigilante raids on *pachuco* hangouts.

As the zoot-suit riots spread throughout California, to cities in Texas and Arizona, a new dimension began to influence press coverage of the riots in Los Angeles. On a day when 125 zoot-suited youths clashed with Marines in Watts and armed police had to quell riots in Boyle Heights, the Los Angeles press concentrated on a razor attack on a local mother, Betty Morgan. What distinguished this incident from hundreds of comparable attacks was that the assailants were girls. The press related the incident to the arrest of Amelia Venegas, a woman zoot-suiter who was charged with carrying, and threatening to use, a brass knuckleduster. The revelation that girls were active within *pachuco* subculture led to consistent press coverage of the activities of two female gangs: the Slick Chicks and the Black Widows.[17] The latter gang took its name from the members' distinctive dress: black zoot-suit jackets, short black skirts and black fish-net stockings. In retrospect the Black Widows, and their active part in the subcultural violence of the zoot-suit riots, disturb conventional understandings of the concept of *pachuquismo*.

As Joan W. Moore implies in *Homeboys*, her definitive study of Los Angeles youth gangs, the concept of *pachuquismo* is too readily and unproblematically equated with the better known concept of *machismo*.[18] Undoubtedly, they share certain ideological traits, not least a swaggering and at times aggressive sense of power and bravado; but the two concepts derive from different sets of social definitions. Whereas *machismo* can be defined in terms of male power and sexuality, *pachuquismo* predominantly derives from ethnic, generational and class-based aspirations, and is less evidently a question of gender. What the zoot-suit riots brought to the surface was the complexity of *pachuco* style. The Black Widows and their aggressive image confounded the *pachuco* stereotype of the lazy male delinquent who avoided conscription for a life of dandyism and petty crime, and reinforced radical readings of *pachuco* sub-culture. The Black Widows were a reminder that ethnic and generational alienation was a pressing social problem and an indication of the tensions that existed in minority, low-income communities.

Although detailed information on the role of girls within zoot-suit sub-culture is limited to very brief press reports, the appearance of female *pachucos* coincided with a dramatic rise in the delinquency rates amongst girls aged between 12 and 20. The disintegration of traditional family relationships and the entry of young women into the labour force undoubtedly had an effect on the social roles and responsibilities of female adolescents, but it is difficult to be precise about the relationships between changed patterns of social experience and the rise in delinquency. However, wartime society brought about an increase in unprepared and irregular sexual intercourse, which in turn led to significant increases in the rates of abortion, illegitimate births and venereal diseases. Although statistics are difficult to trace, there are many indications that the war years saw a remarkable increase in the numbers of young women who were taken into social care or referred to penal institutions, as a result of the specific social problems they had to encounter.

Later studies provide evidence that young women and girls were also heavily involved in the traffic and transaction of soft drugs. The *pachuco* sub-culture within the Los Angeles metropolitan area was directly associated with a widespread growth in the use of marijuana. It has been suggested that female zoot-suiters concealed quantities of drugs on their bodies, since they were less likely to be closely searched by male members of the law-enforcement agencies. Unfortunately, the absence of consistent or reliable information on the female gangs makes it particularly difficult to be certain about their status within the riots, or their place within traditions of feminine resistance. The Black Widows and Slick Chicks were spectacular in a sub-cultural sense, but their black drape jackets, tight skirts, fish-net stockings and heavily emphasised make-up, were ridiculed in the press. The Black Widows clearly existed outside the orthodoxies of wartime society: playing no part in the industrial war effort, and openly challenging conventional notions of feminine beauty and sexuality.

Towards the end of the second week of June, the riots in Los Angeles were dying out. Sporadic incidents broke out in other cities, particularly Detroit, New York and Philadelphia, where two members of Gene Krupa's dance band were beaten up in a station for wearing the band's zoot-suit costumes; but these, like the residual events in Los Angeles, were not taken seriously. The authorities failed to read the inarticulate warning signs proffered in two separate incidents in California: in one a zoot-suiter was arrested for throwing gasoline flares at a theatre; and in the second another was arrested for carrying a silver tomahawk. The zoot-suit riots had become a public and spectacular enactment of social disaffection. The authorities in Detroit chose to dismiss a zoot-suit riot at the city's Cooley High School as an adolescent imitation of the Los Angeles disturbances.[19] Within three weeks Detroit was in the midst of the worst race riot in its history.[20] The United States was still involved in the war abroad when violent events on the home front signalled the beginnings of a new era in racial politics.

Official fears of fifth-column fashion

Official reactions to the zoot-suit riots varied enormously. The most urgent problem that concerned California's State Senators was the adverse effect that the events might have on the relationship between the United States and Mexico. This concern stemmed partly from the wish to preserve good international relations, but rather more from the significance of relations with Mexico for the economy of Southern California, as an item in the *Los Angeles Times* made clear. 'In San Francisco Senator Downey declared that the riots may have "extremely grave consequences" in impairing relations between the United States and Mexico, and may endanger the program of importing Mexican labor to aid in harvesting California crops.'²¹ These fears were compounded when the Mexican Embassy formally drew the zoot-suit riots to the attention of the State Department. It was the fear of an 'international incident'²² that could only have an adverse effect on California's economy, rather than any real concern for the social conditions of the Mexican-American community, that motivated Governor Warren of California to order a public investigation into the causes of the riots. In an ambiguous press statement, the Governor hinted that the riots may have been instigated by outside or even foreign agitators:

> As we love our country and the boys we are sending overseas to defend it, we are all duty bound to suppress every discordant activity which is designed to stir up international strife or adversely affect our relationships with our allies in the United Nations.²³

The zoot-suit riots provoked two related investigations: a fact-finding investigative committee headed by Attorney General Robert Kenny, and an un-American-activities investigation presided over by State Senator Jack B. Tenney. The un-American-activities investigation was ordered 'to determine whether the present zoot-suit riots were sponsored by Nazi agencies attempting to spread disunity between the United States and Latin-American countries'.²⁴ Senator Tenney, a member of the un-American Activities committee for Los Angeles County, claimed he had evidence that the zoot-suit riots were 'axis-sponsored', but the evidence was never presented.²⁵ However, the notion that the riots might have been initiated by outside agitators persisted throughout the month of June, and was fuelled by Japanese propaganda broadcasts accusing the North American government of ignoring the brutality of US marines. The arguments of the un-American-activities investigation were given a certain amount of credibility by a Mexican pastor based in Watts, who according to the press had been 'a pretty rough customer himself, serving as a captain in Pancho Villa's revolutionary army'.²⁶ Reverend Francisco Quintanilla, the pastor of the Mexican Methodist church, was convinced the riots were the result of fifth-columnists. 'When boys start attacking servicemen it means the enemy is right at home. It means they are being fed vicious propaganda by enemy agents who wish to stir up all the racial and class hatreds they can put their evil fingers on.'[27]

The attention given to the dubious claims of nazi-instigation tended to obfuscate other more credible opinions. Examination of the social conditions of *pachuco* youths tended to be marginalized in favour of other more 'newsworthy' angles. At no stage in the press coverage were the opinions of community workers or youth leaders sought, and so, ironically, the most progressive opinion to appear in the major newspapers was offered by the Deputy Chief of Police, E. W. Lester. In press releases and on radio he provided a short history of gang subcultures in the Los Angeles area and then tried, albeit briefly, to place the riots in a social context:

> The Deputy Chief said most of the youths came from overcrowded colorless homes that offered no opportunities for leisure-time activities. He said it is wrong to blame law enforcement agencies for the present situation, but that society as a whole must be charged with mishandling the problems.[28]

On the morning of Friday, 11 June 1943, the *Los Angeles Times* broke with its regular practices and printed an editorial appeal, 'Time For Sanity', on its front page. The main purpose of the editorial was to dispel suggestions that the riots were racially motivated, and to challenge the growing opinion that white servicemen from the Southern States had actively colluded with the police in their vigilante campaign against the zoot-suiters:

> There seems to be no simple or complete explanation for the growth of the grotesque gangs. Many reasons have been offered, some apparently valid, some farfetched. But it does appear to be definitely established that any attempts at curbing the movement have had nothing whatever to do with race persecution, although some elements have loudly raised the cry of this very thing.[29]

A month later, the editorial of July's issue of *Crisis* presented a diametrically opposed point of view:

> These riots would not occur – no matter what the instant provocation – if the vast majority of the population, including

more often than not the law enforcement officers and machinery, did not share in varying degrees the belief that Negroes are and must be kept second-class citizens.[30]

But this view got short shrift, particularly from the authorities, whose initial response to the riots was largely retributive. Emphasis was placed on arrest and punishment. The Los Angeles City Council considered a proposal from Councillor Norris Nelson, that 'it be made a jail offense to wear zoot-suits with reat pleats within the city limits of LA',[31] and a discussion ensued for over an hour before it was resolved that the laws pertaining to rioting and disorderly conduct were sufficient to contain the zoot-suit threat. However, the council did encourage the War Production Board (WPB) to reiterate its regulations on the manufacture of suits. The regional office of the WPB based in San Francisco investigated tailors manufacturing in the area of men's fashion and took steps 'to curb illegal production of men's clothing in violation of WPB limitation orders'.[32] Only when Governor Warren's fact-finding commission made its public recommendations did the political analysis of the riots go beyond the first principles of punishment and proscription. The recommendations called for a more responsible co-operation from the press; a programme of special training for police officers working in multi-racial communities; additional detention centres; a juvenile forestry camp for youth under the age of 16; an increase in military and shore police; an increase in the youth facilities provided by the church; an increase in neighbourhood recreation facilities and an end to discrimination in the use of public facilities. In addition to these measures, the commission urged that arrests should be made without undue emphasis on members of minority groups, and encouraged lawyers to protect the rights of youths arrested for participation in gang activity. The findings were a delicate balance of punishment and palliative; it made no significant mention of the social conditions of Mexican labourers and no recommendations about the kind of public spending that would be needed to alter the social experiences of *pachuco* youth. The outcome of the zoot-suit riots was an inadequate, highly localized and relatively ineffective body of short-term public policies that provided no guidelines for the more serious riots in Detroit and Harlem later in the same summer.

The mystery of the signifying monkey

> The pachuco is the prey of society, but instead of hiding he adorns himself to attract the hunter's attention. Persecution redeems him and breaks his solitude: his salvation depends on him becoming part of the very society he appears to deny.[33]

The zoot suit was associated with a multiplicity of different traits and conditions. It was simultaneously the garb of the victim and the attacker, the persecutor and the persecuted, the 'sinister clown' and the grotesque dandy. But the central opposition was between the style of the delinquent and that of the disinherited. To wear a zoot suit was to risk the repressive intolerance of wartime society and to invite the attention of the police, the parent generation and the uniformed members of the armed forces. For many *pachucos* the zoot-suit riots were simply hightimes in Los Angeles when momentarily they had control of the streets; for others it was a realization that they were outcasts in a society that was not of their making. For the black radical writer, Chester Himes, the riots in his neighbourhood were unambiguous: 'Zoot Riots are Race Riots'.[34] For other contemporary commentators the wearing of the zoot suit could be anything from unconscious dandyism to a conscious 'political' engagement. The zoot-suit riots were *not* 'political' riots in the strictest sense, but for many participants they were an entry into the language of politics, an inarticulate rejection of the 'straight world' and its organization.

It is remarkable how many post-war activists were inspired by the zoot-suit disturbances. Luis Valdez of the radical theatre company El Teatro Campesino, allegedly learned the 'chicano' from his cousin the zoot-suiter Billy Miranda.[35] The novelists Ralph Ellison and Richard Wright both conveyed a literary and political fascination with the power and potential of the zoot suit. One of Ellison's editorials for the journal *Negro Quarterly* expressed his own sense of frustration at the enigmatic attraction of zoot-suit style:

> A third major problem, and one that is indispensable to the centralization and direction of power, is that of learning the meaning of myths and symbols which abound among the Negro masses. For without this knowledge, leadership, no matter how

correct its program, will fail. Much in Negro life remains a mystery; perhaps the zoot-suit conceals profound political meaning; perhaps the symmetrical frenzy of the Lindy-hop conceals clues to great potential powers, if only leaders could solve this riddle.[36]

Although Ellison's remarks are undoubtedly compromised by their own mysterious idealism, he touches on the zoot suit's major source of interest. It is in everyday rituals that resistance can find natural and unconscious expression. In retrospect, the zoot suit's history can be seen as a point of intersection, between the related potential of ethnicity and politics on the one hand, and the pleasures of identity and difference on the other. It is the zoot suit's political and ethnic associations that have made it such a rich reference point for subsequent generations. From the music of Thelonious Monk and Kid Creole to the jazz-poetry of Larry Neal, the zoot suit has inherited new meanings and new mysteries. In his book *Hoodoo Hollerin' Bebop Ghosts*, Neal uses the image of the zoot suit as the symbol of Black America's cultural resistance. For Neal, the zoot suit ceased to be a costume and became a tapestry of meaning, where music, politics and social action merged. The zoot suit became a symbol for the enigmas of Black culture and the mystery of the signifying monkey:

But there is rhythm here
Its own special substance:
I hear Billie sing, no Good Man, and dig Prez, wearing the Zoot suit of life,
the Porkpie hat tilted at the correct angle; through the Harlem smoke of beer
and whisky, I understand the mystery of the Signifying Monkey.[37]

Notes

The author wishes to acknowledge the support of the British Academy for the research for this article.

1. Ralph Ellison, *Invisible Man*, New York, 1947, p. 380.
2. *Invisible Man*, p. 381.

3. 'Zoot Suit Originated in Georgia', *New York Times*, 11 June 1943, p. 21.
4. For the most extensive sociological study of the zoot-suit riots of 1943, see Ralph H. Turner and Samuel J. Surace, 'Zoot Suiters and Mexicans: Symbols in Crowd Behaviour', *American Journal of Sociology*, 62, 1956, pp. 14–20.
5. Octavio Paz, *The Labyrinth of Solitude*, Harmondsworth, Penguin, 1967, pp. 5–6.
6. *Labyrinth of Solitude*, p. 8.
7. As note 6.
8. See K. L. Nelson (ed.), *The Impact of War on American Life*, New York, 1971.
9. O. E. Schoeffler and W. Gale, *Esquire's Encyclopaedia of Twentieth-Century Men's Fashion*, New York, 1973, p. 24.
10. As note 6.
11. 'Zoot-Suiters Again on the Prowl as Navy Holds Back Sailors', *Washington Post*, 9, June 1943, p. 1.
12. Quoted in S. Menefee, *Assignment USA*, New York, 1943, p. 189.
13. Details of the riots are taken from newspaper reports and press releases for the weeks in question, particularly from the *Los Angeles Times*, *New York Times*, *Washington Post*, *Washington Star* and *Time Magazine*.
14. 'Strong Measures Must be Taken Against Rioting', *Los Angeles Times*, 9 June 1943, p. 4.
15. 'Zoot-Suit Fighting Spreads On the Coast', *New York Times*, 10 June 1943, p. 23.
16. As note 15.
17. 'Zoot-Girls Use Knife in Attack', *Los Angeles Times*, 11 June 1943, p. 1.
18. Joan W. Moore, *Homeboys: Gangs, Drugs and Prison in the Barrios of Los Angeles*, Philadelphia, 1978.
19. 'Zoot Suit Warfare Spreads to Pupils of Detroit Area', *Washington Star*, 11 June 1943, p. 1.
20. Although the Detroit Race Riots of 1943 were not zoot-suit riots, nor evidently about 'youth' or 'delinquency', the social context in which they took place was obviously comparable. For a lengthy study of the Detroit riots, see R. Shogun and T. Craig, *The Detroit Race Riot: a study in violence*, Philadelphia and New York, 1964.
21. 'Zoot Suit War Inquiry Ordered by Governor', *Los Angeles Times*, 9 June 1943, p. A.
22. 'Warren Orders Zoot Suit Quiz: Quiet Reigns After Rioting', *Los Angeles Times*, 10 June 1943, p. 1.
23. As note 22.
24. 'Tenney Feels Riots Caused by Nazi Move for Disunity', *Los Angeles Times*, 9 June 1943, p. A.

25. As note 24.
26. 'Watts Pastor Blames Riots on Fifth Column', *Los Angeles Times*, 11 June 1943, p. A.
27. As note 26.
28. 'California Governor Appeals for Quelling of Zoot Suit Riots', *Washington Star*, 10 June 1943, p. A3.
29. 'Time for Sanity', *Los Angeles Times*, 11 June 1943, p. 1.
30. 'The Riots', *The Crisis*, July 1943, p. 199.
31. 'Ban on Freak Suits Studied by Councilmen', *Los Angeles Times*, 9 June 1943, p. A3.
32. As note 31.
33. *Labyrinth of Solitude*, p. 9.
34. Chester Himes, 'Zoot Riots are Race Riots', *The Crisis*, July 1943; reprinted in Himes, *Black on Black: Baby Sister and Selected Writings*, London, 1975.
35. El Teatro Campesino presented the first Chicano play to achieve full commercial Broadway production. The play, written by Luis Valdez and entitled *Zoot Suit*, was a drama documentary on the Sleepy Lagoon murder and the events leading to the Los Angeles riots. (The Sleepy Lagoon murder of August 1942 resulted in 24 *pachucos* being indicted for conspiracy to murder.)
36. Quoted in Larry Neal, 'Ellison's Zoot Suit', in J. Hersey (ed.), *Ralph Ellison: A Collection of Critical Essays*, New Jersey, 1974, p. 67.
37. From Larry Neal's poem 'Malcolm X: an Autobiography', in L. Neal, *Hoodoo Hollerin' Bebop Ghosts*, Washington DC, 1974, p. 9.

2
Second-Hand Dresses and the Role of the Ragmarket

Angela McRobbie

> Miss Brooke had that kind of beauty which seems to be thrown into relief by poor dress. Her hand and wrist were so finely formed that she could wear sleeves not less bare of style than those of which the Blessed Virgin appeared to Italian painters.
>
> *Middlemarch*, George Eliot

> She's dressed in old European clothes, scraps of brocade, out-of-date old suits, old curtains, odd oddments, old models, moth-eaten old fox furs, old otterskins, that's her kind of beauty, tattered, chill, plaintive and in exile, everything too big, and yet it looks marvellous. Her clothes are loose, she's too thin, nothing fits yet it looks marvellous. She's made in such a way, face and body, that anything that touches her shares immediately and infallibly in her beauty.
>
> *The Lover*, Marguerite Duras

Introduction

Several attempts have been made recently to understand 'retro-style'. These have all taken as their starting point that accelerating tendency in the 1980s to ransack history for key items of dress, in a seemingly eclectic and haphazard manner. Some have seen this as part of the current vogue for nostalgia while others have interpreted it as a way of bringing history into an otherwise ahistorical present. This article will suggest that second-hand style or 'vintage dress' must be seen within the broader context of post-war subcultural history. It will pay particular attention to the existence of an entrepreneurial infrastructure within these youth cultures and to the opportunities which second-hand style has offered young people, at a time of recession, for participating in the fashion 'scene'.

Most of the youth subcultures of the post-war period have relied on second-hand clothes found in jumble sales and ragmarkets as the raw material for the creation of style. Although a great deal has been written about the meaning of these styles little has been said about where they have come from. In the early 1980s the magazine *iD* developed a kind of *vox pop* of street style which involved stopping young people and asking them to itemise what they were wearing, where they had got it and for how much. Since then many of the weekly and monthly fashion publications have followed suit, with the result that this has now become a familiar feature of the magazine format. However, the act of buying and the processes of looking and choosing still remain relatively unexamined in the field of cultural analysis.

One reason for this is that shopping has been considered a feminine activity. Youth sociologists have looked mainly at the activities of adolescent boys and young men and their attention has been directed to those areas of experience which have a strongly masculine image. Leisure spheres which involve the wearing and displaying of clothes have been thoroughly documented, yet the hours spent seeking them out on Saturday afternoons continue to be overlooked. Given the emphasis on street culture or on public peer-group activities, this is perhaps not surprising, but it is worth remembering that although shopping is usually regarded as a private activity, it is also simultaneously a public one and in the case of the markets and second-hand stalls it takes place in the street. This is particularly important for girls and young women because in other contexts their street activities are still curtailed in contrast to those of their male peers. This fact has been commented upon by many feminist writers but the various pleasures of shopping have not been similarly engaged with.[1] Indeed, shopping has tended to be subsumed under the category of domestic labour with the attendant connotations of drudgery and exhaustion. Otherwise it has been absorbed into consumerism where women and girls are seen as having a particular role to play. Contemporary feminism has been slow to challenge the early 1970s orthodoxy which saw women as slaves to consumerism. Only Erica Carter's work has gone some way towards dislodging the view that to enjoy shopping is to be passively feminine and incorporated into a system of false needs.[2]

Looking back at the literature of the late 1970s on punk, it seems strange that so little attention was paid to the selling of punk, and the extent to which shops like the *Sex* shop run by Malcolm McLaren and Vivienne Westwood functioned also as meeting places where the customers and those behind the counter got to know each other and met up later in the pubs and clubs. In fact, ragmarkets and second-hand shops have played the same role up and down the country, indicating that there is more to buying and selling subcultural style than the simple exchange of cash for goods. Sociologists of the time perhaps ignored this social dimension because to them the very idea that style could be purchased over the counter went against the grain of those analyses which saw the adoption of punk style as an act of creative defiance far removed from the mundane act of buying. The role of McLaren and Westwood was also downgraded for the similar reason that punk was seen as a kind of collective creative impulse. To focus on a designer and an art-school entrepreneur would have been to undermine the 'purity' or 'authenticity' of the subculture. The same point can be made in relation to the absence of emphasis on buying subcultural products. What is found instead is an interest in those moments where the bought goods and items are transformed to subvert their original or intended meanings. In these accounts the act of buying disappears into that process of transformation. Ranked below these magnificent gestures, the more modest practices of buying and selling have remained women's work and have been of little interest to those concerned with youth cultural resistance.[3]

The literature on youth culture provides by no means the only point of entry to the question of second-hand fashion. It retains a usefulness, however, in its emphasis on the wider social and historical factors which frame youth cultural expressions and in the emphasis on the meaning and significance of the smallest and apparently most trivial of gestures and movements. Second-hand style has, in fact, a long history in British culture, but it was Peter Blake's sleeve for the Beatles' *Sgt Pepper* album which marked the entrance of anachronistic dressing into the mainstream of the pop and fashion business. In their luridly-coloured military uniforms, the Beatles were at this point poised midway between the pop establishment and hippy psychedelia. The outfits, along with John Lennon's 'granny' spectacles and the other symbols of 'flower power' depicted on the cover, comprised a challenge to the grey conformity of male dress and an impertinent appropriation of official regalia for civilian anti-authoritarian, hedonistic wear.

Military uniforms were first found alongside the overalls and great-coats in army surplus stores and on second-hand rails of shops such as 'Granny Takes a Trip', in the King's Road. Metal-rimmed glasses added a further element to that theme in the counter-culture suggesting an interest in the old, the used, the overtly cheap and apparently unstylish. Standard male glasses had been until then black and horn-rimmed. National Health Service gold-coloured rims retained the stigma of poverty and the mark of parental will imposed on unwilling children. Lennon's cheap, shoddy specs became one of his trade marks. At the same time they came to represent one of the most familiar anti-materialist strands in hippy culture. They suggested a casual disregard for obvious signs of wealth, and a disdain for 'the colour of money'.

Stuart Hall saw in this 'hippy movement' an 'identification with the poor', as well as a disavowal of conventional middle-class smartness.[4] His comment touches on issues which are still at the heart of any analysis of second-hand style because the relationship to real poverty, or to particular stylised images of poverty, remains central. At an early point in its evolution the hippy subculture denounced material wealth and sought some higher reality, expressing this choice externally through a whole variety of old and second-hand clothes. None the less, these clothes were chosen and worn as a distinctive style and this style was designed to mark out a distance both from 'straight' and conventional dress, and from the shabby greyness of genuine poverty. A similar thread runs right through the history of post-war second-hand style. This has raised questions engaged with at a journalistic level by Tom Wolfe and then more recently by Angela Carter[5] . . . Does rummaging through jumble sales make light of those who search in need and not through choice? Does the image of the middle-class girl 'slumming it' in rags and ribbons merely highlight social class differences? Wolfe poked fun at the *arriviste* young middle classes of America in the 1960s who were so well off that they could afford to look back and play around with the *idea* of looking poor. Almost twenty years later Angela Carter made the same point in relation to the 'ragamuffin look' favoured by post-punk girls, an image which held no attraction, she claimed, for working-class girls whose role-model was Princess Diana. Each of these writers see in second-hand style a kind of unconsciously patronising response to those who 'dress down' because they have to. It is an act of unintended class condescension.

While it is still the case that students and young 'bohemians' who possess what Pierre Bourdieu has called 'cultural capital' can risk looking poor and unkempt while their black and working-class counterparts dress up to counter the assumption of low status, there have been crucial social shifts which confuse this simple divide. Not all students in the 1980s are white, affluent and middle-class. Nor is it any longer possible to pose the world of street style or second-hand style against that of either high fashion or high street fashion. A whole range of factors have intervened to blur these divisions. For example, the street markets have themselves come into prominence and have been subjected to greater commercial pressure, while high street retailing has been forced to borrow from the tactics of the street trader. The sharpest illustration of these overlaps and cross-fertilisations lies, at present in the wardrobes of the so-called young professionals, male and female. Those 'new' items which now make up his or her wardrobe were almost, to the last sock or stocking, discovered, restored and worn by the young men and women who worked in, or hung around, Camden Market and a whole series of provincial ragmarkets, in the late 1970s and early 1980s.

The ladies' suit announced as the high fashion item of summer 1988, is a reworking of the early 1960s Chanel suit worn by Jackie Kennedy and others. A bouclé wool version in pink and orange can be found on the rails of Next this season, but it is not simply a 1980s revamp of the Chanel original, because it was in the late 1970s, as part of her war on conventional femininity, that Poly Styrene first wore this most unflattering of outfits, the ladies' two-piece found in the jumble sale or ragmarket in abundance for 50p. Exactly the same process can be seen at work in the recent 'respectabilisation' of the classic gents' lightweight poplin raincoat. Designed by Jasper Conran and retailing at £350 in expensive department stores, with the cuffs turned up to reveal a quality striped lining, these were first found by great numbers of second-hand shoppers on the rails at Camden or even cheaper in the charity shops. Finally, there is the so-called 'tea dress', heavily advertised in the summers of both 1987 and 1988 by Laura Ashley, Next, Miss Selfridge and Warehouse. These are new versions of the high quality 1930s and 1940s printed crêpes sought out by girls and young women for many years, for the fall of their skirts and for their particularly feminine cut.

The parasitism of the major fashion labels on the post-punk subcultures is a theme which will be returned to later in this chapter. While fashion currently trades on the nostalgia boom, it also, more specifically, reworks the already recycled goods found in the street markets. It produces new and much more expensive versions of these originals in often poor quality fabrics and attempts to sell these styles, on an unprecedented scale, to a wider section of the population than those who wander round the ragmarkets. To understand more precisely the mechanisms through which this predatory relation reproduces itself, it would be necessary to examine questions which are beyond the scope of this article. In the concluding section they will be referred to briefly. They include the dependence of the fashion industry on media 'hype' and the consequent prominence of the 'designer' fresh out of college and surviving, in fact, on the Enterprise Allowance Scheme but none the less featured regularly in *Elle*; the huge explosion of the media industries in the 1980s and their dependence on an endless flow of fashion images again on an unprecedented scale; and finally, with this, a broader process sometimes described as 'the aestheticisation of culture'. This refers to the media expansion mentioned above, and with it the renunciation by some young people of the grey repertoire of jobs offered in the traditional fields of youth opportunities, and their preference for more self-expressive 'artistic' choices . . . part time or self-employed work which offers the possibility of creativity, control, job satisfaction and perhaps even the promise of fame and fortune in the multi-media world of the image or the written word.

The role of the ragmarket

Second-hand style owes its existence to those features of consumerism which are characteristic of contemporary society. It depends, for example, on the creation of a surplus of goods whose use value is not expended when their first owners no longer want them. They are then revived, even in their senility, and enter into another cycle of consumption. House clearances also contribute to the mountain of bric-à-brac, jewellery, clothing and furniture which are the staple of junk and second-hand shops and stalls. But not all junk is used a second time around. Patterns of taste and discrimination shape the desires of second-hand shoppers as much as they do those who prefer the high street or the fashion showroom. And those who work behind the stalls and counters are skilled in choosing their stock with a fine eye for what will sell. Thus although there seems to be an evasion of the mainstream, with its mass-produced goods and marked-up prices, the 'subversive consumerism' of the ragmarket is in practice highly selective in what is offered and what, in turn, is purchased. There is in this milieu an even more refined economy of taste at work. For every single piece rescued and restored, a thousand are consigned to oblivion. Indeed, it might also be claimed that in the midst of this there is a thinly-veiled cultural élitism in operation. The sources which are raided for 'new' second-hand ideas are frequently old films, old art photographs, 'great' novels, documentary footage and textual material. The apparent democracy of the market, from which nobody is excluded on the grounds of cost, is tempered by the very precise tastes and desires of the second-hand searchers. Second-hand style continually emphasizes its distance from second-hand clothing.

The London markets and those in other towns and cities up and down the country cater now for a much wider cross-section of the population. It is no longer a question of the *jeunesse dorée* rubbing shoulders with the poor and the down-and-outs.[6] Unemployment has played a role in diversifying this clientele, so also have a number of other less immediately visible shifts and changes. Young single mothers, for example, who fall between the teen dreams of punk fashion and the reality of pushing a buggy through town on a wet afternoon, fit exactly with this new constituency.[7] Markets have indeed become more socially diverse sites in the urban landscape. The Brick Lane area in London, for example, home to part of the Bangladeshi population settled in this country, attracts on a Sunday morning, young and old, black and white, middle-class and working-class shoppers as well as tourists and the merely curious browsers. It's not surprising that tourists include a market such as Brick Lane in their itinerary. In popular currency, street markets are taken to be reflective of the old and unspoilt, they are 'steeped in history' and are thus particularly expressive of the town or region.

The popularity of these urban markets also resides in their celebration of what seem to be pre-modern modes of exchange. They offer an oasis of cheapness, where every market day is a 'sale'. They point back in time to an economy unaffected by cheque cards, credit cards and even set prices. Despite the lingering connotations of wartime austerity, the market today promotes itself in the language of natural freshness (for food and dairy produce) or else in the language of curiosity, discovery and heritage (for clothes, trinkets and household goods). There is, of course, a great deal of variety in the types of market found in different parts of the country. In London there is a distinction between those markets modelled on the genuine fleamarkets, which tend to attract the kind of young crowd who flock each weekend to Camden Lock, and those which are more integrated into a neighbourhood providing it with fruit, vegetables and household items. The history of these more traditional street markets is already well documented. They grew up within the confines of a rapidly expanding urban economy and played a vital role in dressing (in mostly second-hand clothes), and feeding the urban working classes, who did not have access to the department stores, grocers or other retail outlets which catered for the upper and middle classes. As Phil Cohen has shown, such markets came under the continual surveillance of the urban administrators and authorities who were concerned with 'policing the working class city'.[8] The streetmarkets were perceived by them as interrupting not only the flow of traffic and therefore the speed of urban development, but also as hindering the growth of those sorts of shops which would bring in valuable revenue from rates. These were seen as dangerous places, bringing together unruly elements who were already predisposed towards crime and delinquency; a predominantly youthful population of costermongers had to be brought into line with the labour discipline which already existed on the factory floor.

The street market functioned, therefore, as much as a daytime social meeting place as it did a place for transactions of money and goods. It lacked the impersonality of the department stores and thrived instead on the values of familiarity, community and personal exchange. This remains the case today. Wherever immigrant groups have arrived and set about trying to earn a living in a largely hostile environment a local service economy in the form of a market has grown up. These offer some opportunities for those excluded from employment, and they also offer some escape from the monotony of the factory floor. A drift, in the 1970s and 1980s, into the micro-economy of the street market is one sign of the dwindling opportunities in the world of real work. There are now more of these stalls carrying a wider range of goods than before in most of the market places in the urban centres. There has also been a diversification into the world of new technology, with stalls offering cut-price digital alarms, watches, personal hi-fis, videotapes, cassettes, 'ghetto-blasters' and cameras. The hidden economy of work is also supplemented here by the provision of goods obtained illegally and sold rapidly at rock-bottom prices.

This general expansion coincides, however, with changing patterns in urban consumerism and with attempts on the part of mainstream retailers to participate in an unexpected boom. In the inner cities the bustling markets frequently breathe life and colour into otherwise desolate blighted areas. This, in turn, produces an incentive for the chain stores to reinvest, and in places such as Dalston Junction in Hackney, and Chapel Market in Islington, the redevelopment of shopping has taken place along these lines, with Sainsbury's, Boots the Chemist and others, updating and expanding their services. The stores flank the markets, which in turn line the pavements, and the consumer is drawn into both kinds of shopping simultaneously. In the last few years many major department stores have redesigned the way in which their stock is displayed in order to create the feel of a market place. In the 'Top Shop' basement in Oxford Street, for example, there is a year-round sale. The clothes are set out in chaotic abundance. The rails are crushed up against each other and packed with stock, which causes the customers to push and shove their way through. This intentionally hectic atmosphere is heightened by the disc jockey who cajoles the shoppers between records to buy at an even more frenzied pace.

Otherwise, in those regions where the mainstream department stores are still safely located on the other side of town, the traditional street market continues to seduce its customers with its own unique atmosphere. Many of these nowadays carry only a small stock of second-hand clothes. Instead, there are rails of 'seconds' or cheap copies of high street fashions made from starched fabric which, after a couple of washes, are ready for the dustbin. Bales of sari material lie stretched out on counters next to those displaying make-up and shampoo for black women. Reggae and funk music blare across the heads of shoppers from the record stands, and hot food smells drift far up the road. In the Ridley Road market in Hackney the hot bagel shop remains as much a sign of the originally Jewish population as the eel pie stall reflects traditional working-class taste. Unfamiliar fruits create an image of colour and profusion on stalls sagging under their weight. By midday on Fridays and at weekends the atmosphere is almost festive. Markets like these retain something of the pre-industrial gathering. For the crowd of shoppers and strollers the tempo symbolises time rescued from that of labour, and the market seems to celebrate its own pleasures. Differences of age, sex, class and ethnic background take on a more positive quality of social diversity. The mode of buying is leisurely and unharassed, in sharp contrast to the Friday afternoon tensions around the checkout till in the supermarket.

Similar features can be seen at play in markets such as Camden Lock on Saturday and Sunday afternoons. Thousands of young people block Camden's streets so that only a trickle of traffic can get through. The same groups and the streams of punk tourists can be seen each week, joined by older shoppers and those who feel like a stroll in the sun, ending with an ice cream further along Chalk Farm road. Young people go there to see and be seen if for any other reason than that fashion and style invariably look better worn than they do on the rails or in the shop windows. Here it is possible to see how items are combined with each other to create a total look. Hairstyles, shoes, skirts and 'hold-up' stockings; all of these can be taken in at a glance. In this context shopping is like being on holiday. The whole point is to amble and look, to pick up goods and examine them before

Street selling. *Photo: Celia Hall*

putting them back. Public-school girls mingle with doped-out punks, ex-hippies hang about behind their Persian rug stalls as though they have been there since 1967, while more youthful entrepreneurs trip over themselves to make a quick sale.

Subcultural entrepreneurs

The entrepreneurial element, crucial to an understanding of street markets and second-hand shops, has been quite missing from most subcultural analysis. The vitality of street markets today owes much to the hippy counter-culture of the late 1960s. It was this which put fleamarkets firmly back on the map. Many of those which had remained dormant for years in London, Amsterdam or Berlin, were suddenly given a new lease of life. In the years following the end of World War Two the thriving black markets gradually gave way to the fleamarkets which soon signalled only the bleakness of goods discarded. For the generation whose memories had not been blunted altogether by the dizzy rise of post-war consumerism, markets for old clothes and jumble sales in the 1960s remained a terrifying reminder of the stigma of poverty, the shame of ill-fitting clothing, and the fear of disease through infestation, rather like buying a second-hand bed.

Hippy preferences for old fur coats, crêpe dresses and army great-coats, shocked the older generation for precisely this reason. But they were not acquired merely for their shock value. Those items favoured by the hippies reflected an interest in pure, natural and authentic fabrics and a repudiation of the man-made synthetic materials found in high street fashion. The pieces of clothing sought out by hippy girls tended to be antique lace petticoats, pure silk blouses, crêpe dresses, velvet skirts and pure wool 1940's-styled coats. In each case these conjured up a time when the old craft values still prevailed and when one person saw through his or her production from start to finish. In fact, the same items had also won the attention of the hippies' predecessors, in the 'beat culture' of the early 1950s. They too looked for ways of by-passing the world of ready-made clothing. In the rummage sales of New York, for example, 'beat' girls and women bought up the fur coats, satin dresses and silk blouses of the 1930s and 1940s middle classes. Worn in the mid-1950s, these issued a strong sexual challenge to the spick and span gingham-clad domesticity of the moment.

By the late 1960s, the hippy culture was a lot larger and much better off than the beats who had gone before them. It was also politically informed in the sense of being determined to create an alternative society. This subculture was therefore able to develop an extensive semi-entrepreneurial network which came to

Traditional hippy items on sale in Camden

be known as the counter-culture. This was by no means a monolithic enterprise. It stretched in Britain from hippy businesses such as Richard Branson's Virgin Records and Harvey Goldsmith's Promotions to all the ventures which sprang up in most cities and towns, selling books, vegetarian food, incense, Indian smocks, sandals and so on. It even included the small art galleries, independent cinemas and the London listings magazine *Time Out*.

From the late 1960s onwards, and accompanying this explosion of 'alternative' shops and restaurants, were the small second-hand shops whose history is less familiar. These had names like 'Serendipity', 'Cobwebs' or 'Past Caring' and they brought together, under one roof, all those items which had to be discovered separately in the jumble sales or fleamarkets. These included flying jackets, safari jackets, velvet curtains (from which were made the first 'loon' pants) and 1920s flapper dresses. These second-hand goods provided students and others drawn to the subculture, with a cheaper and much more expansive wardrobe. (The two looks for girls which came to characterise this moment were the peasant 'ethnic' look and the 'crêpey' bohemian Bloomsbury look. The former later became inextricably linked with Laura Ashley and the latter with Biba, both mainstream fashion newcomers.) Gradually hippie couples moved into this second-hand market, just as they also moved into antiques. They rapidly picked up the skills of mending and restoring items and soon learnt where the best sources for their stock were to be found. This meant scouring the country for out-of-town markets, making trips to Amsterdam to pick up the long leather coats favoured by rich hippy types, and making thrice-weekly trips to the dry cleaners. The result was loyal customers, and if the young entrepreneurs were able to anticipate new demands from an even younger clientele, there were subsequent generations of punks, art students and others.

The presence of this entrepreneurial dynamic has rarely been acknowledged in most subcultural analysis. Those points at which subcultures offered the prospect of a career through the magical exchange of the commodity have warranted as little attention as the network of small-scale entrepreneurial activities which financed the counter-culture. This was an element, of course, vociferously disavowed within the hippy culture itself. Great efforts were made to disguise the role which money played in a whole number of exchanges, including those involving drugs. Selling goods and commodities came too close to 'selling out' for those at the heart of the subculture to feel comfortable about it. This was a stance reinforced by the sociologists who also saw consumerism within the counter-culture as a fall from grace, a lack of purity. They either ignored it, or else, employing the Marcusian notion of recuperation, attributed it to the intervention of external market forces.[9] It was the unwelcome presence of media and other commercial interests which, they claimed, laundered out the politics and reduced the alternative society to an endless rail of cheesecloth shirts.

There was some dissatisfaction, however, with this dualistic model of creative action followed by commercial reaction. Dick Hebdige[10] and others have drawn attention to the problems of positing a raw and undiluted (and usually working-class) energy, in opposition to the predatory youth industries. Such an argument discounted the local, promotional activities needed to produce a subculture in the first place. Clothes have to be purchased, bands have to find places to play, posters publicising these concerts have to be put up . . . and so on. This all entails business and managerial skills even when these are displayed in a self-effacing manner. The fact that a spontaneous sexual division of labour seems to spring into being is only a reflection of those gender inequalities which are prevalent at a more general level in society. It is still much easier for girls to develop skills in those fields which are less contested by men than it is in those already occupied by them. Selling clothes, stage-managing at concerts, handing out publicity leaflets, or simply looking the part, are spheres in which a female presence somehow seems natural.[11]

While hippy style had run out of steam by the mid-1970s the alternative society merely jolted itself and rose to the challenge of punk. Many of those involved in selling records, clothes and even books, cropped their hair, had their ears pierced and took to wearing tight black trousers and Doctor Martens boots. However, the conditions into which punk erupted and of which it was symptomatic for its younger participants were quite different from those which had cushioned the hippy explosion of the 1960s. Girls were certainly more visible and more vocal than they had been in the earlier subculture, although it is difficult to assess exactly how active they were in the do-it-yourself entrepreneurial practices which accompanied, and were part of, the punk phenomenon. Certainly the small independent record companies remained largely male, as did the journalists and even the musicians (though much was made of the angry femininity of Poly Styrene, The Slits, The Raincoats and others). What is less ambiguous is the connection with youth unemployment, and more concretely, within punk, with the disavowal of some of the employment which was on offer for those who were not destined for university, the professions or the conventional career structures of the middle classes.

Punk was, first and foremost, cultural. Its self-expressions existed at the level of music, graphic design, visual images, style and the written word. It was therefore engaging with and making itself heard within the terrain of the arts and the mass media. Its point of entry into this field existed within the range of small-scale youth industries which were able to put the whole thing in motion. Fan magazines (fanzines) provided a training for new wave journalists, just as designing record sleeves for unknown punk bands offered an opportunity for keen young graphic designers. In the realm of style the same do-it-yourself ethic prevailed and the obvious place to start was the jumble sale or the local fleamarket. Although punk also marked a point at which boys and young men began to participate in fashion unashamedly, girls played a central role, not just in looking for the right clothes but also in providing their peers with a cheap and easily available supply of second-hand items. These included 1960s' cotton print 'shifts' like those worn by the girls in The Human League in the early 1980s (and in the summer of 1988 'high fashion' as defined by MaxMara and others), suedette sheepskin-styled jackets like that worn by Bob Dylan on his debut album sleeve, (marking a moment in the early 1960s when he too aspired to a kind of 'lonesome traveller' hobo look), and many other similarly significant pieces.

This provision of services in the form of dress and clothing for would-be punks, art students and others on the fringe, was mostly participated in by lower middle-class art and fashion graduates who rejected the job opportunities available to them designing for British Home Stores or Marks and Spencer. It was a myth then, and it is still a myth now, that fashion houses are waiting to snap up the talent which emerges from the end-of-term shows each year. Apart from going abroad, most fashion students are, and were in the mid-1970s, faced with either going it alone with the help of the Enterprise Allowance Schemes (EAS), or else with joining some major manufacturing company specialising in downmarket mass-produced fashion. It is no surprise, then, that many, particularly those who wanted to retain some artistic autonomy, should choose the former. Setting up a stall and getting a licence to sell second-hand clothes, finding them and restoring them, and then using a stall as a base for displaying and selling newly-designed work, is by no means unusual. Many graduates have done this and some, like Darlajane Gilroy and Pam Hogg, have gone on to become well-known names through their appearance in the style glossies like *The Face*, *Blitz* and *iD*, where the emphasis is on creativity and on fashion-as-art.

Many others continue to work the markets for years, often in couples and sometimes moving into bigger stalls or permanent premises. Some give up, re-train or look round for other creative outlets in the media. The expansion of media goods and services which has come into being in the last ten years, producing more fashion magazines, more television from independent production companies, more reviews about other media events, more media personalities, more media items about other media phenomena, and so on, depends both on the successful and sustained manifestation of 'hype' and also on the labour power of young graduates and school leavers for whom the allure of London and metropolitan life is irresistible. For every aspiring young journalist or designer there are many thousands, however, for whom the media remains tangible only at the point of consumption. Despite the lingering do-it-yourself ethos of punk, and despite 'enterprise culture' in the 1980s, this bohemian world is as distant a phenomenon for many media-struck school-leavers as it has always been for their parents. 'Enterprise subcultures' remain small and relatively privileged metropolitan spaces.

Baby dresses and girls in men's suits

Nonetheless, the 'implosionary' effect of the mass media means that in the 1980s youth styles and fashions are born into the media. There is an 'instantaneity' which replaces the old period of subcultural incubation. The relentless forces of consumerism now operate at the style-face with teams of stylists being sent out by the magazines each month to scour the market places and end-of-term fashion shows for commercial ideas. Students who start off working on the stalls move, often to their own labels, within a year of leaving college, with the help of the EAS and a bank loan. They provide magazines and journalists with strong images and lively copy and the whole system reproduces itself at an increasingly frenzied speed. Thanks to the vitality of the style glossies, the fashion business becomes more confident about and more conversant with fashion language. As more column inches are given over to fashion in the daily and weekly quality newspapers (adding a dash of colour to the black and white format and catering for the 'new' women readers at the same time) fashion learns to talk about itself with a new fluency, it can even mock itself.[12]

Mainstream fashion has a lot to thank youth subcultures for. It can gesture back in time knowing that its readers have been well educated, through the media, in post-war pop culture history. Often it is enough just to signal Brian Jones's hairstyle, or Jimi

Hendrix's hat and scarf, or Cathy McGowan's floppy fringe, as though they have already been immortalised as Andy Warhol prints. They remain recognisable as traces, signs or even as fragments of signs. This instant recall on history, fuelled by the superfluity of images thrown up by the media, has produced in style a non-stop fashion parade in which 'different decades are placed together with no historical continuity'.[13] Punk do-it-yourself fashion has transformed fashion into pop art, and collecting period fashion pieces into a serious hobby.

From the mid-1970s punk girls salvaged shockingly lurid lurex minis of the sort worn in Italian 'jet-set' films of the mid-1960s. They reinstated the skinny-rib jumper and plastic earrings (worn by Pauline of Penetration and Fay Fife of The Rezillos) as well as any number of 'shift' dresses into the fashion mainstream. They also reclaimed tarty fishnet stockings, black plastic mini skirts and, of course, ski pants. When Debbie Harry first appeared in this country she was dressed in classic New York hooker style with white, knee-length, 'these boots are made for walkin' boots, micro skirt and tight black jumper. Television shows, even puppet TV shows, as well as 1960s movies such as *Blow Up* and, of course, all the old James Bond films, were continually raided by the 'new' stylists in search of ideas. Paul Weller, for example, joined this rush in the early 1980s and uncovered old pieces of 1960s 'Mod' clothing which were then installed as part of the 1980s 'soulboy' wardrobe . . . Jon Savage has described this plundering of recent style history displayed each week at Camden Lock as follows: 'Fashion, cars, buildings from the last hundred years piled up in an extraordinary display . . . a jungle where anything could be so worn, driven, even eaten as long as it was old.'[14] Savage reinforces Frederic Jameson's gloomy prognosis of the post-modern condition in this 'mass flight into nostalgia'.[15] Loss of faith in the future has produced a culture which can only look backwards and re-examine key moments of its own recent history with a sentimental gloss and a soft focus lens. Society is now incapable of producing serious images, or texts which give people meaning and direction. The gap opened up by this absence is filled instead with cultural bric-à-brac and with old images recycled and reintroduced into circulation as pastiche.

It is easy to see how this argument can be extended to include

Street selling.   *Photo: Celia Hall*

second-hand style, which in the early and mid-1980s did indeed appear to the observer like a bizarre pantomime parade where themes and strands from recognisable historical moments seemed to be combined at random. Against Savage and Jameson however, it might be argued that these styles are neither nostalgic in essence nor without depth. Nostalgia indicates a desire to recreate the past faithfully, and to wallow in such mythical representations. Nostalgia also suggests an attempt at period accuracy, as in a costume drama.

While both of these are true, for example, of Laura Ashley fashions, they are certainly not apparent in contemporary second-hand style. This style is marked out rather by a knowingness, a wilful anarchy and an irrepressible optimism, as indicated by colour, exaggeration, humour and disavowal of the conventions of adult dress.

The best known examples of this are the two girl groups, Bananarama and Amazulu, and the pop presenter Paula Yates. The wardrobes of Yates and the others are still drawn in spirit, if not in practice, from the jumble sale or the second-hand market. Paula Yates's 'silly' dresses and gigantic hair bows are like outfits salvaged from a late 1950s children's birthday party. The huge baggy trousers worn by Bananarama, tied round the waist 'like a sack of potatoes', their black plimsolls and haystack hairstyles caught up with straggly cotton headscarves are equally evocative of an urchin childhood or a 'Grapes of Wrath' adolescence. It is as though the Bananarama girls tumbled out of bed and put on whatever came to hand without their mothers knowing. Amazulu's gypsy dresses worn with cascades of hair ribbons and Doctor Martens boots creates a similar effect. Again and again they gesture back to a childhood rummage through a theatrical wardrobe and the sublime pleasure of 'dressing up'. There is a refusal of adult seriousness and an insistence on hedonism and hyperbole. The 1950s ball-gown glamour sought out by Paula Yates is undercut by the sheer excessiveness of it. Paula Yates's wardrobe exists within the realms of high camp. Her style of presentation and style of dress create an image of pure pastiche.

However this pastiche is celebratory rather than reflective of a sterile and depthless mainstream culture. It plays with the norms, conventions and expectations of femininity, post feminism. Each item is worn self-consciously with an emphasis on the un-natural and the artificial. Madonna remains the other best-known examplar of this rags, ribbons and lace style. She wore her mid-1980s image like a mask and with what Kaja Silverman has described as a sense of 'ironic distance'.[16]

The other most influential image in the fashion horizons of the 1980s which also drew on second-hand style flirted with the idea of androgyny. Punk androgyny was never unambiguously butch or aggressive, it was slim, slight and invariably 'arty'. The Robert Mapplethorpe cover of Patti Smith's first album made a strong impression on those who were less keen on studs, chains and bondage trousers. Smith appeared casual, unmade-up with a jacket slung over her shoulders and a tie loosened at her neck. The cuffs of her shirt were visibly frayed and she faced the camera direct with a cool, scrutinizing gaze. This cautious but somehow threatening androgyny had a much greater resonance than, for example, Diane Keaton's very feminine take-up of the male wardrobe in the Woody Allen film *Annie Hall*. She too ransacked the traditional gents' wardrobe but her image was New York 'kooky' and eccentric (ex-hippy), and not even vaguely menacing. Smith was unmistakably from the New York underground. She was pale-faced, dark, undernourished, intense and 'committed'.

Patti Smith sent bohemian girls off in search of these wide, baggy and unflattering clothes, while *Annie Hall* alerted others to the feminine potential of the male wardrobe. She made the do-it-yourself look attractive to those less familiar with the ragmarket, and balanced her shirts and ties with a soft, floppy, feminine hat. Suddenly all those male items which had lain untouched for years in second-hand shops, charity shops and street markets came to life. Nothing was left untouched including cotton pyjama tops, shirts, jackets, evening suits and tuxedos, overcoats, raincoats, trousers and even the occasional pair of shiny black patent evening shoes, small enough to fit female feet. Men's jackets replaced early 1970s figure-hugging jackets with an inverted pyramidic line. The exaggerated shoulders narrowed slowly down to below the hips creating a strong but none the less slimming effect. This was immediately taken up by fashion writers as 'liberating'. It covered all 'irregularities' in size, imposing instead a homogenously baggy look. It was a style open to all, not just the size 10s and 12s. As a result these jackets began to appear 'new', in chain stores and exclusive boutiques up and down the country. They were soon being worn by high-flying businesswomen as well as by secretaries, professionals and others. These 'new' jackets imitated what had been a necessary alteration on those bought second-hand. Instead of shortening male-length sleeves, these had simply been turned up revealing the high quality, soft, striped silk lining. Again, the effect of this was to lighten an otherwise dark and fairly heavy image. The same feature appeared in the second-hand winter coats found in 'Flip' and in markets like that at Camden Lock. The huge surplus of tweed overcoats kept prices low and the range of choice extensive. These too were adapted for female use by turning up the sleeves, as were their summer equivalents, the lightweight cotton raincoats of which there was, and still is, a vast discarded 'mountain'. This effect was soon copied in new overcoats for both men and women. It can be seen in outlets as exclusive as Joseph's and Paul Smith's and also in Warehouse and Miss Selfridge. However, the cost of such garments in fabric comparable to that found in their second-hand equivalents makes them prohibitively expensive. This in itself forces a much wider range of shoppers, including the so-called young professionals, back towards Flip and Camden Lock.

These items of male clothing never conferred on girls and women a true androgyny. There was instead a more subtle aesthetic at work. The huge, sweeping greatcoats imposed a masculine frame on what was still an unmistakably feminine form. All sorts of softening devices were added to achieve this effect – diamante brooches, lop-sided berets, provocatively red lipstick, and so on. A similar process took place round the appropriation of the male shirt. It too seemed baggy and egalitarian and thus in keeping with 1970s feminist critiques of fashion. But these shirts were tightly tucked into a thick waistband which just as surely emphasised the traditional hour-glass figure. Men's shirts ushered in the new shape for female clothing. Their sleeve line fell far below the shoulder on women, often connecting with the body of the garment half-way down the arm. This produced a 'batwing' effect which in turn was taken up by manufacturers and marketed as such. The inverted pyramid shape here took the form of an elongated arm and shoulder line narrowing down at each side to a small and feminine waist.

Alongside these, other 'stolen' items began to appear in the high street. Tuxedos (favoured by Princess Diana), bow ties, silk evening shirts, and for everyday wear, flat, black patent, lace-up shoes. For two consecutive winters these were as ubiquitous as leggings were in the summer. And in both cases the point of origin was the man's wardrobe. Indeed, leggings offer a good example. These first appeared alongside the gent's vests, in a cream-coloured knitted cotton fabric, as winter underpants, again in places like Camden Market. They had an elasticated waistband and button opening at the front. Punk girls began to buy them as summer alternatives to their winter ski pants. Dyed black, they created a similar effect. Then, the stall-holders dyed them and sold them in a dark, murky, grey-black shade. But they still suffered from the design faults which arise from adapting male lower garments for women. They were cut too low at the waist and frequently slid down. The fly front cluttered the smooth line across the stomach and they were often too short at the crotch. It was not long, therefore, before the same stall-holders were making up their own models in the professionally-dyed brushed cotton fabric popularised through consumer demand for track suits and sweatshirts. By the summers of 1985 and 1986 these were being worn by what seemed to be the entire female population aged under thirty. They were combined with wide, baggy male-shaped shirts, headscarves knotted on top 1940s munitions-worker style, children's black plimsolls (or else smart walking shoes) and lightweight cotton jackets.

The popularity of the male wardrobe therefore reflects a similar confusion of meanings as those thrown up by second-hand 'baby' dressing. In this apparently androgynous context these meanings highlight an appreciation of high-quality fabrics of the sort rarely found in mass-produced goods, a desire also to reinstate them to their former glory, and even a desire to wear something 'socially useful'. By recycling discarded pieces of clothing new wearers are not only beating the system by finding and defining high fashion cheaply, they are also making good use of the social surplus. An ecological ideal thus resides alongside the desire for artifice, decoration and ambiguous, double-edged femininity.

The death of the designer

Writing in the early 1970s Tom Wolfe offered one of the few fragments on the subject of second-hand dress when he labelled this style, along with that ethnic look made fashionable for whites by the Black Panthers, 'radical chic'. This meant dressing down, looking righteous and wearing 'jeans of the people . . . hod carrier jeans . . . and woolly green socks, that kind you get at the Army surplus at two pair for twenty nine cents'.[17] For those seeking to achieve the white equivalent of Afro-style this meant going natural:

'God knows Panther women don't spend thirty minutes in front of the mirror shoring up their eye holes with contact lenses, eyeliner, eye shadow, eyebrow pencil. . . .'[18]

Wolfe went on to suggest that on a grander scale *'nostalgie de la boue'* marked the arrival of a thrusting new middle class sufficiently confident culturally and socially to outrage their stuffier class equals by asserting in an upfront way where they have come from, through dressing in the 'styles of the lower orders'. These 'Peter, Paul and Mary' hippy types and with their apparently unwashed appearance and preference for old, discarded clothes brought out, on the part of the urbane Wolfe, a tone of slight disdain: 'She didn't wear nylons, she didn't wear make up, she had bangs and long straight hair down below her shoulders . . .'[19] The point which Wolfe made is one commonly enough asserted, that this 'poverty dressing' is both insulting to 'the people' and ill judged: '. . . today the oppressed, the hard core youth of the ghetto, they aren't into . . . Army surplus socks. If you tried to put one of those lumpy lumberjack shirts on them, they'd vomit.'[20]

In a much more recent piece in *New Society*, Angela Carter makes the same point.[21] The focus here is on an image widely displayed in the city centre hoardings and in the London Underground in 1983 to advertise the magazine *19*. The model is dressed in an assortment of wide, baggy clothes, in this case new but drawn in spirit from the ragmarket: 'But if you didn't know she was a fashion model, the girl in the poster . . . would in fact look like nothing so much as a paper bag lady (or rather person), in her asexually shaped jacket, loose trousers, sagging socks, with a scarf of dubious soiled colour wrapped round her head like a bandage, beneath a hat jammed firm down. . . .'[22] Carter sees this as a style favoured, once again, by the rich who can afford to play at looking poor: '. . . it is ironic that rich girls (such as students) swan about in rancid long johns with ribbons in their hair, when the greatest influence on working class girls would appear to be Princess Di. . . .'[23] Both Angela Carter and Tom Wolfe recognise that for working-class people the structure of the working day, the tyranny of the clock, and the monotony of work, with its uniforms, overalls and aprons, conspire to produce in leisure an overwhelming desire to mark out distance from the factory floor. In contrast, the middle classes, who can achieve individuality in dress on a day-to-day basis, have no need for a 'Sunday best'. Likewise, because they have to dress up during the working day for their professional roles, they are able to dress down in leisure and to 'slop about' as students.

The problem is that this is now being changed by forces beyond the control of either of the two groups. In the 1980s, for old and young alike, the discipline of the factory clock no longer prevails. The unemployed and semi-employed have been cast adrift, and for many young men and women their attention has turned inwards towards the body. Wild peacock punk dressing of the type seen on the streets in the early 1980s signified this body politics, this making strange through an excessive masquerade, a 'quotidien marvellous'.[24]

There have been changes on both sides of the class divide. Students are not, as Angela Carter suggests, 'rich girls'. Many are barely scraping along on their grants with no parental back-up. This is even more true for the ranks of the student body who would once have proceeded into training or an apprenticeship but are now finding their way into further and higher education. This too marks the increasing fluidity across the old class lines which previously distinguished working-class from middle-class youth. Of course, it does not mean that all young people now dress in what Carter labelled 'recession style'. There are as many girls who still aspire to the Princess Di look as there are boys who model themselves on the 'casual' elegance of Italian style. It does mean however that there is a much wider constituency for ragmarket shopping than was once the case.

This fluidity is reflected across all the other social sites and fashion spheres engaged with here. The high street emulates the style of the market-place and takes up the ideas of those who produce for the markets. At the same time, for the do-it-yourself 'designers' and stall-holders the lure of the mainstream is not altogether unattractive. Many sell simultaneously to the department stores and to the passing crowds at Camden or Kensington Market. Self-employment of this sort is both an attempt to participate in an economy unwilling to open itself up to school leavers and graduates alike and an act of evasion, an evasion of those sorts of dull jobs which are promised at the end of a work experience programme.

All of the styles described above have been seen as part of the contemporary interest in 'retro'. They have therefore been linked with other visual images which draw on and 'quote' from past sources or earlier genres. These are now most prominent in the world of advertising and in pop videos where some nebulous but nonetheless popular memory is evoked in the swirl of a petticoat or the sweep of a duster coat. It is unwise however to place second-hand style unproblematically within that cultural terrain marked out by Frederic Jameson as the sphere of post modernity. This would be to conflate retro-dressing as merely yet another cultural re-run, no different from the nostalgic re-makes of 1940s 'B' movies, or the endless re-releases and revivals of old hit records.

These trends, including that of second-hand dress, require much more specific analysis. While pastiche and some kind of fleeting nostalgia might indeed play a role in second-hand style, these have to be seen more precisely within the evolution of post-war youth cultures. Second-hand style in this context reveals a more complex structure offering, among other things a kind of internal, unofficial job market within these 'enterprise subcultures'. Girls and young women have played a major role, not just in providing youth subcultures with their items of style and dress, but also in re-discovering these items and imaginatively re-creating them. Despite being at the vanguard of style in this respect, these young women have been passed over and eclipsed in the fashion pages by the young 'geniuses' of fashion in the 1980s like John Galliano or John Flett. In fact fashion designers play a much less central role in setting fashion trends than is commonly imagined. There is even a case to be made for the 'death of the designer', since the main impetus for changes in fashion and in contemporary consumer culture, as this article has argued, comes from below, from those who keep an eye open for redeemable pieces which are then re-inscribed into the fashion system.

Notes and References

1. P. Cohen, 'Policing the Working Class City' in B. Fine *et al.*, *Capitalism and the Rule of Law*, London, Hutchinson, 1979.
2. E. Carter, 'Alice in Consumer Wonderland' in A. McRobbie and M. Nava (eds), *Gender and Generation*, London, Macmillan, 1979.
3. S. Hall *et al.*, *Resistance Through Rituals*, London, Hutchinson,

1977 and D. Hebdige, *Subculture: The Meaning of Style*, London, Methuen, 1979.
4. S. Hall, 'The Hippies: An American Moment', CCCS Stencilled Papers, University of Birmingham, 1977.
5. T. Wolfe, *Radical Chic and Man Maning the Flak Catchers*, New York, Bantam Books, 1974, and A. Carter, 'The Recession Style', *New Society*, January, 1983.
6. Paddy's Market in Glasgow, in the early 1970s, offered one of the best examples of absolute social polarity in second-hand shopping.
7. The Birmingham Ragmarket in the late 1970s provided many similar examples of social diversity in second-hand shopping.
8. P. Cohen (1979).
9. J. Clarke, 'Style' in S. Hall (ed.) *et al.*, *Resistance Through Rituals*, London, Hutchinson, 1977.
10. D. Hebdige (1979) and A. McRobbie, 'Settling the Accounts with Subcultures: A Feminist Critique' in *Screen Education* no. 34, reprinted in T. Bennett (ed.), *Culture, Ideology and Social Process*, London, Academia Press, 1981.
11. A. McRobbie and J. Garber, 'Girls and Subcultures: An Exploration' in S. Hall *et al.*, *Resistance Through Rituals*, London, Hutchinson, 1977.
12. Sally Ann Lasson reviewed Nicholas Coleridge's *The Fashion Conspiracy* by poking fun at her own profession which specialises in lines like 'Paris was awash with frothy femininity', *Observer*, 20 March 1988.
13. J. Savage, 'Living In The Past', *Time Out*, February 1983.
14. J. Savage (1983).
15. F. Jameson, 'Postmodernism, the Cultural Logic of Capital' in H. Foster (ed.) *Postmodern Culture*, London, Pluto Press, 1985.
16. K. Silverman, 'Fragments of a Fashionable Discourse', in T. Modeleski *Studies in Entertainment: Critical Approaches to Mass Culture*, Bloomington and Indianapolis, Indiana University Press, 1986.
17. T. Wolfe (1974).
18. Ibid.
19. Ibid.
20. Ibid.
21. A. Carter (1983).
22. Ibid.
23. Ibid.
24. A. Breton, *What is Surrealism?*, London, Pluto Press, 1981.

3

Monster Metaphors: Notes on Michael Jackson's 'Thriller'*

Kobena Mercer

Michael Jackson, Megastar. His LP, *Thriller*, made in 1982, has sold over 35 million copies worldwide and is said to be the biggest selling LP in the history of pop. Jackson is reputed to have amassed a personal fortune of some 75 million dollars at the age of 26. Even more remarkably, he's been a star since he was 11 and sang lead with his brothers in the Jackson Five, the biggest selling group on the Tamla Motown label in the 1970s. The Jackson Five practically invented the genre of 'teeny-bopper' pop cashed in upon by white pop idols like Donny Osmond. While such figures have faded from memory, classic Jackson Five tunes like 'I Want You Back' and 'ABC' can still evoke the pride and enthusiasm which marked the assertive mood of the 'Black Pride' cultural movement.

After he and his brothers left Motown in the mid-1970s and took more artistic control over their own productions, Jackson developed as a singer, writer and stage performer. His *Off The Wall* LP of 1979, which established him as a solo star, demonstrates the lithe, sensual texture of his voice and its mastery over a diverse range of musical styles and idioms, from romantic ballad to rock. Just what is it that makes this young, black man so different, so appealing?

Undoubtedly, it is the voice which lies at the heart of his appeal. Rooted in the Afro-American tradition of 'soul', Jackson's vocal performance is characterised by breathy gasps, squeaks, sensual sighs and other wordless sounds which have become his stylistic signature. The way in which this style punctuates the emotional

---

* Originally published in *Screen*, Vol. 27, No. 1, 1986.

resonance and bodily sensuality of the music corresponds to what Roland Barthes called the 'grain' of the voice – 'the grain is the body in the voice as it sings'.[1] The emotional and erotic expressiveness of the voice is complemented by the sensual grace and sheer excitement of Jackson's dancing style: even as a child, his stage performance provoked comparisons with James Brown and Jackie Wilson.

But there is another element to Jackson's success and popularity – his image. Jackson's individual style fascinates and attracts attention. The ankle-cut jeans, the single-gloved hand and, above all, the wet-look hairstyle which have become his trademarks, have influenced the sartorial repertoires of black and white youth cultures and been incorporated into mainstream fashion.

Most striking is the change in Jackson's looks and physical appearance as he has grown. The cute child dressed in gaudy flower-power gear and sporting a huge 'Afro' hairstyle has become, as a young adult, a paragon of racial and sexual ambiguity. Michael reclines across the gatefold sleeve of the *Thriller* LP, dressed in crisp black and white on a glossy metallic surface against a demure pink background. Look closer – the glossy sheen of his complexion appears lighter in colour than before; the nose seems sharper, more aqualine, less rounded and 'African' and the lips seem tighter, less pronounced. Above all, the large 'Afro' has dissolved into a shock of wet-look permed curls and a new stylistic trademark, the single lock over the forehead, appears.

What makes this reconstruction of Jackson's image more intriguing is the mythology built up around it, in which it is impossible or simply beside the point to distinguish truth from falsehood. It is said that he has undergone cosmetic surgery to adopt a more white, European look, although Jackson denies it.[2] But the definite sense of racial ambiguity writ large in his new image is at the same time, and by the same token, the site of a sexual ambiguity bordering on androgyny. He may sing as sweet as Al Green, dance as hard as James Brown, but he looks more like Diana Ross than any black male soul artist. The media have seized upon these ambiguities and have fabricated a 'persona', a private 'self' behind the image, which has become the subject of speculation and rumour. This mythologisation has culminated in the construction of a Peter Pan figure. We are told that behind the star's image is a lonely, 'lost boy', whose life is shadowed by morbid obsessions and anxieties. He lives like a recluse and is said to 'come alive' only when he is on stage in front of his fans. The media's exploitation of public fascination with Jackson the celebrity has even reached the point of 'pathologising' his personality:

> Even Michael Jackson's millions of fans find his lifestyle strange. It's just like one of his hit songs, Off The Wall. People in the know say –
> His biggest thrill is taking trips to Disneyland.
> His closest friends are zoo animals.
> He talks to tailor's dummies in his lounge.
> He fasts every Sunday and then dances in his bedroom until he drops of exhaustion. So showbusiness folk keep asking the question: 'Is Jacko Wacko?'
> Two top American psychiatrists have spent hours examining a detailed dossier on Jackson. Here is their on-the-couch report.[3]

Jackson's sexuality and sexual preference in particular have been the focus for such public fascination, as a business associate of his, Shirley Brooks, complains:

> He doesn't and won't make public statements about his sex life, because he believes – and he is right – that is none of anyone else's business. Michael and I had a long conversation about it, and he felt that anytime you're in the public eye and don't talk to the press, they tend to make up these rumours to fill their pages.[4]

Neither child nor man, not clearly either black or white and with an androgynous image that is neither masculine nor feminine, Jackson's star-image is a 'social hieroglyph', as Marx said of the commodity form which demands, yet defies, decoding. This article offers a reading of the music video *Thriller* from the point of view of the questions raised by the phenomenal popularity of this star, whose image is a spectacle of racial and sexual indeterminacy.

Kobena Mercer 53

Remake, remodel: video in the marketing of 'Thriller'

In recent years the 'new', hybrid medium of music video has come to occupy a central importance in the sale and significance of pop music. As 'adverts' to promote records, pop videos are now prerequisites to break singles into the charts. As industrial product, the medium – institutionalised in America's cable network MTV, owned by Warner Communications and American Express – has revitalised the economic profitability of pop by capitalising on new patterns of consumption created by the use, on a mass scale, of video technology.[5] From its inception, however MTV maintained an unspoken policy of excluding black artists. Jackson's videos for singles from the *Thriller* LP were the first to penetrate this racial boundary.

The videos for two songs from that LP, 'Billy Jean' and 'Beat It', stand out in the way they foreground Jackson's new style. 'Billy Jean', directed by Steve Barron, visualises the 'cinematic' feel of the music track and its narrative of a false paternity claim, by creating through a 'studio-set' scenario, sharp editing and various effects an ambience that complements rather than illustrates the song. Taking its cue from the LP cover, it stresses Jackson's style in his dress and in his dance. Paving stones light up as Jackson twists, kicks and turns through the performance, invoking the 'magic' of the star. 'Beat It', directed by Bob Giraldi (who made TV adverts for MacDonald's hamburgers and Dr Pepper soft drinks) visualises the anti-macho lyric of the song. Shots alternate between 'juvenile delinquent' gangs about to begin a fight, and Michael, fragile and alone in his bedroom. The singer then disarms the gangs with superior charm and grace as he leads the all-male cast through a dance sequence that synthesises the cinematic imagery of *The Warriors* and *West Side Story*.

These videos, executed from designs by Jackson himself, and others in which he appears such as 'Say, Say, Say' by Paul McCartney and 'Can You Feel It' by The Jacksons, are important aspects of the commercial success of *Thriller* because they breached the boundaries of race on which the music industry has been based. Unlike stars such as Lionel Richie, Jackson has not 'crossed over' from black to white stations to end up in the middle of the road: his success has popularised black music in white rock and pop markets, by actually playing with imagery and style which have always been central to the marketing of pop. In so doing,

Jackson has opened up a space in which new stars like Prince are operating, at the interface between the boundaries defined by 'race'.

'Thriller', the LP title track, was released as the third single from the album. The accompanying video went beyond the then-established conventions and limitations of the medium. According to Dave Laing, these conventions have been tied to the economic imperative of music video:

> first, the visuals were subordinated to the soundtrack, which they were there to sell; second, music video as a medium for marketing immediately inherited an aesthetic and a set of techniques from the pre-existing and highly developed form of television commercials.[6]

Thus one convention, that of fast-editing derived from the montage codes of TV advertising, has been overlaid with another: that of an alternation between naturalistic or 'realist' modes of representation (in which the song is performed 'live' or in a studio and mimed to by the singer or group), and 'constructed' or fantastic modes of representation (in which the singer/group acts out imaginary roles implied by the lyrics or by the 'atmosphere' of the music). 'Thriller' incorporates the montage and alternation conventions, but organises the flow of images by framing it with a powerful *story-telling* or *narrational* direction which provides continuity and closure. Since 'Thriller', this story-telling code has itself become a music video convention: director Julien Temple's 'Undercover of the Night' (Rolling Stones, 1983) and 'Jazzin' for Blue Jean' (David Bowie, 1984) represent two of the more imaginative examples of this narrativisation of the music by the direction of the flow of images. 'Thriller' is distinguished not only by its internal and formal structure, but also by the fact that it is 'detached' from a primary economic imperative or rationale. The LP was already a 'monster' of a commercial success before the title track was released as a single: there was no need for a 'hard sell'. Thus the 'Thriller' video does not so much seek to promote the record as a primary product, but rather *celebrates the success the LP has brought Michael Jackson* by acting as a vehicle to showcase its star. In the absence of a direct economic imperative, the video can indulge Jackson's own interest in acting: its use of cinematic codes and structures provides a framework for Jackson to act as a 'movie-star'. Jackson himself had acted before, in *The Wiz* (1977), an all-black remake of *The Wizard of Oz* in which he played the Scarecrow. He professes a deep fascination with acting:

> I love it so much. It's escape. It's fun. It's just neat to become another thing, another person. Especially when you really believe it and it's not like you're acting. I always hated the word 'acting' – to say, 'I am an actor'. It should be more than that. It should be more like a believer.[7]

In 'Thriller', Jackson acts out a variety of roles as the video engages in a playful parody of the stereotypes, codes and conventions of the 'horror' genre. The inter-textual dialogues between film, dance and music which the video articulates also draw us, the spectators, into the *play* of signs and meanings at work in the 'constructedness' of the star's image. The following reading of the music video considers the specificity of the music track, asks how the video 'visualises' the music and then goes on to examine the internal structure of the video as an inter-text of sound, image and style.

'Thriller': a reading

Consider first the specificity of the music track. The title, which gives the LP its title as well, is the name for a particular genre of film – the 'murder-mystery-suspense' film, the detective story, the thriller. But the lyrics of the song are not 'about' film or cinema. The track is a mid-tempo funk number, written by Rod Temperton, and recalls similar numbers written by the author for Michael Jackson such as 'Off the Wall'. The lyrics evoke allusions and references to the cinematic culture of 'terror' and 'horror' movies but only to play on the meaning of the word 'thriller'. The lyrics weave a little story, which could be summarised as 'a night of viewing some . . . gruesome horror movies with a lady friend'.[8] The lyrics narrate such a fictional-scene by speaking in the first person:

> It's close to midnight and somethin' evil's lurkin' in the

> dark / . . . . You try to scream, but terror takes the sound before you make it / You start to freeze, as horror looks you right between the eyes / You're paralysed.

Who is this 'you' being addressed? The answer comes in the semantic turn-around of the third verse and chorus in which the pun on the title is made evident:

> Now is the time for you and I to cuddle close together / All thru' the night, I'll save you from the terror on the screen / I'll make you see, that [Chorus] This is thriller, thriller-night, 'cause I could thrill you more than any ghost would dare to try / Girl, this is thriller . . . so let me hold you tight and share a killer, thriller tonight'.[9]

Thus the lyrics play a *double-entendre* on the meaning of 'thrill'. As Iain Chambers has observed,

> Distilled into the metalanguage of soul and into the clandestine cultural liberation of soul music is the regular employment of a sexual discourse.[10]

Along with the emotional complexities of intimate relationships, physical sexuality is perhaps *the* central preoccupation of the soul tradition. But, as Chambers suggests, the power of soul as a cultural form to express sexuality does not so much lie in the literal meanings of the words but in the passion of the singer's voice and vocal performance. The explicit meanings of the lyrics are in this sense secondary to the sensual resonance of the individual character of the voice, its 'grain'. While the 'grain' of the voice encodes the contradictions of sexual relationships, their pleasures and pain, the insistence of the rhythm is an open invitation to the body to dance. Dance, as cultural form, and sexual ritual, is a mode of decoding the sound and meaning articulated in the music. In its incitement of the listener to dance, to become an active participant in the texture of voice, words and rhythm, soul music is not only 'about' sexuality, but is itself a musical means for the eroticisation of the body.[11] In 'Thriller' it is the 'grain' of Jackson's voice that expresses and plays with this sexual sub-text and it is this dimension that transgresses the denotation of the lyrics and escapes analytic reduction. Jackson's interpretation of Temperton's lyric inflects the allusions to cinema to thematise a discourse on sexuality, rather than film, and the 'story' created by the lyrics sets up a reverberation between two semantic poles: the invocation of macabre movies is offset by the call to 'cuddle close together'.

The element of irony set in motion by this semantic polarity is the 'literary' aspect of the sense of parody that pervades the song. Special sound effects – creaking doors and howling dogs – contribute to the pun on the title. Above all, this play of parody spreads out in Vincent Price's rap, which closes the record. The idea of a well-established white movie actor like Price delivering a 'rap', a distinctly black urban cultural form, is funny enough. But the fruity, gurgling tones of the actor's voice, which immediately invoke the semi-comic self-parody of 'horror' he has become, express the affectionate sense of humour that underpins the song:

> Darkness falls across the land. The midnight hour is close at hand. Creatures crawl in search of blood, to terrorise y'awl's neighbourhood. And whosoever shall be found, without the soul for getting down, must stand and face the hounds of hell, and rot inside a corpse's shell.

The parody at play here lies in the quotation of soul argot – 'get down', 'midnight hour', 'funk of forty thousand years' – in the completely different context of horror movies. The almost camp quality of refined exaggeration in Price's voice and his 'British' accent is at striking odds with the discourse of black American soul music.

As we 'listen' to the production of meanings in the music track the various 'voices' involved in the production (Temperton, Jackson, Price, Quincy Jones, etc.) are audibly combined into parody. One way of approaching the transition from music to video, then, would be to suggest that John Landis, its director, brings aspects of his own 'voice' as an 'author' of Hollywood films into this dialogue. It seems to me that Landis's voice contributes to the puns and play on the meaning of 'thriller' by drawing on conventions of mainstream horror movies.

Story, plot and parody

Landis introduces two important elements from film into the medium of music video: a narrative direction of the flow of images and special-effects techniques associated with the pleasures of the horror film. These effects are used in the two scenes that show the metamorphosis of Michael into, first, a werewolf, and then a zombie. The use of these cinematic technologies to create the metamorphoses is clearly what distinguishes 'Thriller' from other music video. 'Thriller' gives the video audience *real thrills* – the 'thrill' of tension, anxiety and fear associated with the pleasure offered by the horror genre. The spectacle of the visceral transformation of cute, lovable Michael Jackson into a howlin' wolf of a monster is disturbing, because it seems so convincing, 'real' and fascinating. As Philip Brophy remarks,

> The pleasure of the (horror) text is, in fact, getting the shit scared out of you – and loving it: an exchange mediated by adrenalin.[12]

Both special effects and narrative return us to the direction of John Landis, who also directed *An American Werewolf in London* (1979). *American Werewolf* is a horror comedy; it retells the traditional werewolf myth, setting its protagonists as tourists in England attacked by a strange animal, into which one of them then turns during the full moon. The film employs pop tunes to exacerbate its underlying parody of this mythology – 'Moondance' (Van Morrison), 'Bad Moon Rising' (Creedence Clearwater Revival) and 'Blue Moon' (Frankie Lymon and the Teenagers). And this humour is combined with special-effects and make-up techniques which show the bodily metamorphosis of man to wolf in 'real time', as opposed to less credible 'time-lapse' techniques. The 'Thriller' video not only refers to this film, but to other generic predecessors, including *Night of the Living Dead* (1968) by George Romero and *Halloween* (1978) by John Carpenter. Indeed, the video is strewn with allusions to horror films. As Brophy observes:

> It is a genre which mimics itself mercilessly – because its statement is coded in its very mimicry . . . It is not so much that the modern horror film refutes or ignores the conventions of

genre, but it is involved in a violent awareness of itself as a saturated genre.[13]

Thus cinematic horror seems impelled towards parody of its own codes and conventions.[14] With hindsight it is tempting to suggest that 'Thriller's' music track was almost made to be filmed, as it seems to cue these cinematic references. Certain points within the video appear to be straightforward transpositions from the song: 'They're out to get you, there's demons closin' in on ev'ry side / . . . Night creatures call and the dead start to walk in their masquerade', and so on. But it is at the level of its *narrative structure* that the video engages in an inter-textual dialogue with the music track. The following synopsis aims to outline this structure:

> The video opens with a car driving through woods at night. The engine cuts out and a teenage couple, 'Michael' (played by Michael Jackson) and an unnamed girl (played by Ola Ray), get out of the car and walk. Michael tells the delighted girl that he would like to be her boyfriend, but then confesses that he is 'different from other guys'. The girl's puzzled look turns into terror as Michael undergoes a metamorphosis into a werewolf. She flees and a chase ensues culminating in Michael as monster pouncing on the girl.
>
> The scene then shifts to Michael and the girl as a couple in a cinema audience, watching (by implication) what we have just seen. The girl becomes frightened and leaves. Michael is enthralled and remains seated but then gets up to join her in the foyer. As they walk away from the cinema the music track fades up and he begins to sing, darting around the girl as they walk.
>
> After the first two verses Vincent Price's rap comes on to the soundtrack as corpses rise from a graveyard and shuffle onto the street. Michael and the girl return into frame, to be encircled by the ghouls. The music track fades down and the girl turns to Michael to find him transformed into a zombie. Michael leads the Living Dead through a dance sequence, accompanied by the music track, culminating in the chorus (in which Michael returns to normal). The music fades down again and the girl flees to a deserted house, pursued by the zombies who violently break into the room in which she is hiding. Led by Michael as zombie, they close in on her.

As the girl screams, Michael is revealed as her boyfriend. He calms her and offers to take her home. As they exit, Michael turns to camera to show two yellow eyes and Vincent Price's laugh is heard.[15]

Unlike most pop videos, 'Thriller' does not begin with the first notes of the song, but with a long panning shot and the 'cinematic' sound of recorded silence. This master-shot, establishing the all-seeing but invisible 'eye' of the camera, is comparable to the discursive function of third-person narration. The shot/reverse-shot series which frames the dialogue between the two protagonists in the opening sequence establishes 'point-of-view' camera angles, analogues to 'subjective', first-person modes of enunciation. It is the use of these specific cinematic codes of narration that structures the entire flow of images and gives the video a beginning, a middle and an end. 'Thriller' incorporates the pop video convention of switching from 'realist' to 'fantastic' modes of representation, but binds this into continuity and closure through its narrative. The two metamorphosis sequences are of crucial importance to this narrative structure; the first disrupts the 'equilibrium' of the opening sequence, and the second repeats but differs from the first in order to bring the flow of images to its end and re-establish equilibrium. Within the story-telling conventions of the horror genre the very appearance of the monster/werewolf/vampire/alien signals the violation of equilibrium: the presence of the monster activates the narrative dynamic whose goal or end is achieved by an act of counter-violence that eliminates it.[16]

In the opening sequence of 'Thriller' equilibrium is established and then disrupted.

LS/Pan	Large 1950s-looking car drives slowly along the road through woods at night.
MCU/shot-reverse shot	Michael (M) and girl (G) in front seats of the car, framed in profile. As car stops G looks at M in disbelief. M looks back and smiles to himself, laughs: 'Honestly, we're out of gas.' G turns her head coquettishly: 'So what are we going to do now?'. M smiles.
MS/shot-reverse shot	M and G walk side by side, camera gradually tilts from ground to eye level.

> G hangs onto M's arm: 'I'm sorry I didn't believe you.' M stops and turns to face G: 'Can I ask you something? ... You know I like you, don't you?' ('Yes.') ... And I hope you like me the way I like you ... ('Yes.') ... I was wondering if you would be my girl?' G cries out 'Michael!' and rushes to embrace him. M proffers a ring and places it on her finger. She looks at it, gleaming. G: 'Its beautiful!' M: 'Now it's official ... I have something I want to tell you.' M's facial expression changes and 'creepy clarinets' fade up on the music score. G: 'Yes, Michael?' M: 'I'm not like other guys', G: 'Of course not, that's why I love you.' M: 'No, I mean I'm different.' G: 'What are you talking about?'.
>
> The music score swirls up in volume and the shot-reverse shot series is broken by an insert of clouds across a full moon. G looks at M with a puzzled expression. M holds his stomach and contorts his face, letting out gasps and squeaks. G: 'Michael, are you all right?' M raises his head to reveal two yellow eyes: 'Go away' he/it cries. G screams in terror. Metamorphosis I.

The dialogue and exchange of glances between Michael and the girl as the male and female protagonists of the story establish 'romance' as the narrative pre-text. The girl's look at Michael as the car stops hints at a question, answered by the expression of bemused incredulity on his face. Did he stop the car on purpose? Was it a romantic ruse, to lure her into a trap? The girl's coquettish response to Michael's defence ('Honestly, we're out of gas') lingers sensually on the syllables, '*So* . . . what are we going to do now?' Her question, and his smile in return, hint at and exacerbate the underlying erotic tension of romantic intrigue between the two characters. Michael's dialogue gives a minimal 'character' to his role as the boyfriend: he appears a somewhat shy, very proper and polite 'boy next door'. The girl, on the other hand, is not so much a 'character' as the 'girlfriend' type. At another level, their clothes – a pastiche 1950s retro style – connote youthful innocence, the couple as archetypical teen lovers. But this innocent representation is unsettled by Michael's statement: 'I'm not like other guys.' The statement implies a question posed on the terrain of gender, and masculinity in particular: why is he different from 'other guys'?

The sequence provides an answer in the boyfriend's transformation into a monster. But, although the metamorphosis resolves the question, it is at the cost of disrupting the equilibrium of 'romance' between the two protagonists, which is now converted into a relation of terror between monster and victim. The chase through the woods is the final sequence of this 'beginning' of the narrative. The subsequent scene, returning to Michael and the girl as a couple in a cinema, re-establishes the equation of 'romance' and repositions the protagonists as girlfriend and boyfriend, but at another level of representation.

MS	M and G in third row of cinema. Audience screams. G, looking with horror at the screen, clings to M.
CU	G hugs M, who stares at the screen chewing popcorn and laughing.
LS	Audience screams.
CU	G turns her head away and steals a look back at the screen. Voices off-frame, from the screen – 'Sheriff, he's over here. God, look at that thing!' (gun-shot) 'Look out!' G: 'Can we get out of here?'
CU	M: 'No, I'm enjoying this'. Continues grinning at the screen.
CU	'Well . . . I can't watch.'
MCU	G gets up to leave, exits right.
CU	M continues grinning, munching and staring at the screen. Voices off-frame, from the screen: '. . . scrawled in blood . . . What does it say? . . . See you next Wednesday.' Screams from cinema audience.

MS	M gets up and exits right.
LS	Panning shot from high angle moving downwards revealing the words 'Palace Cinema' with 'Vincent Price/Thriller' on marquee. Music track fades up. Camera gradually frames cinema facade.
LS	G walks out of the cinema; M runs after her – both framed by the title 'Thriller' on awnings. M: 'It's only a movie' (laughing).
MCU	G: 'It's not funny.' M: 'You were scared, weren't you?' G: 'I wasn't that scared'. M: 'Naw . . . you were scared'. M laughs. G turns and exits right. M follows. Beginning of song-sequence.

In structural terms this shift in modes of representation, from a fantastic level (in which the metamorphosis and chase take place) to a realist level (in which the song is performed) is important because it retrospectively implies that the entire opening sequence was a film within a film, or rather, a film within the video. More to the point, the 'beginning' is thus revealed to be *a parody of 1950s B-movie horror*. This has been signalled in the self-conscious 'acting' mannerisms Jackson employs and by the pastiche of 1950s teenager styles. The shift from a parody of a 1950s horror movie to the cinema audience watching the film and the long shot of the cinema showing the film, visually acknowledge this 'violent awareness of itself as saturated genre'.

While Hammer were reviving the Universal monsters . . . American International Pictures began a cycle whose appreciation was almost entirely tongue-in-cheek – a perfect example of 'camp' manufacture and reception of the iconography of terror.

The first film in this series bore the (now notorious) title *I Was A Teenage Werewolf* (1957). . . . The absurdity of the plot and acting, and the relentless pop music that filled the soundtrack, gave various kinds of pleasure to young audiences and encouraged the film-makers to follow this pilot movie with *I Was a Teenage Frankenstein* and with *Teenage Monster* and

Teenage Zombie creations that were as awful to listen to as they were to see.[17]

Parody depends on an explicit self-consciousness: in 'Thriller' this informs the dialogue, dress-style and acting in the opening sequence. In its parody of a parody it also acknowledges that there is no 'plot' as such: the narrative code that structures the video has no story to tell. Rather it creates a simulacrum of a story, a parody of a story, in its stylistic send-up of genre conventions. But it is precisely at the level of its self-consciousness that 'Thriller's' mimicry of the *gender roles* of the horror genre provides an anchor for the way it visualises the sexual discourse, the play on the meaning of the word 'thriller' on the music track.

Genre and gender: 'Thriller's' sexual subtext

As the video switches from fantastic to realist modes of representation, the roles played by the two protagonists shift accordingly. The fictional film within the video, with its narrative pretext of 'romance', positions Michael and the girl as boyfriend and girlfriend, and within this the fantastic metamorphosis transforms the relation into one of terror between monster and victim. If we go back to Michael's statement made in this scene, 'I'm not like other guys', we can detect a confusion about the role he is playing.

The girl's initial reply, 'Of course not. That's why I love you', implies that it is obvious that he is 'different' because he is the real Michael Jackson. When, in her pleasure at his proposal, she calls him by his proper name she interpellates him in two roles at once – as fictional boyfriend and real superstar. This ambiguity of reference acknowledges Jackson's self-conscious acting style: we, the video audience, get the impression he is playing at playing a role and we 'know' that Jackson, the singer, the star, is playing at the role of a 'movie-star'. In 'Thriller', Michael's outfit and its stylistic features – the wet-look hairstyle, the ankle-cut jeans and the letter 'M' emblazoned on his jacket – reinforce this meta-textual superimposition of roles. If Michael, as the male protagonist, is both boyfriend and star, his female counterpart in the equation of 'romance' is both the girlfriend and at this meta-textual level, the fan. The girl is in two places at once: on screen and in the audience.

As spectator of the film within the video she is horrified by the image on the screen and gets up to leave. 'Fooled' by the violent spectacle of the metamorphosis, she mistakes the fantastic for the real, she forgets that 'it's only a movie'. The girl's positions in the fictional and realist scenes mirror those of the video spectator – the effects which generate thrills for the audience are the events, in the story-world, that generate terror for the girl.

The girl occupies a mediated position between the audience and the image which offers a clue to the way the video visualises the music track. In the middle section, as the couple walk away from the cinema and Michael begins the song, the narrative roles of boyfriend and girlfriend are re-established, but now subordinated to the song's performance. This continuity of narrative function is underlined by the differentiation of costume style: Michael now wears a flashy red and black leather jacket cut in a 'futuristic' style and her ensemble is also contemporary – t-shirt, bomber jacket and head of curls like Michael's own. This imagery echoes publicity images of Jackson the stage performer. As the song gets under way Jackson becomes 'himself', the star. The girl becomes the 'you' in the refrain 'Girl, I could thrill you more than any ghost would dare to try'.

On the music track, the 'you' could be the listener, since the personal and direct mode of enunciation creates a space for the listener to enter and take part in the production of meanings. In the video, it is the girl who takes this place and, as the addressee of the sexual discourse enunciated in the song, her positions in the video-text create possibilities for spectatorial identification. These lines of identification are hinted at in the opening scene in which the girl's response to Michael's wooing enacts the 'fantasy of being a pop star's girlfriend', a fantasy which is realised in this section of the video.[18]

Beauty and the beast-masks, monsters and masculinity

The conventions of horror inscribe a fascination with sexuality, with gender identity codified in terms that revolve around the symbolic presence of the monster. Women are invariably the victims of the acts of terror unleashed by the werewolf/vampire/alien/'thing': the monster as non-human Other. The destruction of the monster establishes male protagonists as heroes, whose object and prize is of course the woman. But as the predatory force against which the hero has to compete, the monster itself occupies a 'masculine' position in relation to the female victim.

'Thriller's' rhetoric of parody presupposes a degree of self-consciousness on the part of the spectator, giving rise to a supplementary commentary on the sexuality and sexual identity of its star, Michael Jackson. Thus, the warning 'I'm not like other guys' can be read by the audience as a reference to Jackson's sexuality. Inasmuch as the video audience is conscious of the gossip which circulates around the star, the statement of difference provokes other meanings: is he homosexual, transsexual or somehow presexual?

In the first metamorphosis Michael becomes a werewolf. As the recent *Company of Wolves* (directed by Neil Jordan, 1984) demonstrates, werewolf mythology – lycanthropy – concerns the representation of male sexuality as 'naturally' bestial, predatory, aggressive, violent – in a word, 'monstrous'. Like 'Thriller', *Company of Wolves* employs similar special effects to show the metamorphosis of man to wolf in 'real time'. And like the Angela Carter story on which it is based, the film can be read to rewrite the European folktale of 'Little Red Riding Hood' to reveal its concerns with subjects of menstruation, the moon and the nature of male sexuality. In the fictional opening scene of 'Thriller' the connotation of innocence around the girl likens her to Red Riding Hood. But is Michael a big, bad wolf?

In the culmination of the chase sequence through the woods, the girl takes the role of victim. Here, the disposition of point-of-view angles between the monster's dominant position and the supine position of the victim suggests rape, fusing the underlying sexual relation of 'romance' with terror and violence. As the monster, Michael's transformation might suggest that beneath the boy-next-door image there is a 'real' man waiting to break out, a man whose masculinity is measured by a rapacious sexual appetite, 'hungry like the wolf'. But such an interpretation is undermined and subverted by the final shot of the metamorphosis. Michael-as-werewolf lets out a blood-curdling howl, but this is in hilarious counterpoint to the collegiate 'M' on his jacket. What does it stand for? Michael? Monster? Macho Man? More like Mickey Mouse.

The incongruity between the manifest signifier and the symbolic meaning of the Monster opens up a gap in the text, to be filled with laughter.

Animals are regularly used to signify human attributes, with the wolf, lion, snake and eagle all understood as signs of male sexuality. Jackson's subversion of this symbolism is writ large on the *Thriller* LP cover. Across the star's knee lies a young tiger cub, a brilliant little metaphor for the ambiguity of Jackson's image as a black male pop star. This plays on the star's 'man-child' image and suggests a domesticated animality, hinting at menace beneath the cute and cuddly surface. Jackson's sexual ambiguity makes a mockery out of the menagerie of received images of masculinity.[19]

In the second metamorphosis Michael becomes a zombie. Less dramatic and 'horrifying' than the first, this transformation cues the spectacular dance sequence that frames the chorus of the song. While the dance, choreographed by Michael Peters, makes visual one of the lines from the lyric, 'Night creatures crawl and the dead start to walk in their masquerade', it foregrounds Jackson-the-dancer and his performance breaks loose from the video. As the ghouls begin to dance, the sequence elicits the same kind of parodic humour provoked by Vincent Price's rap on the music track. There humour lay in the incongruity between Price's voice and the argot of black soul culture. Here a visual equivalent of this incongruity is created by the spectacle of the living dead performing with Jackson a funky dance routine. The sense of parody is intensified by the macabre make-up of the ghouls, bile dripping from their mouths. Jackson's make-up, casting a ghostly pallor over his skin and emphasising the contour of the skull, alludes to one of the paradigmatic 'masks' of the horror genre, that of Lon Chaney in *The Phantom of the Opera* (1925).

Unlike the werewolf, the figure of the zombie, the undead corpse, does not represent sexuality so much as asexuality or anti-sexuality, suggesting the sense of *neutral eroticism* in Jackson's style as dancer. As has been observed:

> The movie star Michael most resembles is Fred Astaire – that *paragon of sexual vagueness*. Astaire never fit a type, hardly ever played a traditional romantic lead. He created his own niche by the sheer force of his tremendous talent.[20]

The dance sequence can be read as cryptic writing on this 'sexual vagueness' of Jackson's body in movement, in counterpoint to the androgyny of his image. The dance breaks loose from the narrative and Michael's body comes alive in movement, a rave from the grave: the scene can thus be seen as a commentary on the notion that as star Jackson only 'comes alive' when he is on stage performing. The living dead invoke an existential liminality which corresponds to both the sexual indeterminacy of Jackson's dance and the somewhat morbid lifestyle that reportedly governs his offscreen existence. Both meanings are buried in the video 'cryptogram'.[21]

Metaphor-morphosis

Finally, I feel compelled to return to the scene of the first metamorphosis. It enthralls and captivates, luring the spectator's gaze and petrifying it in wonder. This sense of both fear and fascination is engineered by the video's special effects. By showing the metamorphosis in 'real time' the spectacle violently distorts the features of Jackson's face. The horror-effect of the monster's appearance depends on the 'suspension of disbelief': we know that the monster is a fiction, literally a mask created by mechanical techniques, but repress or disavow this knowledge to participate in the 'thrills', the pleasures expected from the horror-text. Yet in this splitting of belief which the horror film presupposes, it is credibility of the techniques themselves that is at stake in making the 'otherness' of the monster believable.[22]

The Making of Michael Jackson's Thriller (1984) demonstrates the special effects used in the video. We see make-up artists in the process of applying the 'mask' that will give Jackson the appearance of the monster. Of particular interest is the make-up artists' explanation of how the werewolf mask was designed and constructed: a series of transparent cells, each with details of the animal features of the mask, are gradually superimposed on a publicity image of Jackson from the cover of *Rolling Stone* magazine. It is this superimposition of fantastic and real upon Jackson's face that offers clues as to why the metamorphosis is so effective. Like the opening parody of the 1950s horror movie and its confusion of roles that Jackson is playing (boyfriend/star), there is a slippage between different levels of belief on the part of the spectator.

The metamorphosis achieves a horrifying effect because the monster does not just mutilate the appearance of the boyfriend, but plays on the audience's awareness of Jackson's double role; thus, the credibility of the special effects violates the image of the star himself. At this meta-textual level, the drama of the transformation is heightened by other performance-signs that foreground Jackson as star. The squeaks, cries and other wordless sounds which emanate from his throat as he grips his stomach grotesquely mimic the sounds which are the stylistic trademark of Jackson's voice and thus reinforce the impression that it is the 'real' Michael Jackson undergoing this mutation. Above all, the very first shots of the video highlight the make-up on the star's face (particularly the eyes and lips), the pallor of his complexion, revealing the eerie sight of his skull beneath the wet-look curls. The very appearance of Jackson draws attention to the artificiality of his own image. As the monstrous mask is, literally, a construction made out of make-up and cosmetic 'work', the fictional world of the horror film merely appropriates what is already an artifice. I suggest that the metamorphosis be seen as *a metaphor for the aesthetic reconstruction of Michael Jackson's face.*

The literal construction of the fantastic monster-mask refers to other images of the star: the referent of the mask, as a sign in its own right, is a commonplace publicity image taken from the cover of a magazine. In this sense the mask refers not to the real person or private 'self' but to Michael Jackson-as-an-image. The metamorphosis could thus be seen as an accelerated allegory of the morphological development of Jackson's facial features: from child to adult, from boyfriend to monster, from star to superstar – the sense of wonder generated by the video's special effects forms an allegory for the fascination with which the world beholds this star-as-image.

In 1983, Jackson took part in a two-hour TV special to celebrate Motown's twenty-fifth anniversary, in which vintage footage was intercut with each act's performance; the film was then edited and used as a 'support' act on Motown artists' tours in England. This is how the reception of the film was described:

> The audience almost visibly tensed as Michael's voice . . . took complete control, attacking the songs with that increased repertoire of whoops, hiccups and gasps, with which he punctu-

ates the lyric to such stylish, relaxing effect. And then he danced. The cocky strut of a super-confident child had been replaced by a lithe, menacing grace, and his impossibly lean frame, still boyishly gangly, when galvanised by the music, assumed a hypnotic, androgynous sexuality. Certainly, it was the first time in a long, long time I'd heard girls scream at a film screen.[23]

Amid all the screaming elicited by 'Thriller' it is possible to hear a parody of those fans' response. As a pop idol Michael Jackson has been the object of such screaming since he was eleven years old.

In 'The Face of Garbo' Barthes sought to explore the almost universal appeal of film stars like Chaplin, Hepburn and Garbo by describing their faces as *masks*: aesthetic surfaces on which a society writes large its own preoccupations.[24] Jackson's face can also be seen as such a mask, for his image has attracted and maintained the kind of cultural fascination that makes him more like a movie star than a modern rhythm and blues artist. The sexual and racial ambiguity of his image can be seen as pointing to a range of questions about images of sex and race in popular culture and popular music. If we regard his face, not as the manifestation of personality traits but as a surface of artistic and social inscription, the ambiguities of Jackson's image call into question received ideas about what black male artists in popular music should look like. Seen from this angle his experimentation with imagery represents a creative incursion upon a terrain in pop culture more visibly mapped out by white male stars like Mick Jagger, David Bowie and Boy George. At best, these stars have used androgyny and sexual ambiguity as part of their 'style' in ways which question prevailing definitions of male sexuality and sexual identity. Key songs on *Thriller* highlight this problematisation of masculinity: on 'Wanna Be Startin' Somethin'' the narrator replies to rumour and speculation about his sexuality, on 'Billy Jean' – a story about a fan who claims he is the father of her son – he refuses the paternal model of masculinity, and on 'Beat It' – 'Don't wanna see no blood, Don't be a macho man' – he explicitly refuses a bellicose model of manliness.

What makes Jackson's use of androgyny more compelling is that his work is located entirely in the Afro-American tradition of popular music and thus must be seen in the context of imagery of black men and black male sexuality. Jackson not only questions dominant stereotypes of black masculinity,[25] but also gracefully steps outside the existing range of 'types' of black men. In so doing his style reminds us how some black men in the soul tradition such as Little Richard used 'camp', in the sense that Susan Sontag calls 'the love of the unnatural: of artifice and exaggeration',[26] long before white pop stars began to exploit its 'shock-value'. Indeed, 'Thriller' is reminiscent of the 'camp' excesses of the originator of the combination of music and horror in pop culture, Screamin' Jay Hawkins. Horror imagery has fascinated the distinctly white male genre of 'heavy metal' in which acts like Alice Cooper and Ozzy Osbourne (Black Sabbath) consume themselves in self-parody. But like Hawkins, whose 'I Put a Spell on You' (1956) borrowed from images of horror to articulate a scream 'that found its way out of my big mouth *directly* through my heart and guts',[27] Jackson expresses another sort of 'screaming', one that articulates the erotic materiality of the human voice, its 'grain'. Writing about a musical tradition radically different from soul, Barthes coined this term to give 'the impossible account of an individual thrill that I constantly experience in listening to singing'.[28] 'Thriller' celebrates the fact that this thrill is shared by millions.

Notes

1. Roland Barthes, 'The Grain of the Voice', in Stephen Heath (ed.), *Image–Music–Text* (London: Fontana, 1977) p. 188.
2. Robert Johnson, 'The Michael Jackson Nobody Knows', *Ebony* (USA), December 1984.
3. *The Sun*, 9 April 1984.
4. Quoted in Nelson George, *The Michael Jackson Story* (London: New English Library, 1984) p. 106.
5. On music video, see Michael Boodro, 'Rock Videos: Another World', *ZG* ('Breakdown' issue) London 1984; Dessa Fox, 'The Video Virus', *New Musical Express*, London, 4 May 1985; Dave Laing, 'Music Video: Industrial Product – Cultural Form', *Screen*, March/April 1985, vol. 26, no. 2, and Andy Lipman, 'The World of Salvador Disney', *City Limits*, 24 May 1985.
6. Dave Laing, 'Music-Video', p. 81.
7. Quoted in Andy Warhol and Bob Colacello, 'Michael Jackson', *Interview* magazine, October 1982.
8. Nelson George, *Michael Jackson Story*, p. 108.

9. From *The Great Songs of Michael Jackson* (London: Wise Publications, 1984).
10. Iain Chambers, *Urban Rhythms: Pop Music and Popular Culture* (London: Macmillan, 1985) p. 148.
11. Iain Chambers, *Urban Rhythms*, pp. 143–8 *passim*; see also, Richard Dyer, 'In Defence of Disco', *Gay Left*, no. 8, Summer 1979.
12. Philip Brophy, 'Horrality', reprinted in *Screen*, Vol. 27, No. 1, 1988.
13. Ibid.
14. S. S. Prawer, *Caligari's Children: The Film as Tale of Terror*, Oxford University Press, 1980.
15. The 'Thriller' video is generally available as part of *The Making of Michael Jackson's Thriller*, Warner Home Video, 1984.
16. Stephen Neale, *Genre* (London: British Film Institute, 1980) pp. 21, 56, 62.
17. Prawer, *Caligari's Children*, p. 15.
18. On personal modes of enunciation in pop discourse, see Alan Durant, *Conditions of Music* (London: Macmillan, 1984) esp. pp. 201–6. The 'fantasy of being a pop star's girlfriend' is examined in Dave Rimmer, *Like Punk Never Happened: Culture Club and the New Pop* (London: Faber, 1985) p. 112.
19. One of Freud's most famous patients, The Wolf Man, makes connections between animals and sexuality clear. The Wolf Man's dream also reads like a horror film: 'I dreamt that it was night and that I was lying on my bed. Suddenly the window opened of its own accord, and I was terrified to see some white wolves were sitting on the big walnut tree in front of the window.' Cf. Muriel Gardiner, *The Wolf Man and Sigmund Freud* (London: Hogarth Press and Institute of Psychoanalysis, 1973) p. 173. Freud's reading suggests that the terror in the dream manifests a fear of castration for a repressed homosexual desire.
20. Quoted in Nelson George, *Michael Jackson Story*, pp. 83–4.
21. The notion of 'cryptonymy' as a name for unconscious meanings emerges in Nicholas Abraham and Maria Torok's re-reading of Freud's Wolf Man. See Peggy Kamuf, 'Abraham's Wake', *Diacritics*, Spring 1979, vol. 9, no. 1, pp. 32–43.
22. Stephen Neale, *Genre*, p. 45.
23. Geoff Brown, *Michael Jackson: Body and Soul* (London: Virgin Books, 1984) p. 10.
24. Roland Barthes, *Mythologies*, Paladin, 1973.
25. On stereotypes of black men in pop culture (music, film, entertainment and sport) see Isaac Julien, 'The Other Look', unpublished BA dissertation, St Martin's School of Art, 1983.
26. Susan Sontag, 'Notes on Camp' in *Against Interpretation*, Eyre & Spottiswoode, 1969.

27. Jerry Hirshey, *Nowhere to Run: the Story of Soul* (London, Pan, 1984).
28. Roland Barthes, 'The Grain of the Voice' in Stephen Heath (ed.), *Image–Music–Text* (London: Fontana, 1977).

4
The Grain of Punk: An Analysis of the Lyrics*

Dave Laing

Artistic and commercial reasons have combined to support the commonplace that popular music was primarily a recorded music. For both progressive rock bands and teenybop groups the studio was the creative source, while records themselves yielded greater financial rewards than live performances. The latter were places in which to reproduce the recorded sound.

Punk reversed this order of priority. Nearly all the bands established an identity and reputation through the live show. That, of course, is a first stage for most popular musicians (though increasingly in pop the studio came before even the formation of the band – in the case of the Love Affair, a group was created to perform a hit originally recorded by session players). But most musicians approached their transition to recording artists as a move into another mode. For punk rock, it seemed vital to maintain a fidelity to the live context within the recorded one.

This did not, however, mean that punk was an important site for the 'live' album, a recording made at a performance before an audience. The live side of Sham 69's *Tell Us The Truth* album was exceptional in this respect. It meant, rather, that techniques of recording and of arrangement were adopted which were intended to signify the 'live' commitment of the disc. The studio manipulations had the principal aim of convincing the listener that no trickery of editing; double-tracking and so on had 'interfered' with the self-expression of the musicians. The instrumentation on the records was exactly that of the bands in performance, and the

---

* Originally published in Dave Laing, *One Chord Wonders*, Open University Press, 1985.

'positioning' of the instruments and voices 'mimed' that of the group on stage. The sound was 'set back' from the listener, with the voice either buried amongst the other sounds, or placed only a short way in front of them. The contrast is with the mix on records by 'intimate' vocalists, where the singing combines softness with volume in an 'unreal' way. When punk voices are loud it is because the singer is shouting, not because of production technology. This guarantee of the values of the 'live' act is one function too of the many instances where a punk record begins with a non-sung vocal line. The practice goes back to the Beatles (and no doubt beyond), whose first album began with a counting-in of the band: 'One Two Three Four'. Punk is replete with similar effects, Rotten's 'Right now' and his chuckle on 'Anarchy', Poly Styrene's spoken introduction to 'Oh Bondage Up Yours!', The Adverts' whispering of the title as 'Gary Gilmore's Eyes' starts.

Voices

Recordings can be thought of as spaces in which the various sounds are placed in relation to each other. Conventionally, a recording will foreground one particular element, the others arranged behind or around it as supports. Typically in popular music recordings what is foregrounded is the voice. This point can perhaps be supported negatively in that the listener notices (often with a sense of frustration) when the voice 'disappears' into what significantly is called the 'backing'. The frustration comes from a problem of comprehension (not being able to decipher the words) but also from the withdrawal of the opportunity of identification with 'the voice which typically, if not in every case, provides the level of the song which engages our desire most directly'.[1]

The amplified voice can be seen to provide a comparable object for identification to that of the screen image of the film hero or heroine. In addition, the *musicality* of the process is crucial to this sense of perfection and coherence: singing can make a voice extraordinary in a way that everyday speech cannot (though heightened, dramatic speech can – an important point for punk). . . .

Punk voices, to start with, seem to want to refuse the perfection of the 'amplified voice'. In many instances the homogeneity of the singing voice is replaced by a mixture of speech, recitative, chanting or wordless cries and mutterings. Popular music has a small tradition of the monologue, spoken words set against a musical background. It divides into the comic and the portentous, although in most cases (Les Crane's 'Desiderata' or Wink Martindale's 'Deck of Cards') the latter can easily collapse into the former. Philip Tagg has pointed out that recitatives (used here as a generic term for vocalizations that are between ordinary speech and singing) are among those forms 'where the verbal narrative seems often to be more important than the musical discourse'.[2] This would certainly seem to be the case with many punk records which employ recitative with serious intent, though with very different voices from the lugubrious Crane and Martindale. Virtually all the Sex Pistols tracks (with Rotten on lead vocal) and those of Mark Perry's Alternative TV are examples. The implicit logic would seem to involve the conviction that by excluding the musicality of singing, the possible contamination of the lyric message by the aesthetic pleasures offered by melody, harmony, pitch and so on, is avoided. Also avoided is any association with the prettiness of the mainstream song, in its forms as well as its contents: punk has few love songs.

Yet, any hope for the pure message, vocals as reflector of meaning, is doomed. Deprived of the conventional beauties of singing as a place for identification, for distraction, the listener may shift to some other aspect of the voice. What is at stake here is that element which Roland Barthes variously calls the 'third meaning' or the 'geno-song'. The latter is contrasted with the 'pheno-song' which 'describes everything in the performance which john the service of communication, representation, expression'. The geno-song, by contrast is:

> The volume of the singing and speaking voice, the space where significations germinate from within language and in its very materiality. . . . It is that apex (or depth) of production where the melody really works at the language – not at what it says, but the voluptuousness of its sound-signifiers, of its letters.[3]

This is not a distinction between form and content or signifier and signified,[4] with special emphasis being given to form. Barthes is concerned only with the role of singing-forms – are they subordinated to the message or content, there to underline it (as is the case in most of the Stranglers' work), or are there places where elements of form 'exceed' the message, providing a different focus for the listener? Johnny Rotten's vocal style offers some examples. In 'God Save The Queen', the word 'moron' comes out as 'mo-rrrr-on-er', with an exaggerated rolled 'r' in the middle and the addition of the extra 'er' syllable at the end. As pheno-song, two readings are possible. This presentation of the word both gives added emphasis within the narrative to the description of the Queen as a 'moron', and also connotes a relish on the part of the singer in making the comparison. So the sound 'in the service of representation' informs the listener of the most important part of the lyric message and provides information about the 'character' of the singer (and in doing so links up with the extra-musical discourse on the Sex Pistols, Bill Grundy, etc.).

But, as with the famous visual 'illusions' such as the 'duck/rabbit', by refocusing, the listener can hear Rotten's 'moron' as geno-song, as pleasure in the 'voluptuousness of . . . sound-signifiers'. For there is a sense in which the emphasis on the word is gratuitous within the lyric of 'God Save The Queen'. In the next line, for instance, the word 'H-Bomb', which semantically carries greater impact in general discourse, receives no such special emphasis. Additionally, the specific forms of emphasis have connotations in the popular music field which are very distant from the punk protest of his lyric. The rolled 'r' is a feature of 'Tartanry' singing, the heavily Scottish style associated with Harry Lauder and Andy Stewart (in the latter's 'Scottish Soldier' for instance). The 'er' effect is part of an equally archaic singing style which Richard Hoggart, writing in 1957, called the 'big dipper':

Each emotional phrase is pulled out and stretched; it is the verbal equivalent of rock-making, where the sweet and sticky mass is pulled to surprising lengths and pounded. . . . The most immediately recognisable characteristic is the 'er' extension to emotionally important work, which I take to be the result partly of the need to draw every ounce of sentiment from the swing of the rhythm, and partly of the wish to underline the pattern of emotional statement.[5]

Physiologically, the 'er' embellishment coincides with the places where the singer needs to draw breath. The 'expert' singer will inhale inaudibly, while the less professional may utter a gulp or gasp, coming out as an 'er'. But, as Hoggart's last phrase indicates, this effect is part of the geno-song in the 'big dipper' style, it 'underlines the pattern of the emotional statement'. Johnny Rotten's use of the effect in a context far removed from the sentimentality of the 'big dipper' can be heard as either shifting it into the area of geno-song, so it no longer functions expressively, or as overturning the connotations which the effect has within the big dipper's pheno-song, as satirizing or ridiculing them.

This satirical effect is then the third possible interpretation of the 'er' at the level of pheno-song, while geno-song offers two possible ways of understanding the effect: the overstated intake of breath or a play with the potential of a consonant when the final syllable of 'moron' can be heard as an attempt to stretch out the 'n' sound.

It is thus possible (if difficult) to find pleasure in this celebrated punk rock song without the necessity of agreeing with its message. This is something which is conventionally the case with mainstream popular song – the listener can take pleasure from a vocal representation of suffering without sharing the emotion. But it is clearly an outcome that 'protest' type songs would try to exclude. If someone who rejects the message can still like the song, a gap has opened which was unintended.

There are especial difficulties here for the songs of subcultures.[6] While the subculture (or more precisely its interpreters) may pride itself on its ability to subvert dominant or established meanings, a listener to a manifestly punk song may be able to miss the point, and avoid reacting either as a punk initiate or as a shocked adherent of dominant social values. The latter should, in principle, recoil from 'Dead Cities' by The Exploited, a 'formalist punk' record. Yet, such is the frenetic pace of the piece, that the enunciation of the title can easily be heard as a kind of 'scat' singing, as 'Deh See', and enjoyed as a form of abstract (wordless) vocalizing. The point of this example is that the potential play of the signifiers will always challenge the idea of a 'pure' oppositional or subcultural music. To minimize this challenge, a subculture intent on preserving itself and its meaning must organize the context of reception (through audience dress and response) to ensure that the subcultural meaning predominates. The only place for this is the live concert; once the music is on radio or record, other meanings, inflected by other ways of listening (usually structured by the priorities of the musical mainstream) may come to the fore.

A further aspect of the recorded voice is what can be called the *vocal stance*. In his study of Abba's 'Fernando', Philip Tagg describes how the singer's mouth is 'placed nearer the listener's ear by means of mike positioning and volume level in relation to accompaniment at the final mix-down. This reflects the actual/imagined distance between two persons (transmitter and receiver) in an intimate/confidential dialogue.'[7] This private and confidential stance is in contrast to a public and declamatory one, which reflects a greater distance between the voice singing and the ears listening. As Tagg indicates, both imply a communicative function for the voice and belong very much to the pheno-song aspect of music.

Indeed, the confidential and declamatory emphases tend to be aligned with specific genres of music, different lyric subject-matter and contrasting 'modes of address' in the lyric. This last term will be elaborated later in this chapter, but the genres most closely associated in popular song with the confidential vocal stance are the lyric ballad deriving from the 'standard' song-writing of Irving Berlin through to Lennon and McCartney and some blues styles. The declamatory mode, by contrast, is generally rooted in mainstream soul music, the 'shouting' style of R&B singing which in turn influenced early rock 'n' roll through Bill Haley, Little Richard and Jerry Lee Lewis and a white narrative ballad style deriving via Bob Dylan from Woody Guthrie and the Carter Family.

While the descriptions 'confidential' and 'declamatory' are meant to indicate tendencies in singing, rather than hard-and-fast categories, it is useful to note that of the Top 50 best-selling singles of 1976, nearly half were clearly confidential in tendency. These included 'If You Leave Me Now' by Chicago and Dr Hook's 'A Little Bit More'. More declamatory in their stance were such records as 'Jungle Rock' by Hank Mizell and The Wurzels' 'Combine Harvester'. In general, there is a connection between the preponderance of love songs and the confidential vocal stance, while lyrics on novelty or song-and-dance themes are delivered in a predominantly declamatory manner.

Within punk rock, the confidential stance was very rare. The Buzzcocks' Peter Shelley was one of the few who presented lyrics in a manner approaching that of the mainstream balladeers. Within the declamatory mode as employed by punk, elements of the soul style were equally scarce: Poly Styrene of X-Ray Spex uses falsetto whoops on 'Oh Bondage Up Yours!', while among the few bands to adopt American vocal accents were the Vibrators, The Damned (on the first album) and the Boomtown Rats, where the debt to Mick Jagger's rock-American intonation was very noticeable.

Simon Frith expresses the general view of the innovation in punk accents by describing how Johnny Rotten 'developed an explicitly working-class voice by using proletarian accents, drawing on football supporter chants'.[8] But the argument that punk imported extra-musical elements into the popular music discourse tends to underplay the previous applications of similar accents in rock music.

Accent influenced punk rock through some of the Vibrators' singing, but several punk bands offered a flatter London accent shorn of the aesthetic 'quaintness' which stage cockney (as exemplified by, for instance, David Bowie in the 1960s) had acquired. Prime examples were the querulous and whingeing tone of Mark P. (notably on 'My Love Lies Limp' and 'How Much Longer') and the morose Malcolm Owen of The Ruts in whose singing the word 'feel' came out as 'feeyuwuh'. But if the intention in using such voices (and the far fewer non-cockney ones, like Fay Fife's Scottish accent) on record was to signify the 'ordinary', the language of the streets, the result was paradoxical. For, in the context of popular music, the mundane and everyday was actually the mainstream American or 'non-accented' (sometimes called 'mid-Atlantic') accent associated in 1976 with singers like Abba or Queen's Freddie Mercury. What was ordinary in the streets became extraordinary on record and on radio.

Here is one point, then, where the 'realism' claimed by *Sniffin' Glue* for punk rock is connected with the exotic and unnatural element in the music emphasized by other commentators. Voices which could be strongly identified with 'real' accents acquired a colourful resonance. The more neutral connotations which were perhaps more suited to naturalistic lyrics – the transparent voice – belonged to vocals such as Joe Strummer's, where the standard mainstream rock voice was not so much replaced as *shifted*. 'White

Riot' had the same phrasing as the breathless singing of The Ramones, but without the pronunciation of key sounds which fully identify The Ramones as American. In the syllable 'White', for example, the American tendency to stretch the vowel towards an 'ah' sound (which is also characteristic of rock singing in general) was resisted by The Clash, who retain the short 'i' sound. And the final 't' was clipped off by the British voice, while most American rock pronunciation would keep it, in whole or in part.

Strummer's vocals share with virtually all punk rock singing a lack of variety. There are no moves within songs from high to low, soft to loud, or from one accent to another. One thing which gives the Johnny Rotten voice a special place within punk rock is its unusual practice of changing direction within a song, a verse or even a line. By 'direction', I refer to a vocal strategy, a general approach to the choice of vocal effects. In punk rock, the basic distinction at this level is between 'straight' and 'embellished' singing. Early Clash records exemplify the straight style, where the project is to subordinate the vocal method to the lyric message – a mode appropriate to Barthes's pheno-song. Now, 'Anarchy In The UK' by the Sex Pistols sets off in this mode, a staccato delivery of words with one syllable assigned strictly to one beat. But something happens to deflect that single-mindedness at the end of the second line: 'I am the Anti-Christ/I am an Anarchist'. The final syllable comes out not as 'kissed' but to rhyme with 'Christ'. The embellishment shifts the attention away from the message to the rhyme-scheme and could momentarily set up an ambivalent signal about the 'sincerity' of the whole enterprise. Can anyone who changes the pronunciation of such a key political word be wholly intent on conveying the message of the lyric? This relish for the signifier emerges in other ways that have already been mentioned (the rolled 'r' etc.), and works in tension with the punk ideal of 'straight' singing in the work of Johnny Rotten. As I have already suggested, such a tension can never be fully eliminated from any vocal performance, but it seems more central to the Sex Pistols' music than to most other punk bands of 1976–8.

An important precursor of the punk vocal was the chorus singing on several hit records of the early 1970s. John Lennon's Plastic Ono Band recordings of 1969–71 ('Give Peace A Chance' etc.) had deliberately introduced a chorus line which mingled the 'singalong' approach of nursery rhymes or pub songs with the kind of community singing or chanting to be found at political demonstrations. The singing of the choruses was deliberately loose on the records, to give the impression of audience participation rather than simply a musician's product. With the hits of Slade (17 between 1971 and 1976), a fusion of the singalong and the chants of football supporters took place in the choruses. This form was taken up again in the male choruses behind the lead vocals of Gary Glitter, whose run of British hits began in 1972. Finally, the 1970s also saw a number of topical novelty hits sung by members of various successful soccer teams, including Arsenal, Liverpool and Leeds as well as Tottenham Hotspur's Cockerel Chorus singing 'Nice One Cyril'.

Punk rock, then, had these vocal resources to draw on, as well as those of another recently successful singer with a sound which stood apart from the majority of 1970s hitmakers. The American singer Alice Cooper had a voice without polish which cracked and bellowed on several British hits like 'Elected' and 'School's Out'. With Cooper as one model of successful rule-breaking, much punk singing promoted to the lead vocal the approach and the accent of the raucous British chorus singing. Punk also allied to these vocals different lyric themes and a considerably faster tempo than that accompanying the dirge-like chants of Lennon or even the rock romps of Slade.

Music

The tempo of punk rock was one of its musical resources most commented on in reviews or eulogies which managed to regard punk as both 'going further' and 'returning' musically. Tom Carson (writing about The Ramones) is characteristic: 'they had defined the music in its purest terms: a return to the basics which was both deliberately primitive and revisionist . . . a musical and lyrical bluntness of approach'.[9]

What were the features of punk music Carson had in mind by describing it first as 'primitive' and undertaking a 'return to the basics'? In the context of the progressive rock music of the mid-1970s, the main aspects involved were a strict guitar and drums instrumental line-up (with a few exceptions, notably The Stranglers and X-Ray Spex), the alleged musical incompetence of punk bands and the consequent lack of importance of virtuosity in instrumental solos.

Punk itself eschewed the growing use of electronic instruments to be found in progressive rock, whether synthesizers or the various adaptations of the electric guitar exemplified by the playing of Jimi Hendrix. It was not, however, strictly the case that punk's reliance on the guitar was an actual return to the roots, at least of rock 'n' roll. To begin with, the rock music of the 1950s had involved a range of lead instruments: saxophones (Bill Haley), piano (Jerry Lee Lewis) as well as guitar. In addition, the guitar techniques deployed by punk players of the 1970s were far more akin to certain guitarists of the 1960s than to Scotty Moore, Buddy Holly or James Burton. Its 'basics' were broadly those of the earlier punk music played by The Kinks, the MC5 and the New York Dolls, as well as other bands like The Who. Unlike the relatively 'clear' tone of the 1950s players, punk guitar was replete with effects based on distortion or feedback. Their use of those elements suggests that the 'incompetence' of punk musicians was more rhetorical than actual. There are a few records where the band's ambition so far exceeds their ability that the result is not a tension between the two but a dislocation. The almost total lack of any rhythmic continuity on The Mekons' 'Never Been In A Riot' ensures the collapse of the song's intended message. Instead it tells listeners that literally anyone can make a record, perhaps more effectively than the lyric exhortations of the Desperate Bicycles, a band who triumphantly prove that limited musical means could be deployed to the limit (but not beyond it) to great effect.

Even at the level of the materiality of the sounds themselves the issue of skill and competence in punk rock remains ideologically charged. In an essay on the New York Dolls, which contains virtually the only attempt at musical analysis of punk style, Robert Christgau remarks that 'they refused to pay their dues'.[10] That last phrase had a particular resonance in the rock music discourse of the 1970s. As applied approvingly to musicians it implied that these people had gone through a long and necessary period of acquiring experience and know-how as performers: that to be a rock musician was to be a certain type of skilled worker who had learned 'on the job'.

That model of self-improvement could then be pitted against the 'instant' nature of many teenybop artists, apparently with little performing experience and apparently manipulated by a producer or a manager. There was no issue in teenybop of 'paying dues', and nor was there in punk rock. In fact, quite a number of the early punk musicians had a lot of previous experience as professional musicians, notably members of the Damned, Stranglers and Clash. But this background did not count to their advantage in the punk milieu.

If progressive rock saw itself as skilled labour of an artistic type (comparable to a potter or an illustrator), punk saw itself as self-expression where skill or virtuosity carried with it a suspicion of glibness. Too much concern with the forms of musical expression could lessen the impact of the substance of the thing expressed. This sort of attitude helped to fix the role of the instrumental solo in recorded punk rock, which was very similar to that of both 1950s rock 'n' roll and of 1960s beat music. In progressive rock, solos had often acquired as much significance as vocalists and occupied as much space and time. They frequently introduced new musical ideas into a number. The contrasting approach, which punk shared, gave the solo the more limited role of reiterating some aspect of the piece already stated. This could be either a riff or chord sequence which moved from the background to the foreground during the instrumental break, a set piece sequence of single notes emphasizing the tempo of the piece or (typically on slower tunes or ballads) an 'atmospheric' solo underlining the emotional tone of the singing.

A classic example of the riff and chord solo comes on The Damned's 'New Rose', while 'Anarchy In The UK' and 'White Riot' contain single note sequences in structures which stretch back to Chuck Berry and Scotty Moore in 1950s rock 'n' roll. There is a noticeable lack of the atmospheric solo in punk rock, however, which reflects punk's lack of concern with melody. The highlighting of the melody line in rock ballads like the Beatles' 'Something' allows the solo to enhance the mood simply by an 'emphatic' repetition of the melody. One possible punk example of an 'atmospheric' solo is Laura Logic's saxophone break on 'Oh Bondage Up Yours!' where the celebratory connotations of the rhythm-and-blues/soul way of playing (in the work of King Curtis and Junior Walker, for instance) can be heard to echo the defiance in Poly Styrene's declamatory vocal stance.

More crucial to punk's sense of difference from other musics is its attitude to rhythm. It is here that the apparent paradox of a music both more 'primitive' and 'revisionist' finds its most appropriate application. Perhaps the most characteristic rhythmic feature of music containing Afro-American elements is syncopation. Indeed, one of Bill Haley's accounts of the formation of his own rock 'n' roll style presents it as the key factor:

> I felt that if I could take, say, a Dixieland tune and drop the first and third beats and accentuate the second and fourth, and add a beat the listeners could clap to as well as dance this would be what they were after.[11]

Syncopated rhythms of this kind accentuate the 'off beat' and in doing so draw the listener into the music to 'supply' the 'missing' first and third beats either mentally or physically, through handclapping, nodding or dancing. The presence of a recognizable syncopation in the music is a precondition for all dancing in the rock-based popular music sphere. The main reason for the 'undanceability' of much punk rock (and for its adoption of the 'pogo' as a suitable dance form) is that, to quote Christgau, it tends to 'submerge' syncopation in its rhythmic patterns.

'Holidays In The Sun' by the Sex Pistols begins with the sound of marching feet, a regular, repetitive, definitely unsyncopated sound. This is followed by the drums falling into the same rhythm. This rhythmic monad (1-1-1-1), as opposed to rock's conventional dyad (1-2-1-2, where the accent is on the second beat), is a state of entropy (or perfection) to which much punk seems constantly aiming.

In effect, many punk recordings contain elements of both the monad and the dyad, either distributed in time (in different parts of the song) or in space (in different parts of the rhythm section). The distribution through time has a place in earlier rock music, where the repetition of the single beat in, say, 'Bits And Pieces' by the Dave Clark Five sets up a tension which is released by a shift into syncopated rhythm. But while the non-syncopated occupies only a small amount of the Dave Clark record, in a punk piece like Alternative TV's 'You Bastard' it is on a par with the emphatically syncopated passages.

More frequently, though, the monad/dyad contrast is distributed among the rhythm instruments, often with the bass and guitar laying a non-syncopated line over the muted syncopation of the drums. Here, Jerry Nolan of the New York Dolls, as described by Christgau, is the archetype of punk drummers: 'although drawn to the backbeat (i.e. syncopation), he submerged it . . . the effects and rhythm changes were there when needed but for the most part held in check'.[12] Even earlier, Christgau also notes, Maureen Tucker of the Velvet Underground had experimented with the elimination of the backbeat: on 'I'm Waiting For The Man', for instance. And much of Ringo Starr's drumming had seemed unsympathetic to syncopation.

The key to what Christgau calls punk's 'forced rhythm' lay in the bass playing. It is here that the monadic rhythm is anchored in a continuous and regular series of single notes which contradict the syncopation of the drumming (one source was John Entwistle's bass line on 'My Generation'). Arthur Kane of the New York Dolls and Sid Vicious were perhaps the 'purest' of punk bass players in that they went furthest in the repetition of notes of the same pitch for as long as possible. Others, such as Clash's Paul Simonon, evolved bass runs or riffs which could shift the rhythmic balance towards the syncopated.

That balance was also affected by the orientation of the lead or rhythm guitar and the tempo of the piece. 'Buzzsaw drone' (Christgau) was the typical punk guitar sound. The 'buzzsaw' tone was achieved by combining rhythm chords of the type pioneered by Pete Townshend of The Who with a tone derived from distortion or feedback. The 'drone', which provided the continuous 'wall of sound' effect, came from the way the riffed chords bled into each other rather than staying separate as in the chopped rhythm chords of 1960s beat group rock. Combined with the monadic bass line, this guitar sound provided a feeling of unbroken rhythmic flow, as the patternings of bar or stanza divisions receded into the background.

That effect of unbroken flow was enhanced by the breakneck eight to the bar rhythm of much punk rock, a feature deriving primarily from the influence of The Ramones on British musicians. Speed, in itself, does not create the impression of 'instant blur' (Christgau). Jerry Lee Lewis's 'Whole Lotta Shakin' Goin' On', after all, was taken at a very fast tempo, but because stanza divisions were clearly signalled it lacks the 'formless' impact of much punk rock.

The fast tempo combined with the anti-syncopation tendency of many punk songs imported the connotation of urgency of utterance which declamatory vocals and their lyrics evoked. For if the pace of a song no longer functions as an impetus to dance it then becomes a sign that the singer needs to get across the message as quickly as possible.

One final point on punk music concerns the balance between monadic and dyadic rhythms. In many recordings, this balance is such that a listener can hear either rhythm as primary. Someone looking for and used to conventional syncopation can align themselves with the drumming, for instance, while a listener concerned to identify with punk's transgressive role in relation to mainstream rock can hear the non-syncopating bass line as foreground, and an incitement to pogo.

Words

Song as communication involves a sender and a receiver, one who addresses and one who is addressed. This process always occurs at two levels. There is an 'external' level where the performer (live or on record) addresses the audience (in the concert hall or beside the record-player or radio). There is also an 'internal' communication taking place within the lyric of the song, between the protagonist of the lyric and its addressee.

On his album *Good Old Boys*, Randy Newman has a song called 'Mr President (Have Pity On The Working Man)'. Externally, this is a communication between Randy Newman the performer and any potential listener to his album. Internally, the lyric's protagonist is a Southern working man and the addressee is the President of the United States. Thus, the lyric itself clearly signals the difference between the two sets of senders and two sets of addressees. Newman is like an actor playing the part of the 'working man', and indeed an actor of the Brechtian school who is required to make a distance between her or himself and the character, rather than fusing with it.

Most popular songs, however, do not have so unambiguous a gap between the external and internal levels of communication.

Those two levels are distinguished in linguistic theory by the terms 'énonciation' and 'énoncé'. They distinguish the two aspects of any utterance: the act of uttering (énonciation) which corresponds to the external level or the performance of a song, and the thing uttered (énoncé) which corresponds to internal level of the statement made by the song lyric.

In most songs, the protagonist of the énoncé, the lyric statement, is identified only by the pronoun 'I', rather than some other feature such as name or occupation. This makes possible the identification by the listener of this subject of the énoncé with the subject of the énonciation – the actual singer delivering the lyric in concert or on record: such was the case of David Bowie and Ziggy Stardust. The likelihood of identification is increased by the ideology of sincerity of performance which permeates attitudes towards much popular singing. This ideology judges vocal performance not by how skilfully a singer can *signify* or present an emotion, such as the frustration of Randy Newman's red neck, but by the listener's idea of how far a singer 'really feels' what is being communicated. This position is intensified as virtually all rock performers write their own material: the assumption being analogous with that of lyric poets – what you write must be what you really feel or think; anything else is bogus or contrived. Explosive moments occur only when the sincerity of a composer of a 'protest' or other song on a broadly political topic is challenged. The issue of 'belief', the accusation of 'bandwagon jumping' arises almost automatically, while it almost never occurs in relation to a love lyric. No performer or composer is made to answer whether they 'really' feel the depth of love or pain attributed to the protagonist of their lyric.

This last point is not quite true, however, if love lyrics are extended to include their obverse, a lyric of hate or degradation addressed to a past or current sexual partner. During the 1960s, a controversy developed over Rolling Stones' songs such as 'Play With Fire', 'Under My Thumb' and 'Out Of Time', which in varying degrees expressed the hatred of a male lyric protagonist for a woman, who was sometimes also the addressee of the lyric.[13] The issue concerned how far the 'I' of the words was identified with the charisma and power of the performer, Mick Jagger. Since the lyrics contained no Newmanesque ironic distancing or internal contradictions, the only ways a listener could avoid assenting to the identification of the lyric protagonist with the performer were by heavily foregrounding the énonciation (so much that the énoncé, the statement itself, was made 'inaudible'), or by what can now be seen as acts of special pleading by critics or commentators.[14]

To hear the énonciation (the performance) separately from the énoncé (the lyric), and to respond in contradictory fashion, with attraction towards the former and repulsion from the latter, was something discussed in some feminist writing on the Rolling Stones and on rock in general.[15] Since the Jagger voice had acquired a generic connotation of affirmation of youth, its affirmative tone on 'Out Of Time' could be heard primarily as meaning that, rather than, or as well as, underlining the triumphal misogyny of the lyric.

A similar controversy arose in punk in relation to The Stranglers, whose output of lyrics with grossly sexist protagonists far surpassed that of the Stones. One difference, however, was that The Stranglers were far more diffuse at the level of énonciation. While the Jagger vocal had established itself as a stable and focal element in any recording, The Stranglers not only employed more than one lead vocalist, but also a variety of accents (mock-cockney, Dylanesque and mid-Atlantic) and 'treated' as well as 'natural' sound. (By treated is meant such effects as phasing or echo which change the sound of the voice.)

The vocal variations in Strangler's recordings were determined by the dramatic demands of the lyric. And énonciation was subordinated to énoncé not in the manner of Randy Newman – to 'place' the lyric protagonist – but to make more overwhelming the message of that protagonist. The Stranglers are the most *literal* of punk vocalists. Their recordings most nearly approach the quality of pure pheno-song, where vocal techniques and embellishments are placed at the service of communicating the lyric message. The result is a popular music equivalent of what Barthes called 'the bourgeois art of song', which 'always wants to treat its consumers as naive customers for whom it must chew up the work and over-indicate the intention, less they be insufficiently gripped'.[16] Even at its most unappetizing, the Stranglers' work is always predigested.

The 'ideology of sincerity' also works to cement énonciation and énoncé for the Stranglers. The invocation of that ideology in relation to punk extended to the 'secondary circulation' of the genre – those texts (reviews, interviews, reports) which were about punk, rather than of it. Especially within interviews, the stated beliefs of musicians, and their congruence with the perceived messages of their lyrics, became routine topics. While the necessity for songs to be seen to be autobiographical was not so crucial for the Stranglers as for, say, Sham 69, their published statements on sexual attitudes made clear their own agreement with the positions presented in their lyrics.

Not every song lyric has a first person as its central figure. Some take the form of a narrative where the main figure or figures are in the third person – he, she, they. This type of lyric is common in the folk ballad tradition, where the énoncé also includes an implicit or explicit first person, the storyteller:

It was of an honest labourer as I've heard people say
He goes out in the morning and he works hard all the day
And he's got seven children and most of them are small
He has nothing but hard labour to maintain them all.[17]

Here the 'I' of the énoncé is no longer the protagonist of the events described there, but a narrator whose position is isomorphic with that of the performer in such a way that the two become virtually indistinguishable. In both énoncé and énonciation, the 'I' is a storyteller and 'you' (the addressees of the communication) are an audience. This is in direct contrast to most lyrics sung in the first person, where the subject of the énoncé is superimposed over that of the énonciation, the 'lover' or 'protester', for instance, over the performer. In a lyric whose 'I' is a narrator and whose protagonist exists in the third person (as 'he' or 'she'), the opposite superimposition occurs: the performer over the storyteller. What each case has in common, though, is that the subject him or herself is a unified one, recognizable as an individual or group of individuals, in whom énoncé and énonciation are reconciled. The characteristics of that individual which allow the recognition to occur can come either from the details of the lyric, from the structural position of the subject of the énoncé (e.g. as narrator) or even from the pre-given features of the performer him or herself.

The unified subject, spanning and uniting both aspects of the utterance (énonciation and énoncé) provides a place for the listener's identification with the amplified voice. But the pull to identification is especially strong because of the homogeneity of the communication, the fully coherent non-contradictory nature of the subject-in-song. This process is common to the majority of performances in every genre of popular song, including punk rock. But what happens if the process of unification of the subject of the utterance does not occur, if no parallel exists between the two 'I's'?

'Holidays In The Sun' by the Sex Pistols contains a lyric with no unified point of origin. The first stanza runs:

> I don't want a holiday in the sun
> I wanna go to the new Belsen
> I wanna see some history
> Cos now I gotta reasonable economy.

An attempt to hear this as the statement of an individual subject could interpret the first three lines as a discussion of a choice of holidays or other journeys, with 'new Belsen' remaining mysterious. The fourth line, however, makes this 'naturalistic' interpretation less tenable. States, not individuals, have 'reasonable economies'. If this is an individual, his idiolect is being signified as exceptionally eccentric. 'Ideolect' is Barthes's term for the 'plurality and co-existence of lexicons in one and the same person, the number and identity of these lexicons forming in some sort a person's ideolect'.[18]

But there is an alternative response to the lyrics of this first verse, one based on recognizing links between words and their connotations across rather than within the linear narrative. That is, words are connected by their membership of the same discourse in the world of communication beyond this particular song. Thus, the presence of 'Belsen' and 'history' suggests Nazism and the Second World War, while the addition of 'reasonable economy' sets up faint echoes of terms like the 'German economic miracle' (a media cliché of the 1960s and beyond to describe the rebuilding of West German prosperity). In this perspective, the lyric becomes something like a collage put together from the discourse of newspaper, advertising, pulp fiction, sensationalized history.

Further verses and the chorus offer more material to support this response: 'Berlin Wall', 'Communist Call', 'World War Three' all make an appearance. To hear the lyric as the product of a unified psychological subject it becomes increasingly necessary to regard the lyric's 'disconnected' narrative form as itself a symptom of a state of psychological disturbance. Verse 3 begins: 'Claustrophobia, too much paranoia/There's too many closets, when will we fall. . . .'

The final vocal passage of the record, delivered in a recitative manner, provides a third dimension to the mode of the énoncé:

I can go over the Wall
This third rate B movie stuff
Cheap dialogue, cheap essential scenery
I'm gonna go over the Berlin Wall
Before they come under the Berlin Wall
I don't understand this bit at all (three times)
Please don't be waiting for me.

While line 1 can be read as part of a skeletal narrative scenario, as a sign of emotional intensity or as an example of Cold War obsessions with the Berlin Wall (including an ironic reversal of the conventional wisdom that people from East Berlin are those determined to climb the Wall), the next lines introduce a new point of reference. What is the 'third rate B movie stuff'? – is this the (barely) unified psychological individual commencing on his own paranoia? Is it the producer of the 'collage' pronouncing on his raw material? Or is it a 'performer', a 'Johnny Rotten' making a comment about the words he has to sing, a comment which is returned to in the penultimate line: 'I don't understand this bit at all'?

There is no 'correct' way to hear this lyric. Where it differs from the bulk of lyrics is that the 'I' of the énoncé is not forced to be unitary. A phrase like 'reasonable economy' can thus *float* towards the complex of meanings suggested by the other political reference points dotted throughout the lyric. While Johnny Rotten's voice, the énonciation, still offers the pleasure of identification with a unified position, a different kind of pleasure – that which enjoys the transgression of the codes through which conventional meanings are constructed – is available for listeners to the lyric.[19]

Punk rock offers two other types of 'mismatch' between the subjects of the énonciation and the énoncé: those where the subject of the latter is presented as contradictory, and those where it shifts within the song in an unsignalled way. The classic example of the first type is 'Oh Bondage Up Yours!' by X-Ray Spex. The verse presents a 'masochistic' subject:

> Bind me, tie me, chain me to the wall
> I wanna be a slave to you all

While the chorus following immediately indicates a rebellious subject:

> Oh Bondage! Up yours!
> Oh Bondage! No more!

Unable to grasp the sense of this contradiction and obsessed with the first verse, the censors of BBC radio refused to broadcast the record. But the lyric worked rather like a classic narrative, with the first sections posing a major enigma – how can these two utterances be reconciled? The next verse offered the solution:

> Chain store, chain smoke, I consume you all
> Chain gang, chain mail, I don't think at all

In this perspective, the first verse became a metaphor for the voluntary servitude of consumers in a 'consumerist' society of chain stores and chain smoking. The chorus became a rallying cry of a consumer who refused to conform.

In a sense, 'Oh Bondage' is the lyric as drama (with two speakers) while 'Holidays In The Sun' can be heard as lyric as collage (many speakers) and the vast majority of lyrics are monologues or poems (one speaker). Siouxsie and the Banshees' song 'Mittagerzen (Metal)' is another example of the dramatic énoncé, where the 'speaking' subject shifts within the lyric. Here are the chorus and final verse:

> Metal is tough, metal will sheen
> Metal won't rust when oiled and cleaned
> Metal is tough, metal will sheen
> Metal will rule in my masterscheme.

> It's ruling our lives, there is no hope
> Thought I'd drop a line, the weather here is fine
> But day and night it blares
> Commanding through loudspeakers.

94 The Grain of Punk: Analysis of Lyrics

The song's origin is a 1930s anti-Fascist montage by John Heartfield, which sardonically depicts a German family eating metal in a Germany where all is sacrificed to re-armament. The first person of the song's chorus is the voice of fascism or totalitarianism in general – part of the lyric's aim is to draw modern parallels with the role of television as 'conditioning'. The subject who communicates the verse, in contrast, is a victim of the metallic masterscheme. The lyrics themselves, like those of 'Holidays In The Sun', link hints of prison or concentration camps ('commanding through loudspeakers') with references to holiday-making ('weather here is fine' – a clichéd postcard message).

Despite those examples of non-unified subjects, there is little difference between most punk rock lyrics and the generality of popular songs in the position of the subject of the énoncé. But the situation of the addressee shows some contrasts. Table 4.1 compares the addressees of the 1976 Top 50 songs with those of the lyrics of songs on the 'first five' punk albums.

Table 4.1 *A comparison of the addressees of the 1976 Top 50 songs and the lyrics of songs on the 'first five' punk albums.*

	Punk	Top 50
2nd person singular: lover etc.	31% (21)	54% (27)
2nd person singular: other	21% (13)	4% (2)
2nd person plural: general	39% (26)	32% (16)
2nd person plural: specific	9% (6)	6% (3)

Two Top 50 records (4%) were instrumentals.

While the overall proportion of lyrics aimed at individual addressees is broadly similar, there is a clear contrast in the types of individual addressed. Nearly all Top 50 songs addressed to a single person are to an actual, former or potential romantic or sexual partner, but only just over half of the punk lyrics in this category are so addressed. Punk introduces a high proportion of lyrics addressed to individuals other than 'lovers'. The two Top 50 lyrics in this category are addressed to an old friend (Abba's 'Fernando') and a dancer (Tina Charles's 'Dance Little Lady

Dance'). The punk addressees include a male friend (The Vibrators' 'She's Bringing You Down'), but are mostly aimed at male enemies.

There had been a sub-genre of American black street culture which filtered into the urban blues music, called the 'dozens'. This involved a competition to see who could invent the most imaginative and most outrageous insult to the other person involved.[20] Apart from a few of Bob Dylan's and the Rolling Stones's lyrics of the 1960s, very few white performers had worked on lyrics of the 'put-down'. Until punk that is, and especially until the Sex Pistols.

Four of the dozen songs on their first album are addressed to individuals as hymns of hate. 'New York' deals with an American, '17' is aimed at a 29-year-old who can't accept that the singer is 'a lazy sod', while 'Liar' and 'Problem' are directed to individuals who are just that. As befitted the notions of directness and authenticity surrounding punk, the targets of these songs were supposed in punk rock and journalistic circles to be actual people (just as Bob Dylan's 'Mr Jones' had been said to be inspired by the critic Ralph J. Gleason). Of the other punk bands, The Damned take aim at a journalist in 'Stab Yor Back' ('You dirty hack'), and The Vibrators pour scorn on a dead person in 'Stiff Little Fingers': 'If it wasn't for your stiff little fingers, nobody'd know you were dead.'

Elsewhere in punk rock lyrics, some individual addressees are defined in terms of their occupation, or place in the social system. But these 'agit-rock' songs – like Clash's 'Tommy Gun' (to a soldier) and Angelic Upstarts' 'Youth Leader' ('You're the one with the double face') – are rare in punk rock. More frequent are songs whose addressees are in the second plural, and correspond to 'Them' in the common ideological couplet of 'Us against Them'. These lyrics are included in the category '2nd person plural: specific' in Table 4.1. The 'general' category refers to those lyrics where the form of the communication is either that of a narrative dealing with a third person (e.g. 'Janie Jones' by The Clash) or a soliloquy, where the first person presents his or her feelings without directing them to any specific listener(s).

Although they form a small proportion of the lyrics, it is significant that the 'plural specific' addresses occur more often among punk songs than among the Top 50. Elsewhere in punk rock, in fact, they are even more prominent. It is equally important to note that the plural addressees in the three Top 50 songs are connected with love ('Young Hearts Run Free') and with music ('Play That Funky Music' and 'Don't Take Away The Music'). That is, they remain defined within the standard topics of popular entertainment. The paucity of collective and specific addressees in mainstream lyrics is explained by the predominance there of love themes, which are only exceptionally addressed to a group of people ('Lovers Of The World Unite' for instance) rather than to one.

Outside the standard areas of lovers, dancers, musicians, what kind of identity can the collective addressees of a lyric be given? Within the stream of music deriving from rock 'n' roll, the overwhelming tendency has been to maintain a parallel between the receiver of the énonciation (the audience of the performer) and the receiver of the énoncé (the addressee in the lyric). The pattern is similar to that already found at the originating end of the musical communication, where the two 'I's' are so often brought together.

In this way, the addressees of the popular song are kept as numerous as possible (by not defining the nature of the listeners, they are not divided), just as in most '2nd person singular' songs, the addressee becomes as unique and as vaguely defined as possible. This clearly locks into the economic imperatives of the popular music institution – the drive for the widest possible appeal of a song would be hindered if its addressees were 'limited' to a specific type of person.

Nevertheless, some song lyrics do specify a type of addressee, usually defined in terms of gender or age. Tammy Wynette's 'Stand By Your Man' is a homily to women only, while Slade's 'Cum On Feel The Noize' is addressed to 'all you girls and boys'. Like lovers and dancers, however, these are roles (heterosexual female partners; 'Young Ones') already established as individual addressees within popular song, and the issues of identification for listeners outside these gender and age groups are to some degree similar (and will be discussed later in this chapter).

More pertinent are the even fewer instances of addressees whose definition is from outside the standard set of roles and themes in song lyrics. The folk tradition provides examples of lyrics addressed to occupational groups ('Come All Ye Bold Miners'), but work is a theme rigorously excluded from popular song.[21] 'Back Home', a Number 1 record in 1970 by the England World Cup Football Team, is a solitary example of addressees defined by nationality. Perhaps the place where these non-standard addressees appear most, however, is in the 'protest' mode. Lyrics with these concerns which have direct addressees (as opposed to general second person plural 'narrative' lyrics), fall into three categories. A small number are addressed to 'us', those already believing in the cause ('We Shall Overcome'). There are then those denouncing the people responsible for the social evil; 'You masters of war' sang Bob Dylan. Finally, there are a greater number whose object is persuasion, and whose addressees are more general, and might be defined in opinion-poll terms as 'don't knows'. Dylan's addressee in 'Blowin' In The Wind' is 'my friend', while John Lennon sings 'I hope someday that you will join us' in 'Imagine'.

While I have at several points suggested certain similarities between punk rock songs and those of the protest mode, it is here that the two diverge most sharply. While punk has its lyrics of denunciation and those addressed to 'us', there are no lyrics aimed at a friendly but non-committal listener. Politics as persuasion has no place in punk rock.

Here are a selection of lyrics addressed to the second person plural, and denouncing those addressees:

> I hate the Civil Service rules / I won't open letter bombs for you.
> (Clash: 'Career Opportunities')

> You sit up there deciding my future
> What the fuck do you think you are
> ... If you like peace and flowers, I'm going to carry knives and chains.
> (Slits: 'Number One Enemy')

> Your future dream is a shopping scheme
> (Sex Pistols: 'Anarchy In The UK')

> We're the people you don't wanna know
> We come from places you don't wanna go.
> (Sham 69: 'Angels With Dirty Faces')

Although only one of these comes near to giving the denouncees

98 The Grain of Punk: Analysis of Lyrics

a name – the 'Civil Service' context suggests the State or the Government – each has a slightly different definition of the enemy according to punk rock. Together, these examples indicate the spectrum of that enemy. The Slits lyric firstly refers to a 'you' who rules and has power over the subordinate group represented by the singer. It could therefore include a range of enemies from the various functionaries of the State to the older parental generation. The second extract from 'Number One Enemy' suggests that the range definitely extends beyond the traditionally defined ruling class of the Clash's lyric: here those espousing and promoting 'hippie' ideals are part of the denouncees. 'Anarchy In The UK' introduces a further aspect. Earlier in the song, the protagonist of the lyric has declared his ambition to 'destroy passers-by', an inspired naming which underlines the clichéd nature of the word and the abject character of the social role to which it refers; a 'passer-by' as a person who avoids involvement in a situation – there is a Biblical root in the story of the Good Samaritan. The 'passer-by' idea is perhaps picked up again in the line quoted above: the kind of 'average person' or 'straight' who would be a passer-by would also be limited to the conventional notion of future improvement in their life being defined as a new shopping centre. To these notions of the enemy as the ruling class, hippies, older people and those adhering to conventional behaviour, Sham 69 adds a notion of class difference based on status and life-style rather than (or as well as) on political power. The geographical dimension ('places you don't wanna go') refers to the districts or estates inhabited by the 'inner city' stratum of the working class with which Sham 69 and many of the bands who came after them were identified.

That identification was explicitly made in the lyrics of Sham 69. 'Angels With Dirty Faces' has a chorus which includes the line 'Kids like me and you', while the strongest example of a lyric where the addressee is directly identified with the peer-group of the protagonist is 'If The Kids Are United'. It is important to establish here that this kind of direct identification of the protagonist with a wider group, including the addressees of the lyric, is almost totally absent from the songs of the earliest punk rock bands, the 'first five'. Unlike Sham 69, the Sex Pistols, Stranglers and Clash rarely concern themselves with establishing the positive existence of a movement to which they belong. Negativity and individuality dominate the lyrics, although the 'friendly' use of the second person is sometimes to be found there. In 'Career Opportunities', Clash use the lines 'Every job they offer you / Is to keep you out of the dock', while 'Anarchy In The UK' has 'Not many ways to get what you want'.

This use of 'you', of course is at one level an alternate version of the first person singular – it equals 'I', just as the word 'one' does when used in more formal or bourgeois discourses. But it also serves to link the addressee with the protagonist, inviting the former to identify with the viewpoint of the latter. In 'linking' the two, it stands between the separation of a lyric which uses 'I' in a similar context, and the total identification expounded by lyrics like those of Sham 69.

It is clear from the lines quoted above that a number of punk lyrics have modes of address that seem to shift from one addressee to another, just as we have seen that some have no constant subject of the énoncé (e.g. 'Holidays In The Sun'). Thus, 'you' in 'Career Opportunities' changes from the Civil Service enemy to the linking of 'you' in 'Every job they offer you'. This shifting is also found in 'Hong Kong Garden', Siouxsie and the Banshees' first hit single from 1979. There, 'you' at some points refers to the Chinese (the title refers to a restaurant) and at others to the Westerners, as customers or tourists.

The vast majority of popular song lyrics have a single, stable point which is addressed, and a stable point from which the lyric is delivered. In standard love songs, of course, these positions are well established before the lyric is written: one lover to his or her partner. In protest songs deriving from folk traditions, such as those of Bob Dylan, a series of positions for addressees are marked out: they can be co-believers, those whom the singer wants to persuade, or those whom the singer is denouncing as the enemy. What happens in many punk lyrics is that two of these addressees appear in the same lyric, while in Dylan there is only one in any song.

There is a precedent for the punk approach in some soul music lyrics of the 1960s. Nina Simone's 'Mississippi Goddam' and 'I'm Talkin' About Freedom', recorded by Syl Johnson, are examples where both fellow blacks and the white power structure are addressed in the same song.[22] Perhaps in each case (civil rights soul and punk rock) this shifting in the lyric connotes the urgency of the message to be transmitted, which the listener is intended to realize overrides the need to observe formal consistency in the construction of the lyric. As we have seen this 'inconsistency' is a feature of other aspects of punk rock, notably Rotten's singing style.

Notes

1. See Sean Cubitt, 'Maybellene: Meaning and the Listening Subject', in R. Middleton and D. Horn (eds), *Popular Music A Yearbook: Vol. 4 Performers & Audiences*, Cambridge University Press, 1984, p. 211.
2. P. Tagg, *Fernando the Flude*, 1981, p. 14, University of Gothenberg Press, 1971.
3. R. Barthes, *Image–Music–Text*, London, Fontana, 1977, p. 182.
4. For an explanation of these terms, see Introduction, D. Laing, *One Chord Wonders*, Open University Press, 1985, p. x.
5. R. Hoggart, *Uses of Literacy*, Penguin, 1957, p. 102.
6. For comments on this concept, see above, D. Laing, *One Chord Wonders*, pp. 107 and 123–5.
7. P. Tagg, *Fernando the Flute*, p. 13.
8. S. Frith, *Sound Effects*, Constable, 1981, p. 161.
9. Tom Carson, 'Rocket to Russia', in G. Marcus (ed.), *Stranded: Rock and Roll for a Desert Island*, New York, 1979, p. 108.
10. Robert Christgau, 'New York Dolls', in G. Marcus (ed.), *Stranded*, p. 135.
11. C. Gillett, *The Sound of the City*, Souvenir Press, 1970, p. 30.
12. Robert Christgau, 'New York Dolls', in G. Marcus (ed.), *Stranded*, p. 139.
13. See the articles by Alan Beckett and Richard Merton in *New Life Review* 47, January–February 1968.
14. See, e.g., Richard Merton in *New Left Review*, 47, January–February 1968, and D. Laing, 1969, p. 144.
15. See, e.g., Susan Hiwatt, 'Cock Rock', in J. Eisen (ed.), *Twenty Minute Fabdangos and Forever Changes*, New York, 1971, pp. 141–7.
16. R. Barthes, *The Eiffel Tower and Other Mythologies*, New York, Hill & Wang, 1979, p. 119.
17. B. Copper, *A Song for Every Season*, London, 1975, p. 275.
18. R. Barthes, *The Eiffel Tower*, p. 47.
19. For a stimulating and related analysis of this song, see Greil Marcus,

'Anarchy in the U.K.', in J. Miller (ed.), *The Rolling Stone History of Rock and Roll*, New York, 1980, pp. 460–1.
20. See P. Oliver, *The Meaning of the Blues*, New York, 1963, pp. 151–2.
21. Even in those few lyrics which do deal with work, the addressee is almost never defined as a 'worker' as such. These songs of work include 'Chain Gang' (Sam Cooke), 'Working Girl' (Merilee Rush), '9 to 5' (Dolly Parton), 'Part of the Union' (Hudson-Ford), 'Right Said Fred' (Bernard Cribbins) and 'Crushed by the Wheels of Industry' (Heaven 17).
22. The lyrics of these songs can be found in A. X. Nicholas (ed.), *The Poetry of Soul*, New York, 1971, pp. 55 and 61.

5

The Shattered Glass: Notes on Bryan Ferry

Ian Penman

I

The initiative of Pop strips away our childish name and enshrines the promise of a future body. The teenaged child, plotting the disposal or dereliction of the Father proper, seeks or stumbles upon an illicit replacement – a Pop who is sexily asexual, unavailable, absent; an approximate Pop.

> A proxy mate, a proxy music
> A finer edition of each and any 'you'

Spun in a voice of such beautiful insincerity: selfishly Utopian, confidently exhausted, brilliantly spent, a natural sibilant snare of langorous cynicism. Somewhere over the confused rainbows of adolescence, but shorn of growing up's obsolete sense. A figure who speaks some special thing or other – the spice of a vaguely revealed life, the warmth of gilded abstraction – to fill your lonely night. Something that cannot or should not be named.
Unclassifiable, *then*.

* * *

> the interminable misfortune of their silence is that their best spokesmen are also those who betray them best.
> (Jacques Derrida)

> So when people ask 'How can you relate to working class kids?' all I can say is, I was one. (Bryan Ferry)

The Shattered Glass: Notes on Bryan Ferry

Your name is Bryan Ferry, as far as we can tell. But we shall have to go much further than is customary in these matters – go all the way through such customs in fact – in order, finally, to ask of you: anything to declare?

To ask something of how you came to lead us on and build us up. How you disappeared – as Fathers will, as others do – only to return, during a succession of later dates, as regular as clockwork, reliable and respectable and as stately as the chimes of a homely midnight.

The glossy toll of it: what we now perceive as a *pre* destination: land without cost, price without object, place without name or accent – Avalon; other world of pure atmosphere, autumn swirl of shrivelled or dying signs (that once were lustrous: 'dance' – 'drug' – 'love'); making solemn play of an immensely empty escape in the facades of an *eternal* tone – windswept, misty, limpidly sensual, banal. Which now, we can but hear, seems to be where you have been trailing us down the years: a litter of precious things, a treasure of references, restored to the peak of antiquity – a brand new old-fashioned 'you' is the disappointing result.

Somehow, it is said, and the tone is accusatory, the *real* or potential Bryan Ferry was lost to us, taken away on a detour without end, now rests in a healthy but depleted serenity, pretty vacant, tinkering and toiling, a shadow of a gargoyle for the new decency, an adult finally orientated. No more than a worriedly graceful old bedroom philosopher, nothing untoward, a part of the scenery, with all the necessary airs of a conclusive and forlorn naturalness.

Having weighed up a world or two in his time, he has sold out, has sold 'us' out; our Pleasure devalued, we are now – now this is rich! – finally nothing more than 'Boys and Girls'. Have you ever heard such elaborate, ornate banality! You think *that* is all our pleasure amounts to these days?

* * *

Then, a time when we were young and in love with the *bright* not-quite of Roxy. *When we were young* – didn't we regard their pleasure with a reasonable amount of innocence? We surely knew sex was involved but not necessarily how it was involved, or how involved it was. Bryan F. and Brian E. were dreams of a sex that was both adult and *other* – indefinably so since nothing specific, no protest, nothing *Play For Today*. Just a play made for today, a flare that promised darker things. Like Science Fiction's attractiveness for the teenaged reader – *pre-* or *post-* Gender without the intermediary details, without the emotional shocks. Creatures whose overstressed and slightly askew conception of glamour was ritually arresting. Glam was a rite of passage for Pop/Rock – retaining the *tackiness* of Hippie garb, but going some way towards an eventual reclamation of pure glamour for its outermost skin. Glam salved the pain of transition in a kind of Panto ineptitude; and it cheered up the '70s.

Roxy wasn't quite as gladrags Camp as the navvies-in-girls'-blouses abrasion of Slade, Gary Glitter, Mud, and never as glum as the more serious fools like Black Sabbath and Led Zeppelin; but they did have a bit of the appeal of both worlds, even if the fit was always *not quite*. 'Non musician' Eno, avant-jazz guitarist Manzanera and Andy McKay's occasional oboe put them in a New York kind of mood/moog lineage to begin with – Blues *incorporated* rather than renovated. Roxy's transgressiveness didn't have that *dark side behind it all* hint of Bolan and Bowie, Stones and Zeppelin. The rhythms in blue may ultimately derive from the same levee, but the water came out scented, distilled, no world of torture (artistic or actual) offstage and out of sight.

Ferry was both less campy *and* less of a man than Jagger or Bowie. The sex was never upfront: it was always – and, step by step, increasingly so – veiled behind some *style* or other. Some other's style . . .

Too many times beautiful!
Too many times sad . . .

The first album alternates between high seriousness and high camp, at its best confusing the two in a mournful twine of sham pain and exaggerated joys. (Here also is the jubilant and un-arch breeze of two-minute Pop that blows through the two singles 'Virginia Plain' and 'Pyjamarama'.) By any unreasonable measure, one might have to say that in terms of a 'pure' unfettered jubilation of Pop, Roxy Music should have existed long enough to give us 'Pyjamarama' and given up, there and then; the rest, you could say – and not cynically – is only the careering history of Ferry's error. The songs of this Roxy Music rejoice in a studied dissolution of the calm clear Pop Song; yet it is always a celebratory (not yet *celebrity*) death of popular song and the always hopeful fears contained by that song.

To begin with: he admits defeat. 'I tried – but I could not find a way! Looking back all I did was look away . . .'

It is a standard ploy of the practised Casanova: his seduction begins with a moment of turning away, of seeming to give up, of a long and weary sigh. '*Now – that – we are lonely* . . .' Then, this is what will seem to be so attractive: he is surely reconciled to this fate, has known Fate, must have been through all this before, eternally perhaps, and knows what's what and what this is all about and therefore *what's to be done*. He must know exactly how those obscure pulleys and levers spin round and around; how to set in motion their ploys and transports . . . back, and forth.

This lounge lizard cries crocodile tears on your shoulder. '*I would do anything for you!*' For *you* and no other. His directness is a sidestep, his remonstrations of bleak loneliness but one step closer to your heart; each obscuring diversion one more step up the ladder to you, for you, for your sake. For your pleasure: his present state.

To begin this seduction his Roxy is done up to the nines, is shining, obtuse, frantic, resplendent, dramatic, confused, all over the place, foggy, insiduous, full of half-remembered airs and graces. But it is most of all *corrupt*: nostalgic, practised, and corrupt. The rough edges of imperfection, the churlishness and excitation of its baptismal innocence – all rely on (are fed by) a secret reserve; this crude charm insinuates oh so much experience. *We've been around a long time –*

In not striving to put anything to us at all *truthfully* 'Roxy Music' could be said to observe the passing-out of Rock as Sixties antagonism and usher in the heated indecision of Seventies flair: entertainment as mass fetish, entertainers as heroic in a conservative rather than a hastily *anti*-Heroic mould. Bowie's Ziggy Stardust and the early Ferrys quite literally *personify* this: Rock returns the glamour of mannerism to itself. Both Bowie and Ferry give themselves to be taken both seriously and serially – the serial cashing-in of personae cancelling out the danger of a too-serious ossification, of arrest; each step is not to be taken seriously as an end, as meaning; but more as a general celebration of *the* end of Rock's most recent tone. The ones nearest to glamour, the ones who burned and were bright (Jones, Morrison, Hendrix) are to be mourned; for what remained in their wake was an 'alternative' society that had become as frumpy and set in its daily routine as 'straight' society.

> I tried – but I could not find a way! Looking back all I did was look away –

It's not clear and never will be whether this 'looking back' of his designates a look back *from* the present; or a past and discarded habit of looking back. Whether, looking back, it was a clearing rush of nihilism, or the remembrance of nostalgia past. Despite Pop's addiction to the Now, it is in transition that Roxy Music will be most definite, definitive, leaving a jagged open-endedness that cannot but continue to resonate. It is as if Ferry were using his Roxy song across 'Roxy Music' and 'For Your Pleasure' to get the End over with, to finish it all off, in order to get on with 'better' things. There are not only no *statements* contained across these songs, but there is no attempt to create a Mood, a scene, a tonal impersonation, of something other than what the Song already is. (Ferry will later denigrate his Song in the name of overall *quality*.) At this stage, during that brief staging of a Pop irony supreme, Ferry is as wary of the alluring patina of aspiration as of Rock's dulled claims to rebellion and authenticity.

The baptism (which marks and mourns the death of another scene) requires a commonplace name.

Where better than the *Roxy*, baptismal name and place, which in the space of a breath makes *Rock sexy* again – makes it once again assertively vulnerable, unfinished, hesitant, latent, makes it once again tremble before the mirror? The *Roxy* passes cleansingly from one insinuation to an other, from class memory to some obscure connotation of classiness. It maybe betrays nothing of the more Classical leanings to come but still manages to evoke something less tawdry than Rock – an abstract world of past quality made presently alive: the Roxy is the space of a screen between mostly American otherworlds of eternal monochrome glamour and your expectant gaze.

Roxy Music itself, as name, as sign, will pass into history *before* it dies: in the late Seventies and early Eighties – when albums

continue to appear, to great success – ex-fans will casually reminisce
... 'Remember Roxy Music?', just as others mourned the passing
not of a cinema but of *'The Roxy'*: metaphor for melancholy and
melancholy metaphor, a childhood seduction, space where desire
was awakened and given its image repertoire, and possibly its
language for ever . . .

*   *   *

Recalling his own seduction at the feet of Art and by the tongues
of others, henceforth he must attempt to make his *own* voice
heard – so that he might catch himself giving voice to that same
sweet effortless seduction.

*How can a body make the voice its own? How to make a voice
lose its self-consciousness? How to make your voice do other than
what it is saying? How to make even the voice's dissimulation your
very own? And how* now *to make it?*

Ferry does it thus: by disowning his voice.

In order to single out the voice that will become his alone above
all others, his calling card, *passe partout*, his seamlessly Pop voice,
he must lose his way. Singing is not speaking, after all.

Must lose his way and find an approach.

And so he keeps his distance – *within these songs* – all the while
keeping his *some-ideal-Song* in the distance – and keeps to singing
the distance. It will be this trick of avoiding a truthful presentation –
and keeping an edge or two of distance within – that excites. He
sings of glamour, but distantly, as of a fable, *it can't be true.* He is
sardonic, he sings from an outside of glamour. He imparts its
form, but is still content to leave his picture unfinished, hanging
in the air. He is not part of it, we keep hearing this sardonic note.
We keep hearing an unruly accent also – which we may choose to
call his, for the sake of economy. The accent is heard as intermittance and so retains an edge, a vibrancy, an element of surprise.
Cool as he tried to keep things, at this stage he still cannot still his
accent, cannot steal it from himself and bury it away.

II

We do not demand of an accent that it give any directions; that it let slip anything of the future. Accent, it is easy to say, speaks only what cannot be eradicated, and gives nothing to be anticipated. It is a vocal track always turning back upon itself, always turning the voice in, freely giving away information about its owners' identities. We can be certain: accent is spoken, without shadows, without a doubt. Accent is taken as giving away someone's origin – not necessarily the entirety of who or what they now consider themselves to be; but still it affixes everywhere an initial, immediate address, and therefore *a partial identity*. We listen for instance, for some sign that might – in making the sung give way – let loose the slippery matter of origin: scree at the end of the word, curvature of a sentence, pressure points, unanticipated flights.

From the first syllable, Ferry's longing for languor is incompatible with the underlying impatience of his accent, the working-class remark which ought to betray some vestigial traces of *industry*. The vigorous, sadistic self-confidence of the stand-up comedian, for instance: a confidence that is a protection against the outside, rather than a movement towards it; even when financially successful the comedian will still *deliver* his jokes as if part of the original community.

If accent is found in song, it is spoken of as lending the song a 'lyrical' air or quality, with an optional 'haunting'. What is 'lyrical' is engaged in *expressing direct usually intense personal emotion*, it belongs to *a personal direct intense style or quality in an art*. And this is surely what we feel of an accent: that its anachronistic fluctuation is more than anything else *direct*. But what does it say? It is far from radical. It opens, each time, directly, intensely, onto a past which we haplessly resonate.

In song, accent is considered a 'lyrical' bonus – something rhythmic, unnecessary, other. An 'accent' is often used to designate something very close to vocal technique – an accent felt as common to Gospel, for instance, by which we mean to say: a *common* technique, a common form of address. It may be that the stresses of an accent are what tie song to a particular idiom or community. In Gospel, what could be considered histrionic is perceived the very opposite: selfless subjugation *to* technique, whereby it is not the Self that gesticulates, but a self given over to the accepted norm. What is most let out holds the self in place – to a place, a time, to an idea best borne by Song, to a constant. To an idea of Time: an oscillation between now and a 'collective' past, between the present 'I' and all others who have previously performed the same scene. An oscillation which is often called tradition. (If an accent is constantly to the fore, is *expected of* the texture of the song – in Folk Musics, for instance – then it is settled, as part of a different system of effects entirely: homogenous, integrated, exaggerated, easy on the ear.)

For accent Webster gives the following definition: fr. Latin *accentus*, fr. *ad-* + *cantus* song, fr. *cantus* pp. of *canere* to sing.

So accent will always be a following definition, will always be coming from the behind or beyond of a 'pp. . . . to sing'.

Then this is what accent must be: to be gone, but still to come. To come back again, unexpectedly. (To be tumbled by your accent.)

Without content as such, an outline, accent will always have to content itself with a definition *to follow:* To have an accent, to speak with an accent, to have to re-present and be representative of an accent, is already to sing; but only given the prospect or ideal of a pure, clear, unblemished, univocality: accent is one more potential obstacle in the way of the purely spoken. It is unnecessary (to a pure notion of communication, to a notion of pure communication), it is unwarranted – it has no authority. It is no longer as noble a voice as could be – it has delivered itself over to the degeneracy of *tone*. And a tone that is not yours, properly speaking; not singular to you; that belongs, forever, elsewhere.

You feel it as a ghost. It is not the accent that is ghostly – it is all too tangible. It is you that feel yourself to be ghostly, the aftereffect or imprint of your accent. But no *one* ghost. Accent, your host, speaks in your place, goes on ahead of you because it has history on its side. History, put to work in the voice, the present mark, the bruise of a long forgotten cut, past that is not mine but is interlaced with mine and is mine to display, to share in, to have shares in. Marking the time spent, elsewhere, by others: the journey before me, that is not me, but whose debt I assume. The rhythm of accent separates – joins the voice to history (voice as history: with its 'moments of intensity, its lapses, its periods of feverish agitation, its fainting spells' – Foucault). Accent as economy: lending prominence, distributing sense, dispensing privileges, imposing penalty or stress. Accent *stresses* identity – but whose? (The question always remains for you, for your time being: what in a voice can you call your own?)

Despite its apparently egalitarian nature one might say that accent is that which Pop Music often has to try to lose or tone down in order to have style or class. True style or true class – the contradiction of *lasting* style, or a mythic Now which reflects the lost stability of all Pasts.

A more becoming accent: this now is what accent must become. Thus *preoccupied* by now, it betokens the accent to become neutral. But accent may be felt a site of loss (of control, self-consciousness, power); of what cannot be lost or jettisoned other than by a protracted and stumbling excommunication. There can be no simple erasure, of course (leaving what?); only a *relatively* convincing recession, tension, holding in, ventriloquism. A covering note.

Ferry's eventual retirement into multi-layered decorum – his forging or forgery of a timeless Englishness, a very carefully soiled and landscaped debilitation – is founded on the loss of accent. The Geordie accent is more elastic and relaxed than many, but Ferry's slackening of the line is something else again, an arch half-parody of elocution-in-progress, apprentice aesthete, see-through, unreliable, still spivvishly shifty. For 'Roxy Music' and 'For Your Pleasure' the mock elocution barely controls the stubborn accent – which subsists, persists, perforates, intervenes, slices at the ends of words. ('Stranded', by comparison – the title forewarns before we commence our hearing – is intermediary, cosmopolitan, plays with an uneven and perplexing variety of accents and voices, is preparatory to a complete phasing out of the northern Ferry.)

An *autographic* voice, signing in the register of song, under an assumed name or an adoptive tone: this, for the time being, is his style. (Even his archness is arch, an effect – he's stalling, playing about, sorting through the effects of others.) For 'Roxy Music' and 'For Your Pleasure' the Northern accent remains very much in evidence. The question is – is it used as evidence? More, does Ferry use it in evidence against himself? In the general tone of proxy theatricality and dissimulation, the accent stands out all the more. But at the cost of appearing to be just another effect?

III

It is, we might have to say, a fine irony for such a visually predisposed artist as Ferry to be working in sound at all. But his every step – supposedly taking him further from the heaven of a pure visual presentation – will be dogged by *how things must look*. On the shoreline of *For Your Pleasure*, beneath it, on the waterfront strand, stands the second of many new models: at first sight the second instalment or installation of the stock Ferry/Roxy woman. Ferry fills out his function as her chauffeur (landlocked ferryman: a sign of the times). He waits in amused admiration, surveying the neatness of his visual pun – the model takes her cat (for a) walk: forming a *uni-form* and uniformly predatory alliance with her black panther, eyes and mouth directed out at the viewer. Imperiously, she takes the air, she fields his grace, takes her anima for a prowl and a stretch. Ferry – to be sure – remains to be seen, smiling manfully behind her back, artfully protected by the fold in his sleeve. He has arranged his own look as both within and outside of the main frame. All done with the loveliest of sharp metallic blues – and this is a modern blues scene after all; it's an obvious point, but we all know what the lady of the house really wants with her chauffeur, what order of hood and drive and ride we are really taking stock of here. It's a polite confusion of pleasures, of who comes where on Pleasure's role, of who is whose pleasure, who is servicing who. In other words of who appears to be serving who.

She is a model woman, to be sure; fashion pushing into abstraction and rarified codification, not there for the benefit of a product as such or altogether in the name of Art; so she appears to be what? She appears, on the condition that she appear to be without attributes. We can attribute nothing to her beyond a certain imaginary realm of wealth, of wealth as fetish, (Helmut) Newton's law of physiques. She is sheerest sharp blue nothingness. (For the cool-and-blue post-Duchamp artist, it seems entirely appropriate for beauty to take the veiled form of the *scissors*.)

His cover, as usual, appears to be a tribute to Woman – to her splendour and glamour; posted on to her, forwarded as an address which she has no say in: a tribute to the not-true of her truth. The artist *sees through* the veil of her: to the frozen peace of glamour. The realm of a certain narcissistic eroticism he is not allowed entrance to without putting his heterosexual *sensibility* in doubt.

Whilst he suffers knowledge as a malady, m'lady is projected as emblematic of a happy, vapid yet calculating (and innoculative)

For Your Pleasure sleeve. Provided by courtesy of E. G. Records Ltd, © 1973

modernity. *She* is moreover at home in it; in a crisis of identity . . . in which she has nothing to add. And you don't ask why.

All his Songs' women (and this will be especially so with 'Stranded' and subsequent plaints) are voiceless sirens who – although wielding the utmost power over the artist's life and sensibility – seem to be without implication (which is to say: eternalised out of existence). Neutered time and place (those perennial spans of Fashion) coalesce naturally into the figure of

Roxy Music sleeve. Provided by courtesy of E. G. Records Ltd, © 1973

the woman. Woman as figure, or scene – war pin-up, cat-woman, amazon, siren, Riefenstahl Maedchen. Myth fits her figure well, myth is draped around her: the artist drapes his model with myth. Her value is immortal (which is almost a device for insuring the degree of disappointment and betrayal her suitor will eventually feel); phrophylactic embodiment of Aesthetics on the condition that she say nothing. She is constantly referred to, always there especially when absent: this is her virtue, her virtual nature. Which she is chiselled out of. A frozen asset. Speak to me, only speechlessly. An always monumental woman, monument to no one woman, various editions of the myth of Woman, editions of 'you', of . . . the stock Roxy body that all of the audience can have shares in – because all of these women share the same roxy body.

He may be the ferryman, the chauffeur, but her job is to deliver the male to himself. He reads the letter of her pleasure as if gazing back into the pool of his own eyes – it makes *his starry eyes shiver*. (It is – and will always appear to be – most of all his eyes that are enraptured – or ruptured – by sex.)

'Do The Strand' launches 'For Your Pleasure' with a fevered antipathy – elaborating its deliberately pointless command into a breathless litany of names not so much dropped as skimmed into the dry electric Roxy texture. 'Do The Strand' is a play with *the idea of* a youth anthem, the perfect dream of a dance step – which (it) is not; an idea of a dance you cannot do – or perhaps we are doing for him what he cannot, or is too cool, to do. We are commandeered to do this step, to act as Pop's young must, are given examples of where it might be done and who with. It's a movement made up only of movements (pop goes the Hegel!), history as self-consuming if not fulfilling appetite. It takes in nature and culture, high and low culture, past atrocity and present glamour: room for everything and . . . *perfectly blank*. (Our instructor has conveniently left out the instructions.)

'Do The Strand': *perhaps* . . . how not to be alone, how to avoid coming face to face with yourself. In our stranded post-Modern age mobility is all, no sign is permanent, no value is fixed, no one Dream is your resting-place for long. But what to *do* now? How to go it alone and blend with the crowd: a primer in Youth Culture. But there are so many strands and styles to choose from now (the Warhol pupil as visionary) that the old Rock dream of a youth totalised (its moments of total youthfulness concentrated into a vague movement of usefulness) has faded. Ferry was, anyway, too old to begin with to pose himself as a 'youth spokesman' (he was in fact 28: 'I came into pop music from a different angle . . . that was one of the strengths, also the cross I sort of impaled myself upon . . . I didn't start doing it until I was a complete person . . . I was me before I started making records') and here sings as if Rock's late '60s dream of wistful social interference were nothing but an unfortunate lapse in good manners. He croons '70s nightmares of *Which?* consumer failure in a language of surfaces: campest Broadway, Tin Pan Alley, rag trade, blank verse. *Style* has now become a given, and so style alone is not sufficient; style must pre-empt and co-opt. (Rock is passing from dreams of *de profundis* to *de rigeur*.)

It ends in debris, not Debrett's – '. . . *and Guernica, did the Strand*.' But even here we sense the well-turned trick, the glint of a two-way-mirror vocabulary. This is not history pure, but history 'after' Picasso, time frozen into the proper name of the revered Art object, history into aesthetic monument. You could say he couldn't be more explicit about what has been lost in the gains of Modernism – '*Lolita and Guernica . . . did the Strand*', even going so far as to leave a final suspending pause between '*the*' and '*Strand*'. It is the point at which Ferry is about to join them all – he is about to turn into a *reference point* himself. He will be forever stranded from the original Beauty of Art, from the old cherished idea of Art as original Beauty.

'*Lolita and Guernica . . .*' He will never have this edge again, up against the rule or the margin where irony can adequately stand in for the lost innocence of Beauty. These en-twinned icons stand in as synecdoches for what Art must become, of what the once genteel artist must genuflect to.

The artist is powerless to do anything (to add anything to the roll-call) without being always already caught up in the work of others, of other artists, other media, other *demands*. He cannot write or paint or sing something which does not include within itself an acknowledgement of the impossibility of being a *pure* work of art.

Ferry's advanced primer in upwardly mobile existentialism is very blithe spirited. He lights up the Strand alone. He alone knows how to un-do the strand, or leave it undone: to isolate the correct detail amongst all the crashing noise of reference. But once the strand has been unravelled, it is endless: through 'the Strand' history is reduced to a guest (or ghost) list, entrance by onamatopaeic resonance only.

The difference is that the later Ferry will be content with a list of last night's flames (whoever the chauffeur had to ferry about that night), where 'Do The Strand' signals a larger disenchantment. This is World Warhol Two – and the acolyte is alight, aflame, burning on all cylinders: despoiling all manors of metaphor.

[These pieces have been edited from a more extensive look at the career of Mr Ferry, entitled 'The Shattered Glass'. I.P.]

Part II

Transgressions

6

'Do You Know How to Pony?': The Messianic Intensity of the Sixties*

Jon Savage

'Do you know how to pony?'[1]

At a time when the 'hit' show, single and LP are called *Fame* (an instruction manual, and of course, pace Ziggy and Sheena, a self-fulfilling prophecy), you might consider that the idea is in the forefront of public consciousness. Paradoxically, this may be so at a time when it is at its most devalued, in traditional terms. Warhol's famous curse has seeped through avant-garde theory into popular practice: as the ritual repetition of the electronic media accelerates into gibberish, then so do those 'fifteen minutes of fame' contract. Yet the spell is not broken: the inertia that keeps aloft so many of our institutions, both political and cultural, also keeps the demand for (super) stars constant, even though the social and economic matrix which fostered *that* particular demand may well have disappeared for ever. Indeed, in a time of monetarist hegemony, our Olympians are chosen for their collusive, bland qualities (fiscal is redacted into spiritual contraction, and any residue channeled into that most obsolete form of worship, patriotism). The secularisation of our daily life is virtually complete: hegemony is a 'fight for survival', our current heroes merely a vacuum in an airless room.

Saints need cash.[2]

To put it bluntly, I think public expectations are too high. We have an end to the language of the Sixties. Today we have got to rid ourselves of these outlooks and look at economic and social matters in a new light.[3]

* This article first appeared in *ZG*, No. 8, 1982.

In this 'fight for survival', the iconography, language and institutions of the Sixties recur with monotonous regularity: simultaneously to be deplored – as in radical punk theory ('Never Trust a Hippie') or Thatcherite ideology – or celebrated as a 'golden age' – in pop ideology and design everywhere. But these 'Swinging Sixties' are now Sanitised Sixties: the messages of a furious and complex time are now reduced, by politicians and disc-jockeys alike, to simplistic elements worthy of a time of retraction. Pop songs were better then weren't they, and yet the ideals and spirit of the age are now perceived as 'unrealistic' – which embraces *both* wage claims and libertarian demands. Fascination for what appears to have been, and what we are constantly told was, a better time – and envy that *we* can't participate – filter our response to what is, after all, living history for many of us. We interpret the Sixties with Eighties antennae: what is missing, is a sense of discovery and possibility; what is remembered, squandered opportunities and having to live through the wreckage; what remains, calculation and despair. Grappling too with the inertia of 60's institutions, we may be in danger of throwing the baby out with the bathwater.

> Because you're young (This is the sixties revolutionary hop)
> Because you're young (This is the eighties revolutionary hop).[4]

It is ironic, or simply fitting, that the sound and colours of 'Pop's Golden Age' are invoked so strongly at a time when the passing of the idea of 'youth culture' has returned pop music to its pristine function of entertainment – showbusiness. The reasons are simple economic and cultural sabotage: punk rock's apocalyptic rhetoric was only a hair's breadth ahead of the reality – namely that for a growing number of school leavers and young adults there really is No Future under the old laws. So used are we to a surfeit of brightly coloured playthings, that we take their availability as a constant rather than as an accident (planned) of history. The consumer enfranchisement of that group which Abrams defined in his classic 1959 marketing study, *The Teenage Consumer*, as 'young people from the time they leave school till they either marry or reach 25' has now been rescinded, as manufacturers and marketers concentrate on the 25–35-year-olds, or the early teens. From being the consumer cuckoo in the Selsdon nest, 'kids' are now seen solely as being a massive social problem: doubly disenfranchised from the right to work, and, more importantly, the right to spend, they riot, hang around listlessly, commit suicide or get packed off to the Falkland Islands. If the Sixties marked the apogee of that ideology of youth, when the Beatles, say, could be courted by Harold Wilson, and given MBEs for export services, when it was mandatory to be young, hip and rich, then the Eighties has marked its final demise, unravelled by punk's ferocious cut-ups and a decayed economy. But you wouldn't have noticed: the pop charts have never been fuller of degutted remakes of 1960s songs, and television producers and radio programmers perpetuate the illusion that to be young is to be part of a swinging, consuming youth community. At a time when a producer can talk about a new pop show as having the 'same impact as 'Ready Steady Go', it is hardly surprising that the White E-Type reappears in pop iconography, that 'love' is the year's most overused word, or that the Rolling Stones play an American tour which nets them millions of dollars and re-establishes them as the heroes of youth. Thus is Chaos redacted into Cash, 'Satisfaction' into 'We'll Meet Again', and the magic lost. The 'Sixties' return, to reinforce radical conservatism.

> and I'd like to see
> her rise again
> her white white bones
> with baby brian jones
> baby brian jones
> like blushing
> baby dolls[5]

Talking about all the people who would try anything twice . . .[6]

In considering these matters during the course of this year, I have been obsessed by two people in particular, Edie Sedgwick and Brian Jones. Their lives are not entirely parallel, yet both may now be seen to typify the age, now that 'the Sixties' are far enough away to be considered in the same terms as 'the Twenties' or 'the Thirties': the media interest evinced by two biographies and related books – *Edie* by Jean Stein ('the summer's hot number' – *Time Magazine*), David Dalton's *The Rolling Stones (The First Twenty Years)'*, Warhol and Hackett's *Popism* – places them in the romantic tradition epitomised, at various times, by Chatterton, Brooke, Dean and Vicious, yet also raises questions about our perception of 'the Sixties' as history and as 'living tradition'.

> Chicks screaming, mania in their eyes, fascinated by their idol BRIAN JONES, with their arms reaching out for him. A photographer rudely pushes aside a beautiful blonde, to snap a picture of Brian, she stumbles and falls. Seeing this, BRIAN takes one step forward, and VOOM in one blow kicks away the equipment with the guy catapulting after it . . . Olympia, Paris 1965.[7]

> The best thing Edie does in Ciao! Manhattan is a scene in the very early dawn. She's walking on a brick wall near the Fort Lee castle. An imaginary aerialist, balancing on an imaginary high wire. The way her muscles are moving, fluid at that time, it's very hydraulic, very much in tune with the wind.[8]

Indeed, at this moment, both Brian and Edie are best seen in terms of *presence* rather than achievement, although Brian Jones's contribution to the Rolling Stones and his 'Pipes of Pan At Jajouka' LP are by no means negligible. They appear as a mad, messianic intensity that wiped out any possibility of past or future and zeroed in on a present that had no end. In this concentration, they may well have crystallised the moment, like a Dean leer from 1955, or a withering Johnny Rotten stare from 1976. They paid for it, of course, as did millions of others, partly encouraged by their example: Edie died in 1971 at 28, Brian Jones in 1969 at 26, both from barbiturates among other things.

This intensity was useful, but by necessity temporary: by the end of 1966, Edie and Brian Jones had outlived their usefulness. Having surrendered both spirit and persona to the psychic vampires, Edie to Andy Warhol, Brian to Mick Jagger, they were left to circle the flame ever closer while the two careerists went on to become 60s institutions in the eighties. In this light, a valid question might be: would you prefer to be dead, or Mick Jagger in 1982? Indeed, would you prefer to be dead or Andy Warhol?

> I write the word
> SUN
> across the dreary palimpsest
> of the world.[9]

We need to give a longer evolutionary perspective to these terms by calling all these types – on occasion – Sonnenkinde – Children of the Sun. This extra dignity is appropriate when these young men types are made the objects of an imaginative cult, when a group of people significant in numbers, talent, or power idolises the young man as the supreme form of life.[10]

In the sixties, many worlds fused, to a degree not seen before or after. If in the 1920s, the Sonnenkinder were figures like Brian Howard and Harold Acton, figures from a most rarified atmosphere whose power, as devalued in Granada's *Brideshead Revisited* is still not lost, then they were far from having a mass audience. These dominant figures, however they moved, like flies in amber, still reproduced the class structure of the time: the mysteries of expression and interpretation were the province of a select few, while the mass were contented with the facsimiles of Hollywood. By 1965 as Greil Marcus had noted in connection with the Rolling Stones, the Bohemian, cultured world of the 1920s Sonnenkinder had merged with all the electronic paraphernalia of the great 'pop' age: the new heroes could not either be simply aristocratic, or simply popular, as the social changes of the time demanded expression in the medium most suited. Thus, for a time, Edie Sedgwick needed Andy Warhol as much as he needed her, and the mix of deracinated aristo and arriviste artist was perfect. If Andy Warhol took A-Heads, transvestites and hustlers uptown with him, then the Rolling Stones took the Bohemian tradition of non-conformism and self-expression that was nurtured by their jazz-club roots to a mass, youth audience of a scale and immediacy hitherto unseen, and unreckoned. For a brief time, from 1964 to 1966, the worlds of the aristocrat and the slum-boy, the straight and the gay, the popular and the arcane fused with a reverberation whose effects we are still feeling, even though that mobility or scale has long disappeared.

Wholeness is not achieved, for frenzy is not freedom.[11]

You really believed that you were going to travel in this bubble right out to the end of the stratosphere. You weren't going to have to cope with the normal structures of life and getting older and making a living. Life was going to be completely different.[12]

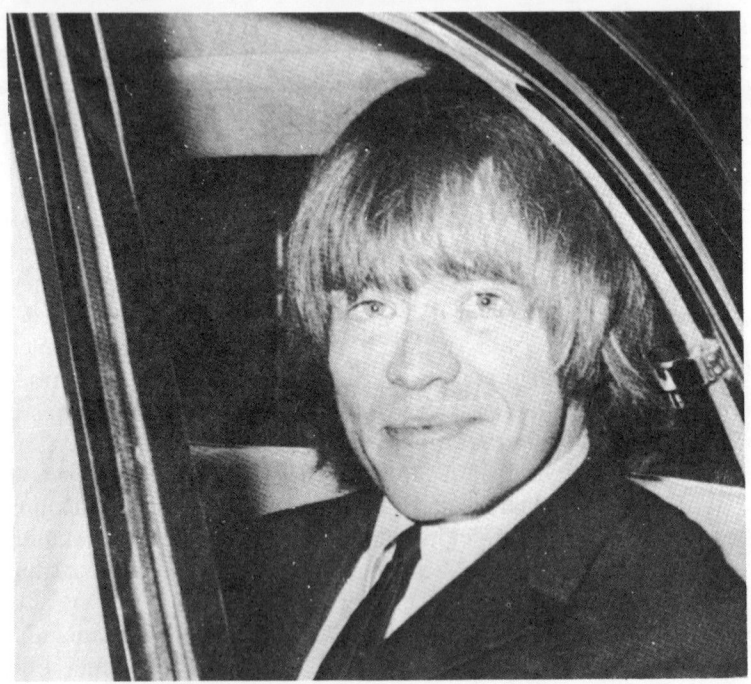

Brian Jones

Certainly, both Brian and Edie were at the epicentre of this hurricane. The sixties have been termed Dionysiac by several commentators, and this would seem apt:

> he is treated and educated like a girl and he grows up to be effeminate. Unable to differentiate feminine from masculine functioning in himself, he scarcely knows who he is. Like an eternal youth he wanders over the world, changing shape, going mad, drinking himself into insensibility, living the abandonment of total nature, and like nature, experiencing the cycles of death and rebirth.[13]

Edie Sedgwick in arabesque. *Photo:* **Enzo Sellerio. Courtesy of** *Vogue.*
Copyright © 1965 by The Conde Nast Publications Inc.

A photo from *Vogue* August 1965 catches Edie in the middle of this dervish dance, 'arabesqueing on her leather rhino to a record of the Kinks'.[14]

(Would that it had been the sublime 'See My Friends'!). An ageless, androgynous mutant, she personifies the spirit of movement and freedom, never once admitting the possibility of falling. The arc of her bare arms and leotarded legs is reproduced by, and framed in a small wall painting of a horse, a motif that recurs, oedipally, in Edie's life and later assumed by quintessential fan-turned-star Patti Smith. She's bathed in grace.

By late 1966, the 'amphetamine spiked negativity' of the last three or four Rolling Stones singles had wound itself up into a pitch of nihilistic chaos not seen again until a good ten years later. Peter Whitehead's film for 'Have You Seen Your Mother, Baby, Standing in the Shadow?' makes explicit the threat of sexual and social chaos implicit in the song's careering momentum and garbled curses: shot in stark black and white, the film cuts up shots of the Stones getting dressed in drag for the cover sleeve photo session in the East Village, and footage from the concert at the Royal Albert Hall on 23 September which ended in a bloody riot after 6 numbers. The drag section ends with an oblique Brian Jones smile to the camera, while, as the momentum of the hysterical stage performance accelerates through violence and frenzy to complete breakdown, Brian Jones appears from camera right, at the centre of the vortex, doubling up in demonic laughter.

> Brian, who had once described his treatment in a Chicago hospital (following an overdose of pills) with 'I had so many tests I felt like a human sacrifice', seems to have had a premonition – in the story by Brian Gysin – that he was to become the scapegoat, whose sacrifice would not renew the world but bring down with him a whole era.[15]

> I was the Girl of the Year and superstar and all that crap. I'd do things like . . . Everything I did was really underneath, I guess, motivated by psychological disturbances. I'd make a mask out of my face because I didn't realise I was quite beautiful, God blessed me so . . . I'd freak out in a very physical way. And it was all taken as a fashion trend.[16]

The events of 1965 and 1966 set a pace that was just too frantic; any synthesis that had occurred was too volatile, its overweening ambitions not based on any real foundation. This was hard on some of our protagonists – Jagger and Richard jailed briefly in July 1967, Warhol shot by Valerie Solanas in June 1968, while the declines of both Brian and Edie can be traced from the photographs – and for those that survived there was retrenchment soon after: by the 1970s, the Rolling Stones were 'the greatest rock 'n' roll band in the world', a term that would have been laughed at in 1966 and is laughed at now, and Andy Warhol the 'world's most famous artist'. If Edie and Andy had met Mick Jagger at the 'Scene' mid-'65, then by 1971 Warhol was busy designing the sleeve for 'Sticky Fingers', the album that, more than any other, turned its back on utopianism for self-indulgence. What a different world.

This utopian synthesis of the mid-60s, however fragile, had had some practical results. What such people as Brian Jones and Edie Sedgwick hinted at by their undoubted glamour and presence in a dramatic form – the breaking-down of social, sexual and psychic barriers – became crystallised in political rhetoric and action, with the rise of the *enragés* in France, the SDS in the United States, and, perhaps most importantly, the gay and women's movements – all of which, at their inception, retained a playful, dervish quality in keeping with the times. Not for nothing did the Situationists spray 'Sous les paves, la plage': there was.

Naturally it would be unwise to push the parallel between Brian Jones and Edie Sedgwick too far, just as it would be unwise to wish to emulate or inflate reputations already furred by pop mythology and ritual: zonked 3am phone calls are simply not glamorous. Their particular tragedy was to act out too soon, and too fast, the enormous changes that were occurring in society; their singular demise meant that others were wary of assuming this vast responsibility. It is interesting to note that, in recent pop history, their presence has been invoked as a kind of touchstone by performers wishing to recapture that dervish spinning motion into synthesis; David Bowie photographed in a Brian Jones T-shirt or Patti Smith titling her first, extraordinary album after Edie's oedipal symbol. It is more interesting to consider, however, that the very severe damage done by Punk Rock to pop mythology has stripped the mythology of death away from Brian Jones and

Edie Sedgwick enough for us to be able to tear away the veil and interpret their current media vogue in terms beyond mere ghoulishness and voyeurism (although the last two cannot be under-estimated): at a time when both Andy Warhol and the Rolling Stones have become figureheads of that '60s hegemony which explicitly shores up the regimes of the new, rabid Right, the concentration on these two skeletons in their closet merely emphasises the bankruptcy of these fraudulent Olympians, whose actions reflect a world that is being trained not to dream. At a time of fragmentation, envy and cultural impotence, the naked trajectory of these two Sonnenkinder, aptly androgynous, point to a wish to recapture possibility and abandon, to restate what still has to be learnt from a complex and maligned age in a new language and a new arena.

After all, consider this dominant cry:

I'm waiting for something
I'm only passing time
And now I'm all alone
And I don't care
And I don't care
And I don't care[17]

Notes

1. Patti Smith from the album *Horses*, 1975.
2. Stephen Koch, *Stargazer: Andy Warhol's World and His Films*, 1973.
3. Francis Pym, Foreign Secretary, quoted in a London speech, 2 February 1982.
4. Theatre of Hate single *The Hop*, 1982.
5. Patti Smith quoted in *Edie* by Jean Stein, Jonathan Cape, 1982.
6. The Rolling Stones' track 'Have You Seen Your Mother, Baby, Standing in the Shadow?' 1966.
7. Sleeve note (anonymous) Rolling Stone bootleg 1975.
8. Huddler Bisby quoted in *Edie* (see above).
9. Harry Crosby, *Assassin*, London, 1929.
10. Martin Green, *Children of the Sun*, 1977.
11. June Singer, *Androgyny: Towards a New Theory of Sexuality*, 1977.
12. Cherry Vanilla, quoted in *Edie* (see above).
13. June Singer, *Androgyny*.
14. Quoted in *Edie* (see above).

15. David Dalton, *The Rolling Stones: The First Twenty Years*, 1982.
16. Edie Sedgwick, quoted in *Edie* (see above).
17. Soft Cell single 'Bedsitter', 1981.

7

Only Dancing: David Bowie Flirts with the Issues*

Simon Frith

In the jealous world of British youth cults, David Bowie is the only star who cannot 'sell out': whatever he does is validated by the fact that he, David Bowie, did it. This is partly because Bowie has never performed on behalf of anyone else; his emphasis has always been on art as the invention of self. What Bowie (and Bryan Ferry) did in the 1970s was redefine the pop object. Their 'texts' – the pieces of art for audiences to interpret – were not simply songs, records, words, images, but all these things *as organized by the pop sales process* (ads, gossip columns, disc jockey patter and so on). To appreciate Bowie was not just to like his music or his shows or his looks, but also to enjoy the way he set himself up as a commercial image. How he was packaged was as much an aspect of his art as what the package contained. The traditional British rock star's dealings in the marketplace were either wary (Van Morrison), cynical (Rod Stewart) or both (John Lennon) – their messages reached their audiences despite the necessary distortions of the hard sell. But Bowie was more interested in the hard sell than in anything else.

Bowie once claimed that 'when you are an artist you can turn your hand to anything, in any style. Once you have the tools, then all art forms are the same in the end.' And all that makes rock and roll specifically interesting is, then, its public presence. Artists in rock, a mass medium, can titillate the public aesthetically in ways that salon stars cannot. Bowie's position is, in art history terms, decadent – an art-for-art's-sake version of shocking the bourgeoisie – and in his Thin White Duke persona Bowie did,

* This article first appeared in *Mother Jones*, 1983.

indeed, flirt with fascism. 'People aren't very bright, you know,' he announced in 1976 as he arrived back in Britain from a world tour with delusions of grandeur and the commanding gestures of a would-be leader. 'They say they want freedom but when they get the chance, they pass up Nietzsche and choose Hitler. . . . A liberal wastes time saying, "Well, now what ideas have you got?" Show them what to do, for God's sake. If you don't, nothing will get done.'

Ask Bowie about this in interviews now and he expresses shame and regret, but I'm chilled, too, by his present pose – the natural aristocrat whose duty it is to make 'helpful' music. Luckily, pop doesn't work like this (and when he's not having to explain himself Bowie knows this as well as anyone).

Intentions don't matter in pop, effects do, and Bowie's career is interesting not because of anything he has stood for specifically but because of what it reveals about the making of pop meaning.

Suburbia and its discontents

David Bowie was a Bromley boy, a '60s mod from the suburbs of south London, the white-collar son of a white-collar father who learned to be clever at school, quiet at home. His brooding place was his bedroom; his audience was selected school friends. He saw his fantasies in his wardrobe mirror and wrote poetry with a sax in his lap. He left school at the age of 16 to work as a commercial artist in an advertising agency and he had the 1960s art student's sensibilities: R&B was the music that mattered, not because Bowie had much need of its power to define adult lust and resignation, but because it was the source of a set of adolescent poses (which he later honoured on the *Pin Ups* LP). As he put it this year, looking back:

> As an adolescent, I was painfully shy, withdrawn. I didn't really have the nerve to sing my songs on stage, and nobody else was doing them. I decided to do them in disguise so that I didn't actually have to go through the humiliation of going on stage and being myself. I continued designing characters with their own complete personalities and environments.

And so, Bowie's first record, as David Jones with the King

Bees, was routine British club R&B, fast and anxious; his second, as David Jones with the Mannish Boys, was a cover of Bobby Bland's 'I Pity the Fool'. As a Mannish Boy, David refused to have his hair cut for a TV show and, instead, formed a 'society' to defend young long-hairs – the BBC still sometimes shows a clip of an earnest Bowie (in his Brian Jones cut) leading the studio discussion that followed his performance.

Even as an ordinarily cocky, would-be R&B star, David Jones was, then, a committed 'modernist'. And, by 1966, as David Bowie, a solo pop singer, he had the knowing London tones, the sophisticated 19-year-old's nostalgia, of a character from Colin MacInnes' youth novel, *Absolute Beginners*, the book that most acutely caught the mood of the new generation of affluent British teen-agers. Bowie was, very specifically, a grammar-school mod. He was less interested in Pete Townshend's ordinary kids or Mick Jagger's hedonistic blues than in the modernist's original French connections – the coffee-bar readings of Sartre, the celebration of private alienation, the dramaturgy of life as a series of lifestyles. Bowie did not make it as a pop star in those days, but he studied mime and Buddhism, ran an 'arts lab' and absorbed some hippie influences (on 'Space Oddity', for example). As his artistic ambitions grew, his lack of pop star status became, paradoxically, his strength – in the 1970s he had the freedom to twist rock expectations to his own ends; most of his famous peers had been, by that time, twisted by them.

By the start of the 1970s, Bowie was working as a self-conscious artist (a songwriter, a poet, a mime, an actor) on the fringes of the new world of the British rock elite and its parasites. And as he slipped in and out of its round of frantic self-indulgence, its mood of nervous contempt for the fans, it was increasingly the idea of stardom itself that interested him – both for its own sake, as the most accessible source of a young man's wealth and cultural power, and for its being a role packed with aesthetic possibilities. Rock stardom was, by this time (post-Woodstock, Altamont and the first round of drug deaths) a complicated, slightly sour affair. Lip-service was paid to the rock 'community' even as it fragmented; rock stars claimed to represent the 'kids' even as the age gap between performers and audiences grew. As the stars got richer, more glamorous, so the fantasies laid on them got heavier; their sense of power was becoming both more ominous and more banal.

The contradictions revolved around sexuality: rock stars were at once the speakers of phallic freedom and the passive objects of consuming desire.

Between 1971 and 1974, using a traditional British blues band (led by Mick Ronson) as his basic power tool, David Bowie made a series of five LPs (*The Man Who Sold the World*, *Hunky Dory*, *The Rise and Fall of Ziggy Stardust and the Spiders from Mars*, *Aladdin Sane*, *Diamond Dogs*) exploring the meaning of stardom. He didn't, in practice, escape its pressures himself – when he finally took his place in L.A.'s lotusland in the mid-'70s, Bowie had made his own additions to rock's more doltish mythology of doom and gloom – but he did also make fun of them.

The unexpected consequence of Bowie's 'serious' pursuit of stardom was Britain's wonderfully trivial glam-rock movement – even such butch young performers as Slade and Sweet had to wear glitter, eye-liner and high-heeled silver hobnail boots. This was a laugh (though I never was sure that Sweet got the joke), but it had far-reaching effects: in disrupting pop certainties about the signs of sexuality, Bowie and the glam-rockers threw the meaning of sexuality itself into question. What entered deep into British youth consciousness, in short, was not Bowie's vision of the future (*2001* meets *1984*) but his panache in the present: singing 'Starman' on *Top of the Pops*, for example, in a psychedelic leotard and orange hair; being photographed in a 'man's dress'; experimenting with bisexuality; having a child (the son he is concerned about now) named Zowie Bowie!

David Bowie was pop star as voyeur. The suburban schoolboy, introverted, arrogant, bright, still lurked beneath the masks. Bowie offered his emotions as poses, to be admired and used, but he didn't risk 'real' feeling. As a record producer (and fan), he was interested in musicians whose styles were conventionally raw and fixedly individual (Lou Reed, Iggy Pop); but as a performer Bowie celebrated the cleverness of his own false positions, and his 1970s switches of style, from glam-star to the disco sounds of *Young Americans* and *Station to Station* to European studio art, were bound by a commitment to stylishness. The settings changed (from stadium to disco to club) but not the sense that every move that Bowie made depended on a purely aesthetic judgment.

Bowie has always been an oddly impersonal singer: there are songs about desire, but not songs of desire. Bowie himself has made the point in recent interviews that only now is he thinking of songs dealing with 'one-to-one relationships'. As it is (and in comparison with, say, Elvis Costello's concern to cut through the *language* of love), Bowie has only skittered across the surface of romantic feeling. He's a singer–songwriter who doesn't work in the confessional mode – an acute observer of 'scene', but an observer whose own position cannot be pinned down.

The club version of such aestheticism became, in the context of punk and the rock recession, a gesture of grace. For the late 1970s' generation of suburban kids, Bowie offered a model not of public stardom but of private dignity; what they learned from him was how to keep cool under pressure.

Hero

Bowie defined for a British pop generation what it means to be an artist. Previously, rock-and-roll fans admired honesty, direct passion, suffering, the ability to transmute feeling into a sort of misty imagery that hints at things that can be known but never said. Bowie's message, by contrast, was that what really mattered was *complete control* – control of the means of artistic production, control of the means of emotional production, too. Bowie had invented himself, so his 'honesty' was not an issue. This account of art drew obviously on ideas of the avant-garde, and Bowie duly had avant-garde concern for form, for experiment, for braininess. But if he thereby refused to 'please the public' (hence RCA's harsh reaction to *Low* – there wasn't enough singing on it!), he never lost sight of the source of rock's aesthetic power – its public accessibility. His avant-garde dabblings have always been smoothly formalist enough to be used by his listeners as a measure of their own position in the pop vanguard. Bowie's fans have always identified with him particularly intensely, because no one else has captured so well their sense of difference.

In his early Ziggy Stardust days, Bowie used to arrive on stage to a recording of the theme from *A Clockwork Orange*, and, indeed, from the start of his career (in the excellent song 'The London Boys', for example) it was clear that he had street as well as stage dreams. This, again, is a suburban norm (nice boys longing for nastiness). But unlike other rockers (Pete Townshend, for example), Bowie fused the two images, stage and street star, aesthetically (in terms of style and gesture) rather than socially (in terms of community). As a star, Bowie never pretended to 'represent' his fans, but he did make available to those fans a way of being a 'star'. Bowie's pop masterpiece from the early 1970s, 'All The Young Dudes' (the record he wrote and produced for Mott the Hoople) was about this, about the way in which youths, by dressing up, construct their own stage, write their own parts, set up their own audience. Glam-rock dissolved the star/fan division not by the stars becoming one of the lads, but by the lads becoming their own stars.

By 1973 there was in most British cities a small but noticeable youth subculture of Bowie-boys – hair dyed green and orange, eyes brushed with glitter, the *Aladdin Sane* flash across their faces. Such making-up (with its stress on sexual shock and ambiguity) was a poetic gesture (adolescent angst had some new forms of visual imagery) but also a semiotic one – the 'sissiness' of the Bowie-boys became a comment on the usual signs of teenage sexuality; their 'unsuitability' (zig-zag streaks and mascara at the bus stop) a comment on the gap between advertising glamour and teen-age routine. Games with hair and clothing had long been a part of subcultural activity, but Bowie offered his fans a more individualized, more theatrical, more *artful* way of refusing to be dourly proletarian. These fans, it should be said, were mostly male. Of course there were Bowie-girls, but the narcissism involved drew upon male youth convention – girls' culture still meant dressing up for other people. It took the combined forces of punk and feminism to shift the iconography of female teenage sexuality.

By 1975–6, the Bowie-boys were ready to make their striking contribution to the scandal of punk (the dyed hair, the semiotic shocks, the sexual dissolve, the studied calm . . .). Punk gigs were soon highly stylized events, but what I still remember most clearly (waiting for the Clash, Penetration, Suburban Stud) is Bowie's driving presence. His version of rock and roll – 'Rebel Rebel', 'The Jean Genie', 'Suffragette City' – fitted into the patterns of dub reggae and thrashed punk in ways that other rock and roll certainly did not. The immediate sound of these records, Mick Ronson's flashy, mannered guitar, simply accentuated Bowie's essential *playfulness* – which I had never appreciated until I heard it in these sweaty settings. His voice had an odd, crooning intimacy, moving confusingly between 'we' and 'they', actor and observer, male and female, harshness and joy. What was equally apparent was that Bowie's dilettante stance needed punk's bitter, scruffy edge to give it social power.

In the end (by 1978) such power dissolved. The punks and the Bowie-boys separated: the punks to pursue their stylized ugliness, social realism as nostalgic anthem; the Bowie-boys to go back underground, to set up their own more exclusive events. Local clubs began to have Bowie nights, the room hired for the occasion, everyone in costume, posing, dancing to the electro-disco beat, Bowie and his influences. This 'rolling club' movement overlapped physically and culturally with the gay disco scene – the same clubs, the same emphasis on stylistic invention, the same music, a parallel breaking of sexual rules – and from it emerged, at the end of the decade, the New Romantics, a new generation of fops and would-be pop stars (as many of them now are – Boy George of Culture Club most prominently). Fops, but working-class fops, whose response to Thatcherism certainly doesn't make left-wing sense like punk did, but which isn't *simply* 'escapist' either.

Sound and vision

David Bowie has never been an obviously 'political' artist. His only explicitly political gestures have been right-wing, and listening to his songs now, it's difficult to spot any clear comments on matters of social concern. 'All the Madmen', an early song, draws on the Laingian politics of madness that swept round hippie London in the late 1960s; 'Panic in Detroit', from the *Aladdin Sane* LP, is a sort of all-purpose flash of urban guerrilla. Both songs work by aestheticizing the issues, turning struggle and suffering into mood and imagery. Bowie has never been the sort of rock star expected to support a cause, open a nuclear disarmament rally, come out for socialism. His current video for 'Let's Dance' is, he says, a comment on Australian treatment of aborigines, on racism and cultural imperialism generally; but the video is cryptic enough, and this message certainly isn't obvious on the record.

The question remains then: Is there any reason to think of David Bowie as a radical pop star? The positive answer to this is based on Bowie's artistic rather than political credentials – as a fringe member of the international avant-garde, it might be argued, Bowie is 'radical' by definition. During his Ziggy days, Bowie and his more learned fans made reference to Brecht, the alienation effect and the like. Here was music that was self-referential, that was about the process of pop stardom itself. The problem with this claim is that it doesn't make a lot of sense of Bowie's place *in* the pop process. If Bowie made rock stardom a problem, he was, nevertheless, a rock star; and his image was familiar – he used hackneyed rock sci-fi ideas about technological alienation, for instance.

The strength of his Ziggy music actually lay in its atmosphere. What Bowie captured was the unearthly desperation of consumer pleasures, the sense of discos, clubs and dance halls apart from 'real life', where people danced urgently because of their fears of what would happen when they stopped, where teenagers, in particular, invented their own transitory social order.

Others suggest that Bowie's real involvement with the avant-garde came after his Ziggy phase, with his move from rock and roll (via the emotional stylization of disco) to the anti-emotionalism of his synthetic collaborations with Brian Eno. What Bowie learned most importantly making *Low* was that music isn't necessarily expressive: it doesn't stand for something else (whether ideas, emotion or atmosphere). The Bowie/Eno trilogy, *Low*, *Heroes* and *Lodger* (Bowie's best work, in my opinion), wasn't about anything. Its interest was musical – the successful attempt to define the terms of electro-pop-funk, the uses of clashing conventions (intimate, familiar vocals, programmed electronic narratives). It was on these records that Bowie really drew attention to the means of musical production (human and inhuman), to the taken-for-grantedness of national soundscapes (*Lodger* plays deliberately with the shorthand signs of ethnic musical identity).

This is an intriguing argument but not completely convincing. Much as I love *Low* and the others – maybe because I love them – I don't hear them as radical. Bowie has neither the intellectual toughness nor the sense of present danger to use art forms, even avant-garde art forms, as anything other than a way of feeling good. There is a remarkable lack of anger and bitterness in his repertoire, and an even more startling absence of confusion. Play his records against those of Captain Beefheart or The Fall, the

Gang of Four or early Au Pairs, Public Image Ltd. or The Birthday Party: what is most obvious is his tidiness, his neatness. Control means order.

And this is, of course, why he is popular and culturally influential in the way the others are not. Bowie sees himself as a photojournalist – recording the popular mood in a series of snapped images, his subjects startled by the light. I see him, rather, as the photographic paper itself, a black sheet on which people develop their own images (and he's certainly the most photogenic rock star ever). Bowie has always been careful, has always disdained mess – in his vulgar guise, in his avant-garde guise, even as a wasted rock star. If he is now, as a result, more popular than ever, then he's a sign of the times – fastidiousness as a measure of the reduced scope of our choices.

8
The Best Uniforms*

Marek Kohn

A film scene: Two young, attractive, hedonist Weimar decadents – the audience's sympathies are with them – chance upon a picturesque scene while motoring on a sunny day. A smart young Brownshirt begins to sing; clean, clear, evocative: 'Gather together to greet the sun / Tomorrow belongs to me.' First his comrades, then the rest of the assembled citizenry join in, swelling the refrain to an uplifting, hopeful climax.

This scene was from *Cabaret*, a film which did much to establish the delightfully decadent image of pre-Nazi Germany for the Glitter (later punk) generation. That cameo stood out from the rest of the film. It was shocking because it showed Nazism as magnetically attractive, as something which looked *better* than decadence.

1981: Actuality: a Saturday afternoon on the Central Line heading east from Liverpool Street. Two skinheads and their girlfriends get into the car, fairly drunk. Everyone else studies their feet or otherwise feigns indifference. The skins soon start up, something about the nigger-lovers. No one knows whether they're going to make anything of it, but they're on the tips of their toes ready to move, and when a bottle is tossed, just for effect, everyone on the right side of the car bolts through the emergency door into the next one. The few left get treated to the British Movement songbook: the skinheads are onto the hard stuff now, not the common, average racist talk. It's specifically Nazi – the wonders of Germany and its erstwhile Leader, and the blacks

---

* This article first appeared in *ZG*, No. 2, 1981.

142 The Best Uniforms

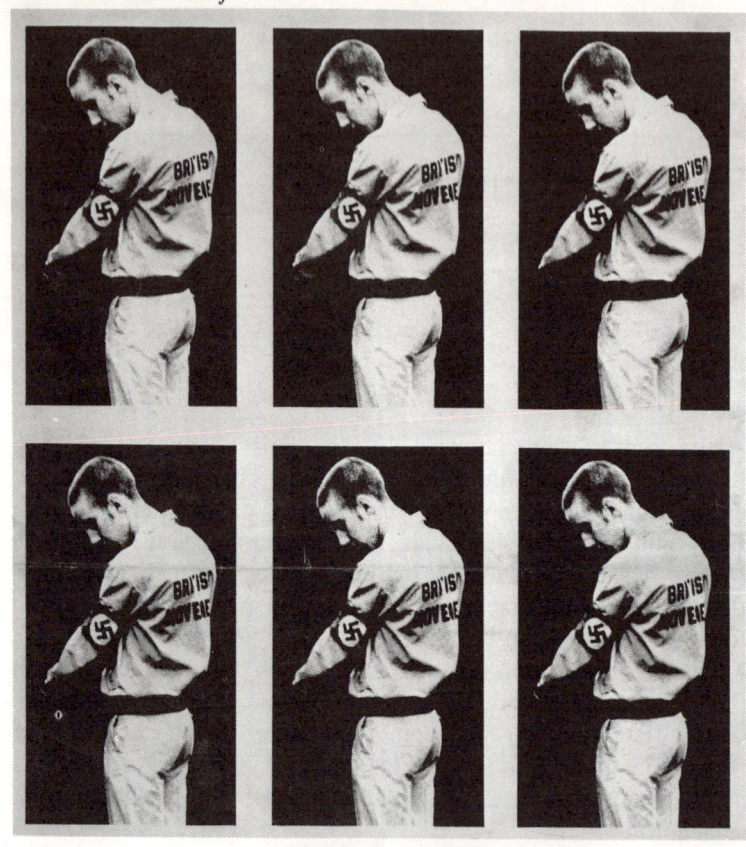

British Nazi signs, 1980

should be gassed. Everyone else is silent, except an elderly lady who complains about the mess of the broken glass, and the girlfriends, who giggle and say I'm not going on a train with him.

                  * * *

Fascism has two lines of influence on contemporary white British youth culture. One is the kitsch of it all, and the visual imagery which is taken as found, but is to some extent separated from the ideas and historical reality behind it: the Cabaret brownshirt's smart uniform, for instance. This operates on a psychological level rather than on a political. It led to the original brouhahas that blew up over punk and early swastika chic, which had nothing to do with Nazi sympathies and was usually excused as being done to shock. The other possible explanation, which was rarely canvassed, was that something about the aesthetic that the Nazis manipulated for its psychological impact had an independent but related appeal to this generation. Other fascist images have subsequently surfaced, like the Rodenstahl-style Olympic cover of the Skids' album *Days in Europa* (the name of the pan-European state envisaged by the Nazis). Here, a stupid tendency to cruise near the boundaries of morality is apparent, but it does not imply that the Skids were fascist. In embracing the ideas of strength and physical idealism, they aligned themselves with a movement that professed to share these ideas. But this is tasteless rather than evil. It only involves an isolated part of the fascist vision – which has picked up an awful lot of motley baggage over the years. There is a danger, when surveying popular imagery, of seeing fascism in every corner. It gets a bit like detecting the yearning for a strong leader in the commuter who complains that the trains don't run on time.

This kind of thinking is pernicious not only because it breeds panic, but because it obscures the second sort of hold that fascism has on youth: the considerable amount of the real thing which has emerged under the wings of the British Movement and the National Front. This series of reactionary thought is moving beyond simple racism and random paranoia and is developing into authentic, brutal, radical, populist fascism.

The shallow opportunism of the fascist organisations shows itself as an elastic, accommodating ability to give their target markets what they want. Without the need to worry about the trappings of statehood and responsibility, these fringe parties merely have to provide a limited group of people with a framework of ideas and organisation. This 'rationalises' and gives direction to tendencies they already have: violence, racial hatred; and the urge to be ordered into a movement. It brings all these together and makes them more than the sum of their parts.

Fascist, and in particular Nazi, symbols account for much of the phoney glory of the current fascist subculture. Obviously, a vital factor in the power of these symbols is their reference to the Third Reich. Enough time has passed, fewer young people's parents fought in the war. The folk-memories are increasingly those of film and Battle Picture Library. The smart visuals take precedence over the blood, sweat and genocide more and more as the years go by; and the sanitizers of National Socialism are more than ready to provide bland assurances that the Holocaust never happened. The war was a mistake, Britain should have ganged up with Germany against Russia: history is seamlessly rewritten. History is made an irrelevance, allowing the choice of allegiance to be made on image. The small boys' judgment that the Germans had the best uniforms looms large (the choice is between theirs, ours, and the Yanks' – the dashing, heroic uniforms of the Red Army remain unknown).

The recent spasms of cross-burning in the Southern backwoods (Plaistow? Enfield? Portsmouth?!) may seem a tiny bit too lurid, too *foreign* for the average dull British racist. But we have a new breed here. This isn't done by the backbone of British bigotry; the Alf Garnett looking up from his beer or whatever else he considers to be truly, forever England, seeing dark skins and bristling with indignation. These are young men, who are the sickening side of the spiky, leathered, dyed, made-up, dandified peculiarity that is the extreme-fixated hip fraction of British youth. The original anti-hippie no-nonsense skinheads would no more have contemplated wearing earrings or having stripes razored into their crops than they would have gone round in Fauntleroy suits. Though the skinhead core style remains around a level labourer/squaddie standard – flying jackets, jeans, Doc Martens – the theatrics predicted in *A Clockwork Orange* are in the embryonic stages of a comeback. The copycat cult which sprang up after the release of that film, the vicious face of Glam, was just an isolated foretaste of a mood which now runs far deeper and wider. In dress, it takes the form of British Movement armbands, Nazi accessories such as Hitler Youth badges (which usually seem to be worn the wrong way up, amusingly), and ultimately the skinhead-stormtrooper or combat-clothed paramilitary look of the BM 'elite' Leader Guard.

This is still Action Man stuff with dashes of red-white-black high-drama Nazi trimmings added. The flaming crosses, even if they are pranks or stunts, represent apocalyptic ritual taking off under its own power. This form of symbolic terrorism may well be contrived, but is none the less an outburst of a radically new form of political expression. Donning the sheets, putting on the hood, is something very different for a white youth whose previous dress style has been the practical, universally understood working-class garb intensified just far enough to suggest aggression and a conventional kind of uniform. All that is potent and striking – but *normal*. Ancient pagan fire ceremonies are something else again, something more than suburban *News Of The World* witchcraft or a bit of 'primitive' for jaded ex-hippie hedonist palates.

Grotesque comedy co-exists with the deep psychological undertow of the Nordic pagan-Nazi subculture. There is something quite disablingly funny about tough, glowering skinheads with West Ham and Madness badges handing around Viking Youth leaflets which urge the nation's youth to rediscover its Nordic heritage, live cleanly and take up hiking (illustrations make it clear that large Aryan shorts and blond short-backs-and-sides are appropriate for this). Viking Youth has also attempted to exert its influence over the Boy Scouts . . . Yet at the same time, its function as the British section of the neo-Nazi Viking-Jugend organisation gives it a more sinister aspect.

The Odinist outer reaches of fascism are probably too crackpot to do more than inject some twinges of theatre into the Nazi twilight world, but there are other sources of symbol. One is the icon of the Fuhrer, a central touchstone. Hitler-reverence, or at least reference, is a major cultural element for, say, the skinhead bawling 'Hilter Was Right' and 'Adolf Hitler Was a Skinhead' when out on the town, and going home to pictures of Adolf and his Reich on the bedroom wall. Perhaps becoming a secular society has some serious drawbacks.

* * *

The 'Fuhrerprinzip' is peculiar to neo-Nazis. Abstract images do not have the same concentrated authority as the legend of a personality, especially when they take the form of dress accessories. These have a currency much wider than that limited group who have the urge to submit to the order of Fronts and Movements. The symbols which identify those organisations retain the associations of coherence, unity and strength. The National Front achieved the effect by combing the letters N and F in its logo. This move boosted the initials' attractiveness, particularly as a graffiti symbol which meant more than simple party allegiance. It became a sign which conferred power by association on the writer; a neat satisfying talisman which allowed the user to become instantly aligned with an attitude, without necessarily having any contact with the actual NF. A weapon and a power symbol, in fact.

The British Movement, being more open about where its ideas come from, adopted the internationally used fascist symbol of the circled cross. This bowdlerised swastika uses two of the most absolutely basic graphic elements. Geometrically satisfying, simple, complete (the circle), strong (the cross bolstering the circle) and unified (the symmetry of the design and the central focus of the intersection of the cross). A sort of modern amulet, with very marked power connotations. Again, it is ideal for personal use, especially for people with 'o's in their names to seal with a cross.

And then there is the real thing, the one that the others are hinting at; the swastika. At this point in history it seems like the ultimate universal symbol: its origins are buried in antiquity but spread among every culture from China to Western Europe (except the ancient Egyptians), and it has thrived perennially down the ages to its last catastrophic revival. Its traditional meanings range wide: good fortune, prosperity, male and female principles, the sun, the Supreme God. These interpretations are by no means the only ones, suggesting that the swastika is both mighty and empty, a graphically forceful symbol onto which meaning can conveniently be projected. It is a compelling sign. School desks were decorated with swastikas idly doodled as effectively meaningless images extracted from films and comics years before anyone would have dreamed that British schoolchildren would one day join neo-Nazi groups. It seems to be almost a graphic reflex which is produced in any culture in which people draw signs. The masterstroke of Nazi opportunism was to appropriate it.

Its Third Reich phase is what fixed the swastika's rank in the post-war, post-rock'n'roll generations' regiments of imagery. Nevertheless, it is still working as it has throughout the ages, as a graphic classic. Its universal, absolute character makes it almost banal. The form in which the Nazis presented it as a banner, over a white circle on a red ground, added the drama of colours to it. This is roughly the form in which it tends to be reproduced as youth style, especially together with a lot of black, metal or leather. The look of those other elements represents a baseline for dress from the late '70s on, the time when the post-rock generations began to claim music and style as their own. It can still be seen now in casual, de-fashioned wear, in high-contrast new romanticism, in punk and in rocker styles. It reflects the visual sensibilities of that portion of youth which seeks to set itself apart in some manner from family or society. A variety of reasons for its popularity present themselves: some important ones are a desire for intensity, a sense of frustration, and the use of clothes as a prime form of personal political expression. Black clothing in itself manages to signal both drama and introversion. Kids today really are growing up peculiar: a demoralised generation with little tradition or faith. The signs and colours exploited by the Nazis are promises of glory, drama: infusions of passion and strength. Those qualities are among those which inspire youth dress styles. They do *not* reflect latent Naziphilia: the styles have similarities but the spirit is different. However, that subgroup which has gone beyond racism and fighting – the preoccupations of those on the BM/NF margins – to a budding espousal of the fascist belief-system, uses Nazi visuals as its own particular warped expression of those image-sympathies common to its generation as a whole.

* * *

An urge to be managed and led, a desire to be a Fuhrer, is an important factor in a person's acceptance of fascism. One funny thing about post-war youth is its reluctance to accept authority. (It throws the baby of solidarity out with the bathwater of authority, which is one way to reduce experience and potential down to self-centredness.) This must drastically restrict any new fascist constituency. A reflexive distaste for taking orders is not the same as an aversion to order, though. The certainty that fascists possess – 'the gas chambers *were faked*', no question – is enviable. It becomes more enviable as stresses accumulate.

* * *

After the suicide of Ian Curtis, Joy Division relaunched themselves with a new name. It signalled completeness, change, strength and spirit: all the dignity and capability implicit in the idealistic and classical name New Order. It is an especially satisfying, calming and inspiring phrase. And, of course, it was the flagship phrase of the Third Reich. As such, it cannot be used innocently and with integrity as a label by anyone anymore. Musically – artistically! – New Order rely on aura, reflected glory from a handle which makes grand promises. The name reflects a pseudo-classical preciousness surrounding the Factory Records coterie, and an 'apolitical' (amoral) streak which imagines it can set itself apart from the evil backing of this name.

New Order brought much richly deserved criticism on their heads for their choice of name. Oddly, no one seems to have picked on the similarly avant-garde and latterly fashionable gig promotion agency with the far more repellent title Final Solution. Like New Order, it has pleasing associations when divorced from history: decisiveness, resolution, completion, and the hint of being the *dernier cri*, or the last word. Both are abstract, simple, and have an air of grandeur.

* * *

The vitriolic but dull-witted 17-year-old lionising the Fuhrer and invoking a Fourth Reich, believing the BM slogan 'We Are Not The Last Of Yesterday But The First Of Tomorrow' (cue for a song!) is only one seeker after grandeur. Posers, fops, the art-rock intelligentsia; it seems as though the whole country's running around putting on airs and graces. The relative success of delusion and giggly fantasy at the moment masks the desire for something bigger than an individual, something to anticipate in hope. Only little strands of this tendency are visible, and it is probably a phenomenon of the medium-term future, somewhere in the middle distance. This is not a vision of the rise of any one political or religious belief. It is a prediction that unemployment, its associated anomie, and the level of social chaos may become so chronic and inescapable that *en masse* youth may just turn against increasingly desperate and peripheral pleasure-seeking, and place a longing for meaning close to the centre of its web of needs. To rephrase, there may be a new tendency to seek order.

Small caricatures of this have been detectable in vanguard fashion recently: the 'purity' of Spandau Ballet sleeve design, the exaggerated and inappropriate dignity (that is, preciousness) of Robert Elm's prose, Willy Brown's claims to classicism in clothes design. All contain certain elements of simplicity and reference to order; all of these are borrowed images which create what our cultured Victorian forebears would have regarded as a burlesque paradox, a romantic vision of classicism. They are concerned less with the effects of 'pure' form and structure, and more with the image of this concern, of classicism. The idea is to *seem* like a person who aspires to classical values.

Willy Brown's raids on British regimental uniforms and the Anglo-Scottish aristo establishment's ceremonial finery provide another hint at the distortions that the idea of classicism may undergo. Some people need no prompting to leap backwards and clutch at the traditional, and almost vanished, British imperial values. We have left behind a world in which a very clear order existed, was extensively justified, had the backing of years, and was made to seem beautiful. As its outdated values recede in importance, its style comes to the fore. However, if those images became more than something in which to dabble for a few weeks, if they meet a need, some of these associated attitudes would be adopted to please the inner eye. A re-interpretation of Establishment serenity, grandeur and culture would be safe, easy and readily integrated into the individualist-bohemian-petty-entrepreneur lifestyle. Very cosy: a youth version of the antique dealer's English tweed-and-brogues look and life. This is a yearning for aristocracy. It is not fascist, although it is reactionary. Stylists who associate the lower classes with bolshevism may, however, profess a sympathy for fascism as a form of snobbery.

Reaction can take a multitude of such forms, all shades and intensities. There is a certain kind of apocalyptic vision with a relentless, paranoic impetus of its own which lurks at the core of fascism – the flaming crosses and the Nuremberg rallies express it. It is the euphoria of contemplating destruction. Anti-fascist thinkers can succumb to it, helping to create the cultural capitulation which assists the rise of the tides of barbarity. The secret, addictive excitement of projecting conditions to their horrific conclusions is an indulgence which, in a small way, can help lead to those conclusions. There is no future in being the Weimar observers watching an unstoppable force engulf the masses beneath them. Better to accept that fascism promises and is fascinated by many gifts of the modern age, and help create a new, committed aesthetic of mechanised civilisation, electricity, speed and electronics. There is no logical barrier to left-wing futurism.

9

Heroin, the Needle and the Politics of the Body*

Martin Chalmers

> From what can we read living thought today – if not from the bodies of the slaves and their resistance?
>
> (Glucksmann)

> So many murders of his own body . . . There was a strange lack of care regarding his fingers, even in spite of his ultimate nightmare of having hands cut off at the wrists. His nails chewed down and indistinguishable from the callouses of his fingers. He could hardly feel his lady properly anymore. Suicide of the hands. So many varieties of murder.
>
> (Ondaatje)

> Some people seem to get addicted to the tattooist's needle . . .
>
> (Ragdon)

I

There are other ways of taking heroin and other substances that are injected, but whoever says or writes 'heroin' also means the syringe, the needle. Means the marking, puncturing of the skin, the flesh, the veins (the meeting with blood), leaving marks, tracks, bruises, abscesses, scars. The syringe, the most familiar emblem of medicine and the prevention of disease, is transformed into an instrument of excessive pleasure and self-destruction. It now threatens dis-ease. The fascination of the needle puncturing the skin, of the needle dipping into one arm after another. Getting under the skin.

* This article was written in 1983.

The needle is used to defy the good sense which aims to make the body a healthy working machine, ready for labour and the conspicuous display of consumer leisure-time. Its transformed use defies the constant injunctions and orders on how to maintain and improve the body. It proclaims an excess of defiance to the healthy order and to good sense.

No doubt, the experience itself is not discursive, that is, it leaves you speechless. What interests me here are significances, correspondences and images involved under the code-word 'heroin' in using and presenting the body.

Heroin appears at the end of a spectrum running from the clean, healthy unmarked body, ready for labour, through all the marks of self-imposed exile, from proletarian tattooing to the safety-pin, to the marks of the fix. Also: the ear-ring, the mohican, the shaved head, the slashed wrists (which ends in suicide 'only' by accident) and the bracelets worn to 'conceal' the scars. They are marks of a defiance, a curiosity, a rage to play with the body, at a time when the body appears as a last proof, a last sign of life. To talk of self-mutilation is to make a premature judgement.

The depth of defiance, the degree of disaffiliation from workaday respectable oppression and its assertion of the desirability of labour – short sharp shock of work – is marked on the surface of the body. Defied too is the smooth and tanned 'natural' healthy body of 'consumer society'.

The unease and the vulnerability of the observed body are denied in the display of bodily imperfection, of the 'unnatural'. Most succinct were the broken and missing teeth of punk.

Defiance is marked on the body as it was by those prisoners in the Gulag, who wrote it, scratched it, primitively tattooed it on their foreheads, cheeks, necks; who risked having the skin cut out without anaesthetic in the camp hospital. 'The communists are hangmen', was the slogan on one prisoner's face. Another prisoner had a black hand squeezing his throat tattooed on his neck. On the back of the hand were the letters 'CPSU', and on the thumb, placed on the adam's apple, were the letters 'KGB'.

The defiance, also, of the working-class German communists whose hands or backs tattooed with hammer and sickle marked them out for Nazi retribution after Hitler came to power.

The tattoos confirmed their politics as those of the dangerous classes of the slums. (Lombroso had seen in tattooing the mark of the born criminal.) They represented dirt, were an unwashable stain. Incomprehensible – degenerate – this self-infliction of pain and risk of disease (hepatitis) by the worker/idler/vagrant/pimp in pursuit of the decoration of the body.

In the eighteenth century, tattoos had been the noble savage's mysterious patterns. In the nineteenth century, they stigmatised the primitiveness, the atavism, of the urban savage and the forbidden temptations of below decks and of the fairground. Dirt and deviance were fixed in certain bodies, as later they were to be in the figure of the addict.

(Yet, the tattoos retained a promise of earthly paradise, the South Seas perhaps, whose bearer was the recurring motif of the palm tree. The tattoo was a claim to that promise which could neither be robbed nor sold.)

II

Play with the body, as opposed to the labour of making it fit, has been at once a sign of oppression and of the subversion of that resistance, ever since – with the ascendancy of the bourgeoisie – power became discreetly dressed in a suit. This play, this waste (of time), was the preserve of women and homosexuals. For women, the decoration and marking of the features and the body are not simply to please and attract men. They also served the need – apart from the direct pleasures of doing and looking – of separating 'work' from 'leisure', since women's work was not recognised.

III

> Four prisoners at Lerida in Spain have sewn their mouths shut with needles and thread in protest against gaol conditions, others are refusing to eat . . .
>
> (Reuter)

The experience of fixing, I said, is not discursive. Like madness it evades discourse. But the act of defiance also evades discourse, or rather it is a speechless discourse amidst the noise of discourse around it. Usage is defined as sickness, or in terms of crime. Or is confined to the transgressions of a certain art, a certain literature, to certain writers and musicians ('artists'). Using the needle, the syringe, escapes the camaraderie, the identification, the understanding of the sociologist, the youth cultural researcher. The user is observed, yet makes what is observed incomprehensible to the observing gaze, is not a victim. Playing with the body with the needle is a means of breaking off speech. For the left and for liberals, defiance and the suffering out of which it comes, has to be brought to talk, to reason, in order to become meaningful suffering. The suffering has to be for something, for an end, for general principles, or for material needs; has to fit into a chain of cause and explanation. But the intensity of this play with pleasure and death, with the individual's own body, with conspicuous waste and an excess of sensation, can't be brought to meaning in that way; it remains illegible and beyond sense. Heroin, perhaps more effectively than any other sub-cultural strategy, evades imposed meanings and understandings.

There are other outlaws, other 'body-politicians'. The urban guerrillas of the Red Army Faction (Baader–Meinhof) also broke off speech, made an equally 'unanswerable closure of relations with the straight world' (Paul Willis). They directed rage and contempt against the left and the left 'speakers' they wanted to exclude, and became enclosed in their defiance and the rules of conspiracy and of carrying a gun. The leftists who did not support the armed struggle, and who kept on thinking and writing, were merely making up fairy tales ('herumfabulieren' – Meinhof).

There was a certain punk heroisation of the RAF, and the link is the latter's total commitment of their bodies. A commitment which found an end with the final silence, first of Ulrike Meinhof, and then of the other suicides in the Stammhein cells, evading the dialogue which the left had longed for. (The guerrilla who talks, is now cured.)

One of the few interesting moments of that largely spurious film, *The German Sisters* (*Die bleierne Zeit*), was the irruption into it of the actors representing the terrorists on the run, bearing silence (non-communication) and leather jerkins.

What I've pointed to, is a correspondence. However, for some of the later members of the RAF and the successor groups, who were also fixing, it was more than a matter of 'mere' correspondence.

IV

The groups, the users, the families of users, like so many *enfants terribles* (on so many *bateaux ivres*) linked together in their rejection.

This sense of a 'community of deviance' perhaps helps to 'explain' why there's no break to be covered up between an act of defiance which escapes from one set of controls, and the knowledge that the individual user stands at the end of a long chain of capitalist organisation and investment. Because it also makes one a participant in an enormous conspiracy, scam, the perfect crime. You and the Mafia, or the Triads, or whoever, threatening the world like monstrous baddies – the Mekon or Dr Mabuse. Outlaws together. (What's the good of being on the same side as the murderous political goodies?)

But what is the relationship between the stories? Between the stories lived in the music scene, or in an Italian small town or by a 14-year-old user in Glasgow – or the slums of Karachi? The mystique of the junkie writer, the tradition of the opium fiend doesn't necessarily carry much weight.

It's impossible at any rate not to think of heroin and the needle in terms of the city. Not to think of it in connection with the intensification of urbanity. The city at night, the city as night, where the ostensibly negative aspects of the city are reversed, and filled with the desire to make the end of the night disappear. As the everyday is tending to disappear in(to) unemployment, bohemia and the search for experiences. Like going to the cinema in the afternoon, a forbidden pleasure which is an only apparently trivial comparison here, as an extending of the night in the search for an intensity of urban living. Perhaps that's why heroin always seemed to have such an attraction in places like Luton. Towns so physically near to and yet so far from the urban experiences promised by London.

Sources

I have principally drawn on (even quoted) the following:

Mike Featherstone: 'The Body in Consumer Culture', *Theory, Culture and Society*, 1, 3 (1983).
André Glucksmann: *La cuisinière et le mangeur d'hommes* (The Cook and the Cannibal), Paris, 1974.
Klaus Günther: 'Hölderlin und die Anderen. Das Ende des Traumes vom vernünftigen Leiden' (Hölderlin and the others. The end of the dream of rational suffering), *Konkursbuch*, 8 (1982).
Helmut Hartwig: 'Spielwut zwischen Identitäts – und Bruchkultur' (Play rage between culture of identity and culture of rupture), in *Ästhetik und Kommunikation*, 49 (Sept. 1982).
Dick Hebdige: *Subculture: The Meaning of Style*, London, 1979; 'Hiding in the Light', *Ten:8*, no. 9 (1982); 'Posing Threats, Striking Poses . . .', *SubStance*, 37/38 (1983).
Anatoly Marchenko: *My Testimony*, London, 1969.
Jonathon Miles: 'Life in the Shadows. "Christiane F." and other excluded images', *ZG*, no. 6 (1981).
Stephan Oettermann: *Zeichen auf der Haut. Die Geschichte der Tätowierung in Europa* (Signs on the Skin. The history of tattooing in Europe), Frankfurt/Main, 1979.
Michael Ondaatje: *Coming through Slaughter*, London, 1984.
Rebecca Ragdon: 'Tattoo You?', *City Limits*, no. 175 (Feb. 8–14, 1985).
Michael Rutschky: *Erfahrungshunger. Ein Essay über die siebziger Jahre* (The Hunger for Experience. An essay on the 70s), Cologne, 1980.
Paul Willis: 'The Cultural Meaning of Drug Use', in Hall and Jefferson, *Resistance through Rituals*, London, 1975.

10
Wild Style: Graffiti Painting*

Atlanta and Alexander

Futura's painting in Notting Hill Gate, designed to be seen from the underground (between Ladbroke Grove and Westbourne Park) is one of a number by Futura and by other New York graffitists. London must seem like virgin territory to Futura and Ali who have both visited London recently. Access to the underground must seem like child's play for graffiti writers who have had to cope with a mounting security campaign directed against them by the New York Transit Authority. Few of the generation who invented the large-scale pictorial graffiti style, which reached its height in New York about two or three years ago, are still able to practice their paintings on the street in the same way. Some are being pursued by the police for their huge acts of joyous vandalism. It must be nostalgic to be creeping through the tunnel again. In a culture where graffiti is restricted to political denunciation and support of football clubs or rock bands, there is a lot of wall space and little to deter its appropriation.

The graffiti painting stars seem to enjoy Europe for the spotlight of attention which they receive here. The clandestine act is videoed. Futura is photographed by music magazines in front of his picture. They are more stars here than at home. They are having a good time. Moving in art circles, music circles, opening rap clubs, Fab Five Freddy, Futura, Lee and Ali have been busy travelling, spreading the culture of graffiti painting, rapping, break dancing and crew style far beyond the ghettos of New York where 'hip hop' culture originated. They are responsible for an expansive ever-proliferating synthesis of word, sound and image in a subculture which embraces painting, poetry, music, dance and fashion.

---

* This article appeared in *ZG*, No. 2, 1981.

Graffiti painting was the first focus of public attention, though many of the painters have since become more involved in rap, the latest (and most economically lucrative) manifestation of hip-hop. The acrobatic break dancing, the disc-flipping of rap DJs, the fantasies and exaggerated stories of rap, the science fiction look of crew style, the jarring fluorescent colours of graffiti painting; the desire always to go over the top is a new assertion of black or ethnic identity. It is a cultural identity which half mocks, half celebrates the excesses of mainstream white culture. The graffiti painter is the Spiderman of the ghettos scaling the walls, projecting pure fantasy. A terminal vantage point on white consumer culture, hip-hop is a subculture which feeds for its material upon the alien culture which needs make no concession to blacks. The spray paints and comic-book images of graffiti painting to the disco beats and found sounds of rapping are diverted from the mainstream domestic use and put out on the streets as celebration. For the white middle-class kid, the comic heroes occupy a space of boredom (passing time). For the black ghetto kid they are transformed by graffiti art into fantastic visions invested with secret meanings.

The origins of graffiti painting are in the foreign language graffiti of the New York immigrant areas. The manifestation of the home tongue and written language of the displaced community, set against the walls of the huge city with its alien public language and sign system, was an assertion of ethnic cultural identity. This function of graffiti is still obvious in the Hispanic community in Chicago. Such graffiti operates as a sign both to insider and outsider demarcating territory.

This function has not been entirely displaced by the development of graffiti writing in New York. The new graffiti writing retains regional shifts of style, e.g. the spikey, almost Oriental style of the South Bronx graffiti or the bubble style more characteristic of writing which hails from Brooklyn. But the style can be practised equally by Puerto Rican or black. It no longer signifies ethnic origin. The new graffiti writing attempts, through stylistic abstraction, to encode its words in the look of a foreign alphabet. (It is tempting to suppose that the source of such abstractions might be the foreign alphabets of the graffiti forefathers, but in reality one need look no further than the Japanese lettering on the Pentel felt-tip pen for the model of some typographical distortions.) Only practice

158 Wild Style: Graffiti Painting

makes 'wild style' legible and so it operates as a non-regional cipher for dividing initiates and outsiders of the subculture.

Fab Five Freddy (so-called after Line 5 on which he lives and which he and Lee have 'worked' as the Fabulous Five) is in many ways the prophet and catalyst of hip-hop. He has run the gamut of cultural activities. Starting as a graffiti painter, he moved into

Graffiti painting, Jean Michel Basquiat. *Photo:* **Tseng Kwong Chi, © 1987**

rapping in 1979 and has since been exploring video. He has tended to open up territory which he leaves others to explore. Always on the move, in many ways he is the embodiment of the outward reaching, ever proliferating subculture whose horizons he has done so much to enlarge.

Blondie's *Rapture* record helped make Fab Five Freddy an international star and put out his rap to a mass audience in 1980.

She also made a video which featured Fab Five Freddy painting to the accompaniment of her song. He admits that his rap made Debbie Harry a lot of money; when it comes to the rip-off, the music business is the fastest. The espousal of the philosophy of street-wise by the music business has meant a new openness about business strategies. The new image of the pop-star/ businessman/street-wise gangster is an open legitimisation of the cultural exploitation on which the music business is based. The rip-off can be more naked (and on both sides). After punk we all know that it's swindle.

But if Fred Braithwaite of Brooklyn made nothing out of his now world-famous rap, he is not licking his wounds. He has turned the situation to his advantage and is making films and videos for rap clubs.

Fab Five Freddy has helped set the trend for an outward-reaching graffiti painting. It had become a new public art. Having set the course it had to keep moving outward. The scope of the subversion had to become bigger. Apart from other considerations, the generation of Lee, Fab Five Freddy and Futura, now in their mid-twenties, could face prison sentences as non-juvenile offenders. In the late '70s, official attitudes to graffiti painting were changing. Mayor Koch's liberal attitude to it as local folk art made it possible for some graffiti painters, like Lee, to paint officially – murals for schools, on handball courts, etc. But judicial attitudes remain fixed as does the Transit Authority's determination to stamp out graffiti painting once and for all. (Under their 5.5 billion dollar improvement programme, the TA is planning the introduction of military-scale security measures for their yards with guard dogs, razor ribbon and electronic surveillance.) The painting of whole trains seems less likely in the future and, whilst the work of artists like Lee has developed in the movement into the open, the prospects of graffitists as public-funded community muralists is depressing. This kind of sponsorship could only separate out a few stars and give them jobs. Anyway, such a development is now inconceivable, as the 'stars' have bigger horizons than another branch of Welfare. Evidence suggests anyway that the level of public acceptance of graffiti painting has done more to wipe out large-scale graffiti paintings than all the security measures of the Transit Authority.

The picto-graphic style put graffiti art on the map. Certain 'masterpieces' have remained intact for years, protected from overpainting or scrubbing down by unspoken neighbourhood law. A new level of acceptance was found outside the community as well. *Village Voice* ran a poster of some of the whole train graffiti paintings by Dondi, Lee, Futura, Seen and Blade. The art-world was beginning to pay attention too. The hassles and hazards of getting into train yards was becoming a diversion in the development of graffiti painting. (An incident which represented a turning-point in the attitudes of graffiti painters to the trains was Ali's near fatal accident when his aerosols inexplicably exploded whilst working in the yards.) As Lee has said: 'We wanted to write not fight.'

The picto-graphic style meant a new enlargement of the scope of graffiti in its co-option of found elements to the ready-made fantasies of American consumer culture. Taken from the fusion of image and word from the covers of American comics, the paintings recycle images from Disney and Marvell magazines, diverting to a street vantage point on the world. Comic heroes viewed through the smack-eyes of black kids, the heroes, who in their original settings promise world salvation through huge feats of daring, become the dark angels of a fearsome cosmology of doom. Lee especially developed this characteristic style, distorting images of comic heroes and monsters into a deathly vision of the fantastic. He emphasises the importance of the high you get from inhaling the chemicals of aerosol paint (the same is true of fumes from felt-tip pens to a much lesser extent). The 'high' allows the painting to go over the top. It is also important in the reading of graffiti names and is part of the encoding process of the obscured name. The indecipherable words in 'wild-style' are rendered legible to the more 'pictorial' perception of the high. Out of a few marks emerges a word. Out of an amalgam of comic-book fragments emerges a space. 'Space' is an important word for the graffiti painters. Graffiti is the individual appropriation of public space. There is a desire to create space for oneself – to give space to the individual's projection and fantasies. 'Space' describes both the state of mind of hallucination and the limit of fantasy in the concrete walls of the city.

But the space created in graffiti paintings is not the private space of individualised vision. The characteristic use of three-dimensional lettering borrowed from comic magazine covers is another way of creating space. The writing is not directly on the wall but illusionistically related to it. It seeks to dominate urban space with the same totality with which drugs dominate perception. Graffiti paintings saturate the senses with their crowded fields of excess, their fluorescent colours and their Hollywood monumentality. But the paintings are not just excessive. They reflect upon excess as it exists in the monsters which underlie consumer culture and which heroin and grass help bring to the surface as fantastic visions. The paintings are like collective hallucinations – the nightmare flip-side of the white consumer culture dream. They feed off the shared fantasy of comic books but direct them from the moral and ideological intentions of the original and relocate the images in the culture of hallucinations of the ghetto world.

Drugs offer rapture and intervention in white culture, a state of being and seeing which is bodily and confronts the familiar spectacular abstractions of white culture with displaced awe and fascination. Living on the street means engaging with what passers-by overlook. Hallucination keeps vision to the here and now of immediate gratification and transforms images which for their intended audience are investments of hopes and plans, into images of immediate joy and dread. The cultural chimera of the comic images become the glittering graffiti painting thundering its apocalyptic vision out of the tunnel. Like the needle in the vein, the metallic crashing of the cars through the underground is a suspension – a sudden spectacle.

For all that it has become public, graffiti remains a cipher, communicating one thing to cultural insiders and another to the rest of the world. Drugs are a part of that cipher which divides a straight 'reading' from the specific associations of drug culture.

Some of the magical associations of language in the origins of writing are found resurfaced in graffiti writing. Overwriting or 'slashing' is to put one's mark on the name slashed. It can be a direct challenge to the sovereignty of the graffiti king. The magic potential of symbols and even the association with the mythic origins of black culture in voodoo, lives on in the hallucinatory weed culture of the black ghettos. The more visionary and contemplative aspects of black weed culture which has its roots in the West Indies is alien to the street wise ideology of hip hop.

Large-scale graffiti painting sacrificed the contemplative aspect of religious icons for the fast spectacularity of the street advertisement. But new situations make new demands and create new possibilities. The entry of graffiti painting into the contemplative spaces of galleries and the dark interiors of drug consumption clubs is certain to evolve new kinds of visual experiences.

It is perhaps symptomatic of the power and speed of communication of the music business in comparison to the art world, that the new graffiti painting was picked up by the music art world before the world. Fab Five Freddy's collaboration with Blondie, and Futura's more recently with the Clash, has brought graffiti painting to a much wider audience than could the usual process of permeating downwards from the art world. A lot of media and music people had their apartment walls painted by graffiti painters before the art world explored these avenues of collecting, and the first time that graffiti was picked up in the art world, it followed the lead of media co-option. Lee and Fab Five Freddy were often simply given paints as in early Fashion Moda shows or else offered an hourly rate to paint the walls of 'White Columns' and the apartment walls of 'collectors'.

The first shows of graffiti-painting were staged in the late '70s either downtown close to the artist community (like 'White Columns') or in the Bronx closer to home in 'Fashion Moda'. 'Fashion Moda' was made famous by graffiti art, though it has done more conventional shows by local black artists like the sculptor John Ahearn, and more conceptual orientated shows like the black Christ show which consisted of a collection of religious images of black Christs to be found in black ghettos all over America. The real breakthrough for graffiti painting was the point at which it was taken as seriously as white painting of the same generation. The 'Fashion Moda' exhibition at the New Museum showed both graffiti painting and the work of white lower Eastside artists who in some cases were either influenced by the black graffiti painters or at least by the ethos of an art so closely associated with the street.

A generation of artists disaffected or at least excluded by the mainstream of recent gallery art, have adopted a method of working which is close in some respects to those of the black graffiti painters. Working in public places usually without official permission, artists like Justen Ladda and Jenny Holzer have started to engage in an art which deliberately transgresses the semi-private spaces of the New York art world. To occupy public space seemed like an escape from the solipsism and self-referential aspects of recent art-history. Some of this generation of artists openly acknowledged the influence of their black counterparts. Keith Haring, for example, produces his drawings as graffiti in white chalk on the 'blacked' empty ad boardings in the subway. But his territory is Manhattan and his 'local' community is that of the art world; the drawings are found in subways, the closest to the galleries and museums. But unlike their black counterparts the lower Eastside artists have found it easier for their work to survive the transition to the up-town galleries. Jenny Holzer's flyposted statements have come to look like official plaques, subverting their surroundings as the billposters had in the lower Eastside. However the black graffiti paintings transposed to the canvas (or more usually the sheet metal) of the marketable painting seem curiously mute. Lee's new paintings have gone beyond the original 'germ' of the word into purely image paintings. His painting of Blondie is sophisticated in technique but is indistinguishable from other air-brush representations of pop-stars.

Fab Five Freddy went to art-school but the product of this experience seems to have been to drop painting for more immediate cultural expressions like rap and more recently video. Perhaps the meaning of graffiti painting for the New York art-world is in its brashness, its directness of expression and its lack of concern for painterly surface. Frank Stella's '70s paintings seem to imitate the brash exuberance of graffiti painting, using aerosol paint, glitter and fluorescence to cover a more deliberately broken surface. More recently artists like Jonathon Borofski and Mike Glier have adopted the method of working directly onto the wall. Perhaps there is something of the influence of graffiti painting in Schnabel's irreverence for conventional painterly surface. The surfaces of his paintings which are most characteristically fragmented by broken plates, are overlooked in the painted image in much the same way as graffiti artists overlook the immediacies of their surfaces (subway cars or bricks) in projecting their image.

The input of 'primitivism' has of course been one of unequal exchange. The art-world promised a way out of the ghetto only to confine the work of the graffiti painters to the more restricted code of the art-world. Coinciding with a crisis in modernist painting, graffiti painting showed a way towards a direct use of public imagery without the irony, pathos and parody to which other re-uses of found imagery seems condemned.

In the process of gallery consumption little of the specific meaning of graffiti art was communicated, or even survived the threshold of the gallery itself. That appropriation of black culture by white culture involves exploitation and manipulation comes as no surprise to artists like Lee. Perhaps the new (gallery-oriented) paintings are fair exchange. The culture in which graffiti art has meaning is doubly separated from the white collector.

But in the process it seems that the large-scale graffiti paintings are a thing of the past. Energy now seems directed more into the word than the image and more into the spoken than the written.

The stylistic distortions and evolutions of graffiti writing which keep the name perpetually at the limit of legibility, means that reading involves an initiation into a history of style changes. In this development from the earlier graffiti writing, motives changed too, from expressions of community solidarity to that of individual identity. Graffiti became more outward moving, embodying a desire to put one's name about town. This seems to be the reason for the focus on the subway system in the late '60s graffiti explosion.

The point at which the city became covered by graffiti, the older functions of graffiti of the type still found mostly in Europe (statements of political or sport affiliation, etc.) died out and were replaced by the pure mark of individuality – the name and sometimes the street number. The preoccupation of the graffiti writers changed from the content to the style of words. People copied others' style and developed their own personal lettering. This was the initiation into the new, rapidly growing subculture of the seventies. Style changes and affiliations themselves became a form of speech of greater and greater complexity in its stylistic divisions and syntheses. Typographical expressionism took writing to further and further limits of abstraction. But with the emergence of the new picto-graphic style of graffiti signature which developed with the use of the paint aerosol and sometimes encompassed whole trains, the more private messages of stylistic currency, the old province of the felt-tip pen, was worked out in the interiors of the train cars. A division between the public graffiti painting and the restricted 'language' of graffiti writing. Futura suggests that the writing in the cars is more about communication to initiates, whilst the exterior paintings are communications to the population as a whole. A glance around a subway car and you can tell who is writing, what lines are cool and a complex of information about individual allegiances and divisions within the subculture:

> You can walk into a car, see everyone's name, you know just from the styles and tell what's really going on in the community. (*Futura*)

In the early seventies Norman Mailer was able to look at graffiti-covered walls as collectively meaningless surfaces, comparable with those of Abstract Expressionist paintings. Clearly, the way that the art-world first came to an appreciation of this urban vandalism was through the interesting surfaces which it created, and the simple humanity of the mark – the pathos of the collective wall. To add one's mark to the rosta of misery must have seemed futile and dwarfing. The graffiti-covered walls seemed to symbolise the overcrowding of the ghettos. But, of course, this was far from the intentions of the graffiti writers whose mark was an assertion of identity. Graffiti had to do more than leave a trace upon the alien surface of the city wall.

Graffiti became more obviously an act of defiance. Signatures became bigger, less often furtive acts with a felt-tip pen, more often large-scale acts of defiance using the scale which paint aerosol made possible. Finally, from this emerged the recent pictorial graffiti which transformed the assertion of self into a public art. Consequently the art of vandalism started to reach the level of a quite substantial criminal operation. Firstly, ripping off the paint in quantities large enough to cover entire trains requires planning and considerable risk. The second part of the operation – access – has meant the need for organisation and strategies for what is more or less a graffiti-army staging permanent guerrilla war with the Transit Authority.

> Getting at the [train] exteriors is no mean feat. It entails infiltrating the various underground and elevated lay-ups and the secured outdoor yards where the trains not in service are stored. The first few trips to the yards and lay-ups tests the mettle of the bravest 'toys', even when accompanied by veteran writers. There are rat-infested tunnels to negotiate, cyclone fences to scale or cut through, transit patrols to dodge and third

rails coursings with 625 volts of juice to sidestep just to reach the trains. Even then, there is constant threat of being vamped or ripped off by such predatory gangs as the 'Ballbusters' and the 'Vamp' Squad, who frequent the yards, stations and lay-ups on their respective turfs. (Bill Mosely, 'Graffiti', *Omni*, Jan., 1982)

The dangers of the occupation are a part of the ethos of graffiti painting. Arguably the means are as important as the ends when a subway car painting has only a life expectancy of about a week before it encounters the Transit Authority's ultimate weapon, the 'Buff'. (Sometimes called the 'Agent Orange Crush', the machine is like a huge carwash which sprays solvents leaving a ghost image of the former painting.) The transcience of the painting means that the cultural meaning is involved with the process of doing, of pulling it off. The scale and the speed of the transformation is an important part of appreciation of the painting. (The incorporation of graffiti painting into recent pop videos like those of Futura and Fab Five Freddy on Blondie and Clash videos continues this emphasis on the process of painting.)

Graffiti for marginalised culture is the ideal crime. It is crime for its own sake. As such perhaps it can be considered 'art'. Few graffiti writers reject the idea that their work involves criminal damage. The criminality of the act is in the subversion of the authority of urban space. Cultural subversion is one thing but most graffiti painters reject the label of vandalism.

Here is a thing that doesn't hurt you. When a train comes out of the darkness, voom!, all it does is excite your heart, make your eyes follow it. It doesn't take your wallet. (Lee, quoted by Bill Mosely, *Omni*, Jan. 82)

Graffiti is certainly an open crime, since the product of the work is nothing but the name of the criminal. The transgression of official appearance is something in which the whole community can enjoin. Awed by the scale of the operation and of the painting, the means and ends are the same – the simple assertion of the triumph of the individual over authority, of the name over the nameless.

Writing one's name across the city, like rapping, is a form of bragging. The manifestation of ego in paintings, participates in a mini-history and mythology of 'graffiti kings'. There is the semi-mythic TAKI 183, amongst whose numerous feats was the 165-foot ceiling of Grand Central Terminal. There have been many since, and there are always several contenders.

As graffiti got bigger, of course, so have the penalties. Some graffitists have been sent to jail so it is unsafe to operate above the age of a minor.

> Graffiti is Art, and if Art is a Crime,
> let God forgive all. (Lee, from '*Roaring Thunder*' mural)

The relation of graffiti painting to criminality is an important one. Crime is the central reality of street life. For ghetto-livers, the Reagan era represents a sort of de-mystification of the democratic false promises of previous administrations. The whole structure is criminal. Everything is up-front. There are the rich and there is the poor. Confronted by corruption in every conceivable political form and by the impotence of radical politics, only direct subversion on the microscope scale of the individual street crime has any meaning. Being street-wise means not being taken in by the abstractions of political rhetoric. Graffiti art is a cultural manifestation of this cynicism. It is politically and culturally subversive as a simple manifestation of civil disobedience: crime. The new culture-hero is the one who can pull off the biggest job. Paradoxically this view of the world finds common ground with the political objectives of the Reagan administration. (There is a surprising amount of support for Reagan in the ghettos.) In Gil Scott Heron's 'B-Movie' rap Reagan is the second biggest cowboy of them all.

The edge of parody and irony is ever-present in the way that the rap is put across. Like rapping, graffiti is rooted in the philosophy of being 'street-wise'. Rapping expounds the virtues of making it, of taking control of one's destiny. Crime is the only way of gaining that control to those condemned to the ghettos. The manifestation of ego on the scale of the whole train graffiti painting, the exaggeration and bragging of raps, are set against an unspoken background of individual powerlessness. The rap tells you that there is only oneself; that there is no one else to rely on. You have to learn to live on your wits. The rap speaks of immediacy of fulfilment. Getting control of oneself and one's destiny, not through hopes and plans but through the ever-present possibilities of the here and now of street life. The stance means living out an openness to the world but being street-wise, i.e. wary without being cautious. Graffiti painting is an immediate realisation of self, through no other mediation than one's name.

> So they say, O.K., I'm going to take to the trains . . . and then they start to get some recognition, start to become someone. (*Futura*)

Graffiti writing for the unemployed black ghetto kid may have developed because there is little else to do but street wisdom tells you to turn it to your advantage. The rap insists on self-realisation but on your own terms, to be unafraid of established channels, but to use them on your own terms, i.e. rip them off. This is the philosophy, though the reality can seem quite different. Graffiti writers like Lee, Futura and Fab Five Freddy have made their names (literally) far beyond their streets and of New York itself, through the established channels of the music industry and the art-world. But whether it is they who are ripping off the establishment or vice versa, is an open question.

11

The Age of Plunder*

Jon Savage

Beatles 12 inch flops onto my desk, sporting a rather fetching colour pic of those well-known faces in their velvet collar Burtons and their famous pink tab collars. The record contains their first – not very good – single 'Love Me Do' with an *alternative take*. Train-spotting sleeve notes and a facsimile of the original label add up to a product that is perfectly anachronistic (they didn't have Beatles' collectors *or* 12 inchers in 1962, but that's another story). It's perfectly aimed: backed up by a clever campaign on the London buses – youthful pics of the Four with the captions 'It Was 20 Years Ago' and 'Did You Know That John Lennon Was In The Beatles?' – the record charted and peaked at number 5. I thought it was shit in 1964, but now?!

This alerts me, and I start noticing things. A few days later, I'm on a quick shoot: Manchester's Christmas lights are being switched on in the City Centre. There's a bit of razzamatazz: a brass band, an electric organ, appearances by the stars of *Coronation Street*. What gets me is the large crowd, and how it's behaving: this is, after all, only a low-key event but there are thousands more out than have been expected and they're ravening.

The crowd is pinched, cold and in sections obviously very poor. As they surge and yell, I catch a note of real desperation and chilling frenzy beneath the surface jollity that could turn any which way. Things are nearly out of control. And, supreme irony, this crowd, which has been ground down by Tory policies reinforcing the divide between the two Nations, starts singing and bawling between the carols; *Beatles songs*, those songs of hope from another age, 'She Loves You' and 'A Hard Day's Night'. 'Help' might have been more appropriate.

* This article was first published in *The Face*, No. 23, January 1983.

You wouldn't catch them singing ABC songs. Back to the wonderful world of pop, I turn to the *Daily Mail* of November 16. A full-page feature trumpets Mari Wilson as 'The Girl Behind The Return Of The Beehive'. The piece adds, revealingly, that 'Mari, 25 . . . is dogged by the fact that her hairstyle has always been bigger than her recording success'. *Quite.* A few days before, she has appeared on *The Old Grey Whistle Test*: a quick interview reveals that she's done all the homework necessary on the beehive and the late Fifties early Sixties, that she rilly wants to emulate Peggy and Judy and that she is going to perform one of her fave songs, 'Cry Me A River'.

She perches on a stool, surrounded by her violinists, the 'Prawn Cocktails' – so *Ealing* – who actually look like punks. It's not bad, but nothing like Julie London. But then Mari is one camp joke that has transcended as things tend to at present: she records for a very studied little label called Compact which has also done all the necessary homework: silly cod sleeve notes by 'Rex Luxore', silly inner sleeves with Fifties curtain patterns and a name taken from a cruddy early Sixties television serial that is hip enough to drop.

The thing that really floors me is that in the same *Daily Mail* of November 16 there is a tiny news item on page 5: *Compact*, the twice-weekly TV serial set in a women's magazine office, is to be brought back by the BBC in the spring of 1984. The original series was killed off 17 years ago. Clearly, we are dealing with something quite complex that is beyond the bounds of parody.

We are inundated by images from the past, swamped by the nostalgia that is splattered all over Thatcherite Britain. Everywhere you turn, you trip over it: films, television series of varying quality, clothes, wars, ideologies, design, desires, pop records. A few more examples, to make your hair really curl: the Falklands War – *so* Empire, *so* Forties war movie; *Brideshead Revisited* and *A Kind Of Loving*, two Granada serials that looked at the Twenties and the Fifties respectively through rose-coloured glasses with the design departments having a field day with all this 'period' nonsense. *The* British film of 1982 that has the Yanks drooling is *Chariots Of Fire*, a 1920s morality play. There's a rush of public-school and working-class boys into the army, an event unthinkable ten years ago and a new respectability and confidence in the middle classes, just like the Fifties, with the rise of formerly moribund magazines like *The Tatler*, and the runaway success of *The Sloane Ranger Handbook*. It's all underpinned by a reinforcement of the old class and geographical divisions by the most right-wing government since the war. And I haven't even *mentioned* the Sixties.

Craving for novelty may well end in barbarism but this nostalgia transcends any healthy respect for the past: it is a disease all the more sinister because unrecognised and, finally, an explicit device for the reinforcement and success of the New Right.

Part of this is a response to increased leisure. Because we don't produce solid stuff any more – with the decline of the engineering industries – we are now all enrolled in the Culture Club. In the gap left by the failure of the old industries comes Culture as a Commodity, the biggest growth business of the lot: the proliferation of television, video (especially in the lower income groups), computers and information. But this flow of information is not unrestricted: it is characteristic of our time that much essential information is not getting out, but is instead glossed by a national obsession with the past that has reached epidemic proportions.

Pop music, of course, reflects power politics, and it is fascinating to see how it has toed the line. As elsewhere, 1982 has been the year of the unbridled nostalgia fetish: consumers are now trained – by endless interviews, fashion spreads, 'taste' guides like the *NME*'s 'Artist As Consumer' or *The Face*'s own arch 'Disinformation' – to spot the references and make this spotting *part of their enjoyment*. It is not enough to flop around to 'Just What I've Always Wanted', no, you have to know that Mari has done her homework and you should be able to put a date to the beehive. Thus pop's increasing self-consciousness becomes part of the product and fills out nicely all the space made available by sleeves, magazines and videos.

These days, it is also not enough to sling out a record: it has to be part of a discrete world, the noise backed up by an infrastructure of promotion, videos, and record sleeves that has become all-important and now is in danger of making the product top-heavy with reference. Basically, it's mutton dressed as lamb: do ABC *really* have to dress up (badly) as country squires to promote 'All Of My Heart'? Of course not: but it sells the product like the wrapping on a chocolate box. But this is ABC's third or fourth

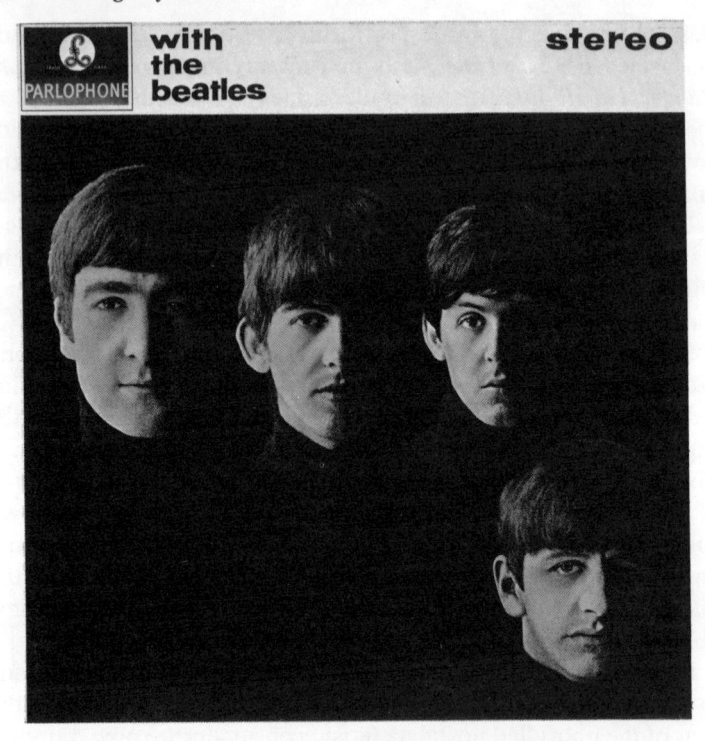

Robert Freeman's famous photograph for *With The Beatles*, 1963

image: when do they stop, and when does the audience have enough?

Record sleeves have been an integral part of this tendency towards mystification and an overloading of meaning: in this Tower of Babel the designer, too, has become all important. Designers even have two books to celebrate their role – the *Album Cover Albums* – and they win design awards and stuff like that. If – like me – you remember when records came in plain white sleeves, it's nice to see people trying, but it is getting a bit silly when the sleeve is more important than the record. Or maybe not: here is perhaps the ultimate recognition of the disposability of today's pop *music*, an acknowledgement of the victory of style over substance.

Here we refer, as always, to Punk Rock: because in those turbulent

Jon Savage 173

Edward Barker's homage to *With The Beatles* for Roogalator, 1976

nine months the ground rules were laid. Punk always had a retro consciousness – deliberately ignored in the cultural Stalinism that was going on at the time – which was pervasive yet controlled. You got the Sex Pistols covering Who and Small Faces numbers and wearing the clothes from any youth style since the war cut-up with safety-pins; The Clash wearing winklepickers and sounding like The Kinks and Mott The Hoople on *better* speed: Vivienne and Malcolm buying up old Sixties Wemblex pin-collars to mutate into Anarchy shirts. Partly this was a use of a deliberate reference point – an age before country-rock, session musicians, and dry ice. It was also a reflection of the revivalist groundwork already put in by labels like Stiff and Chiswick who were the first to reintroduce picture sleeves and customised labels, just like those French or Portuguese Rolling Stones EPs you'd find in Rock On.

174 The Age of Plunder

Thus you will find items like the 'All Aboard With The Roogalator' sleeve at the time much more interesting than the record itself: a direct crib of Robert Freeman's famous picture for 'With The Beatles'. Or, rather more wittily, the sleeve notes written by Paul Morley for 'The Good Time Music Of The Sex Pistols', a 1977 bootleg, which are a word-for-word steal from 'The Pretty Things' album of 1965. Here at least, the disjunctions are quite amusing: 'Exactly one year ago, as we write, the Sex Pistols were raw, unexposed and latent. They were like the atom, ready to ecstatically disclose to the world punk rock, a religion of fast moving people.'

By this time, picture sleeves were, like 'Limited Edition' 12 inch singles or coloured vinyl, an established part of the record company come-on to the consumer and, thanks to designers like Jamie Reid for the Sex Pistols and Malcolm Garrett for Buzzcocks, an integral part of the way the product was put over. Sleeves like Jamie's 'Holidays In The Sun' and 'Satellite', and the Buzzcocks' 'Orgasm Addict' (designed by Garrett around a montage by Linder) complemented perfectly what was inside, as nostalgic and found elements were ripped up and played around with to produce something genuinely new.

The energy that had created punk and, as an unintentional by-product, revitalised the music business couldn't sustain: by the time the channels were fully opened, there wasn't really very much left to say. Punk's quite careful, instinctive constructions were unravelled stitch by stitch in a series of revivals, renewals and plain fads as every youth style since the war was paraded for emulation and consumption. The references that had been a means to an end became an end in themselves. Instead of trashing the past, pop music started to celebrate it – an act formerly unthinkable in such a tawdry, transient medium. The Age of Pillage had begun: so many sleeves to fill, so many images to construct – where better to go than pop's *own* rich past?

This was and is simple enough. Images from pop's un-self-conscious past are invoked as some kind of ritual, or key to a time when pop was still fresh and all a gogo: money, sex and fame beyond measure. Key figures recur: thus you will get the Ray Lowry sleeve for the Clash's 'London Calling' directly imitating that of Elvis Presley's first HMV LP, or the sleeve for 'Armagideon Time' reproducing the blithe young dancers that are to be found

Jon Savage 175

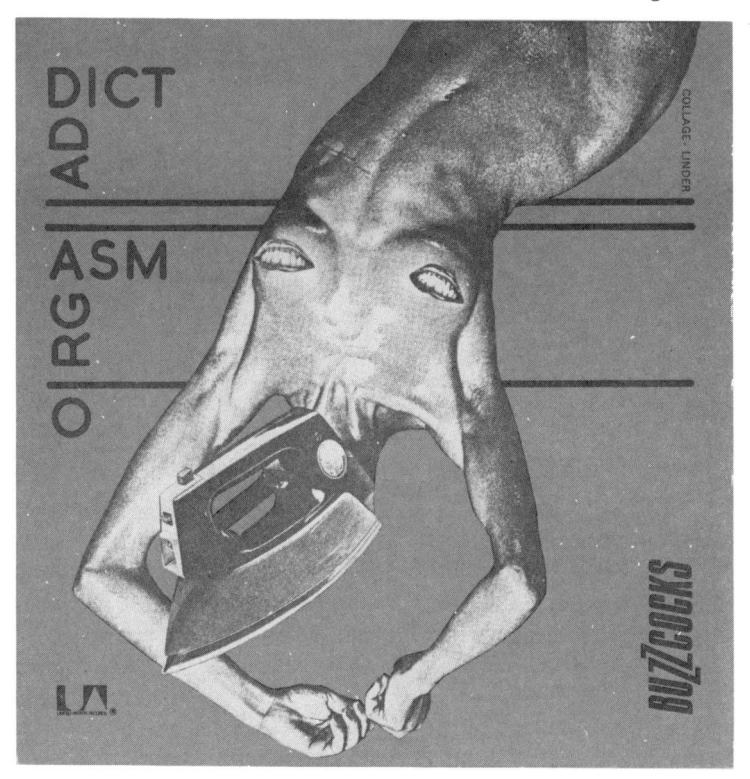

The Buzzcocks' collage cover

on any pre-1958 HMV single sleeve. These references are further compounded by genuine re-issues, like HMV's own 'It's Only Rock 'n' Roll: 1957–62' which reproduces the dancers again, but in a different context: Collectors Corner.

The Beatles are also ripe for plunder. The 'With The Beatles' sleeve, perhaps *the* most famous and monolithic piece of cover art – a symbol from the exact moment when pop went *mass* for the first time – reappears everywhere. Little stylistic devices like the white band on top of the front sleeve, with the name of the group and a mono/stereo designation or silly sleeve notes surrounded by ads for 'Emitex' and notices that this is 'Microgroove' or '$33\frac{1}{3}$ Extended Play' have become so familiar as to be

'Armagideon Time': back sleeve of 'London Calling', Ray Lowry, 1979

hardly worth remarking upon. What the Beatles signify also becomes a matter for comment: thus the Residents felt it necessary to graffiti-ise the 'With The Beatles' sleeve for their own insect ends to make the 'Third Reich 'N' Roll' point: that pop music as epitomised by the Beatles has become a dread, totalitarian hand upon the minds of the youth. Perhaps they protest too much, but then a group like Haircut 100 will invoke the rear sleeve of 'Rubber Soul' to reinforce their 'pure-pop' Monkee pretentions.

It is worth pointing out the difference in meaning between the original and the copy or homage. When 'Rubber Soul' or 'With The Beatles' came out, the design was innovative: not shocking perhaps, but thought-provoking. Its invocation by Haircut 100 or even the Residents shows how the Beatles have taken on, with time, a meaning very different from their original one and how falsely current pop views the past, redefining that past in its own contemporary image. Similarly, when the Elvis HMV sleeve appeared, it was simultaneously surprising and instinctive – not a matter for comment. Lowry's sleeve captures the *feeling* well – mainly because he is a genuine obsessive but there's no getting away from the fact that the Clash are putting themselves in the 'Great Rock'n' Roll Tradition' with all that *that* implies. It's ironic for a group that had said 'No Elvis, Beatles or Rolling Stones in 1977', but even that was giving the past a little too much credence.

1950s' HMV original sleeve cover

Another example of the way this plunder works can be seen in the sleeve for the recent Bauhaus hit, 'Ziggy Stardust'. The group's pretentions in naming themselves after the architectural school –

particularly when their work has no conceivable reference to it – can be dismissed as another example of pop's demented pillage of all Twentieth Century Art, but the mechanics of this particular 'revival' are quite interesting. The record was an unabashed tribute by the group, as they admitted, to glam rock in general and Bowie in particular and an astute choice as the Great Single that Bowie himself never released. The packing reflected this: the Bauhaus 'corporate' logo – another recent trend, this – was overlaid by the 'Aladdin Sane' flash, typically inaccurate and out-of-synch, as 'Ziggy Stardust' came from the previous album. The package was then topped by lettering taken directly from Edward Bell's 'Scary Monsters' sleeve, thus matching three different periods of Bowie into one 'authentic' package. The group made a very good job of it on *Top Of The Pops* – all of David's mimetic gestures, and 'Ronno' lurches – but by then it was all beside the point. This *was* Glam Rock for 1982.

Pop's own past has not been sufficient: perhaps the most irritating manifestation of the Culture Club is the way that the whole of Twentieth Century Art and – more recently – any amount of ethnic material have been used with increasing desperation to tart up a product that has increasingly less meaning. In this, Bauhaus are only weeny offenders.

Take the spearheads of last year's obsession with style, for instance: Spandau Ballet, before they got wise and changed direction, connived in sleeves by Graham Smith that peddled the worst kind of neo-neo-Classical pomposity in their frank debt to John Flaxman's lithographs. Or consider Chris Sullivan's poor Picasso – cubist period, please – pastiches on any Blue Rondo A La Turk sleeve. These were obvious enough and made the mistake of being much too 'fine art': anybody with an Athena poster on the wall could see where they came from: just like all the progressive groups used to do bad Dali in the early Seventies. Much more clever and systematic is the work of Peter Saville, perhaps the best known sleeve designer in England today, and one whose work on the new Ultravox album gained, hardly surprisingly, more comment than the record itself.

Saville began work on designing Factory posters and sleeves, where his frank debt to Futurist posters and typographer Jan Tschichold fitted in perfectly with Factory's 'industrial', 'machine' image. Tschichold published the book that is regarded as the foundation of modern typography in 1928: *Die Neue Typographie* proposed a new, almost classical simplicity and a rejection of Victorian ornament – like the Futurist movement in Italy, it was a celebration of the age of the machine. Thus it comes as no surprise that Saville's brilliant sleeves for Factory Records – 'The Factory Sample', New Order's 'Movement' and 'Everything's Gone Green' – reproduce Futurist and Tschichold designs fairly closely. They gave Factory one of the highest, if not *the* highest, graphic profile and made Saville's name.

If on occasions the sleeve became not an ornament but a prison, then it was because the product didn't come up to the Factory 'specification': a very good example of this occurs on Section 25's tentative, delicate 'Always Now' album, which is all but swamped by a Saville sleeve that is an object exercise in over-design, and a clear indication that the designer has become more important than the group.

With time, this process has become clear as Saville becomes more important and more influential: his recent designs for Ultravox's 'Quartet' and 'Hymn' are perfect examples of cover art that matches the interior product in a way that is far from flattering. Like Ultravox, these sleeves are grandiose, cod neo-classical exercises perfectly executed for the erection of false pillars of worship. Like the ABC sleeve for 'All Of My Heart', which has them parodying the 'classical' grandeur of a Deutsche Grammophon sleeve, they represent some kind of nadir of style over content. Boys, my congratulations!

The Past then, is being plundered in Pop as elsewhere in order to construct a totality that is seamless, that cannot be broken. It is a characteristic of our age that there is little sense of community, of any *real* sense of history, as 'The Present' is all that matters. Who needs yesterday's papers? In re-fashioning the past in our image, in tailoring the past to our own preconceptions, the past is recuperated: instead of being a door *out* of our time, it merely leads to another airless room.

The Past is then turned into the most disposable of consumer commodities, and is thus dismissible: the lessons which it can teach us are thought trivial, are ignored amongst a pile of garbage. A proper study of the past can reveal, however, desires and spirits not all in accordance with Mrs Thatcher's mealy-mouthed ideology, and it is up to us to address ourselves to them. What pop does, or doesn't do, ceases to be important.

Part III

Interiors

12

Sighs and Whispers in Bloomingdales: A Review of a Bloomingdale Mail-Order Catalogue for Their Lingerie Department*

Rosetta Brooks

When, in the late 1970s, Bloomingdale's commissioned Guy Bourdin to take the photographs for their lingerie mail-order catalogue, they must have been aware that overnight it would become a collectors' item. The other major '70s fashion photographers, Helmut Newton and Deborah Turbeville, have both been anthologised; but the Bloomingdale catalogue, *Sighs and Whispers*, is the only book by Guy Bourdin available. It is actually more of a pamphlet, being only eighteen pages long and containing the same number of photographs, including the front and back covers, and placing Guy Bourdin's name only on the back page as a vertical photo-credit. None the less, the double role of *Sighs and Whispers* as a photo-series by Bourdin and as an album for registering consumer choice, was an irony that would not have escaped either Bourdin or Bloomingdales. It is indicative of a split in consumer attitudes and in the consumer product image which, whilst it is characteristic of a tendency in a range of advertising and consumer products now, was first noticeable in fashion photography in the mid-'70s. At this time, at the bodily centre of advertising, the nature of the relationship between product-image and product (form and content) changed.

In 1975, Guy Bourdin did an advert for Charles Jourdan shoes in which the shoes lie discarded on the side of the road on the site

---

* This article appeared in *ZG*, No. 3, 1982.

of what appears to have been a fatal car accident (from the chalk-marked outline of a figure suggested to be the Jourdan shoe wearer). Particular attributes of the shoes are more or less imperceptible in the double-page photograph. The gap between the product and product-image is at its most extended. By the late '70s, it was more usual to see a Bourdin spread advertised as such, at the beginning, with the product name at the end reduced to the size of a credit, almost as if the advertiser was taking on the role of patron for the fashion photography *Auteur*.

As the role of the advertising image moved away from simple affirmation, so the relationship of the advertising photographer with the advertiser becomes more complex. Guy Bourdin achieves a new level of freedom. He can make demands on Bloomingdale's as well as vice-versa. Like Helmut Newton, Bourdin works in *spreads*, occupying sometimes as many as ten pages. But whereas Newton's photo series tend to be unified by a narrative, Bourdin's are suggestive of narrativity but rarely tell a story. His spreads tend to be unified by a formal interest, theme or motif, which is explored across a sequence of double pages. In *Sighs and Whispers*, it is the spatial divide. The setting is often the bedroom because of the lingerie. The pictures are almost all vertically divided at the centre by walls, doors, windows and mirrors. The central cut is used to explore spatial and temporal continuities and discontinuities inside and between pictures, across the double pages. This decentring of the picture is partly for the convenience of the listings of garment details in columns below, but it also reflects upon the act of scanning itself. The images become metaphors for movement from space to space – from picture to picture. In a scan, we move from room to room (divided by wall and door), from inside to outside (with the window), from reality to appearance (the mirror). Double pages often seem to be mirror reflections of one another. The door becomes the turn of the page. His use of pictorial symmetries is both a response to the demand to get two outfits into one picture and a dramatisation of what is at the roots of such demands. Where other photographs of lingerie would use asymmetries (foreground and background) to make a pair of women, one in nightgown and wrapcoat and the other in gown alone, look somehow at ease in the peculiarity of the mail-order catalogue setting, Bourdin uses symmetries to dramatise the unreality of setting, and overtones of lesbianism and narcissism to

Sighs, whispers and mirrors: the Bloomingdale Catalogue

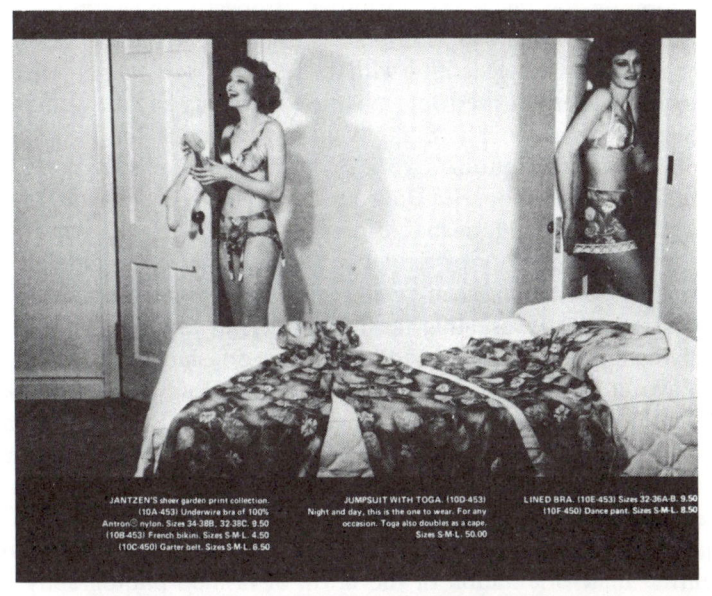

Sighs, whispers and doors: the Bloomingdale Catalogue

emphasize the sexual implication of the oddity of the female consumer's vantage point on her own image. Instead of naturalising the setting, Bourdin makes the image strange, exploiting the peculiarity of the fashion photograph by imposing devices which keep the consumer at a distance from the ostensive content of the image (the product).

In the turning of the pages from slips to nightgowns, we go from reality to appearance, from the female double to the mirror reflection. Expectations are constantly being subverted; a simple relation of access to the picture space constantly denied. The divide of a window frame in the centre of one picture becomes, in the turn of the page, the divide of a wall between rooms. Across the double pages, an intermediary frame is created, like a frame caught out of synch in a cine projection. The process of scanning is arrested. Directed from the centre, from the reality of the product, or from the body of the woman, the point of consumer attachment becomes the frame, the page, i.e. the realities of consumption conventionally traversed in the photographic transparency of the image. Glamour is not the neutral index of sexuality but is spectacularised as falsity. The glossiness and glamour seem to merge in the images as attributes of opacity and as points of closure, rather than as transparent openings upon the desired object(s). (His preoccupation with the female doppelganger reflects this split between desired objects – the commodity and the woman.)

Seventies fashion photography is most famous for its sexual explicitness, and Bourdin's work as much as Newton's has contributed to this reputation. But Bourdin's use of lookalikes is calculated to distance immediate sexual responses to his models. Perhaps this intermediary territory of sexual response, reflects the ambiguity implied in sexual images of women, designed for female consumption. Instead of presenting fashion models as real people whose individuality is seen in the adoption of the fashion, he enhances the aspect of fashion-image-consumption normally suppressed in the fashion photograph – the reduction of women to type (dramatised as identity) by style. The images are undoubtedly erotic, but their all-pervading deathliness (glamour is *old* in Bourdin's pictures) makes it an erotic attachment to the surface of glamour and gloss in all their explicitness. This is in contrast to the more centred male-orientation of the norm of fashion photography in which for all titillating illusion, the body is the centre for male appropriation.

Bourdin found a new point of erotic attachment a little closer to his own concerns – with the photograph itself. Not that photo-fetishism is new to fashion photography. Many photographers claim that one of the hazards of the job is a loss of the erotic impulse in 'real' sexual contact, whilst working. This take on the fashion/sexual image is by no means new, but most fashion photographers put this at the service of straightforward, male-centred erotic imagery, whereas in Bourdin, it intrudes and takes over as the object of attention from the body/commodity. Snapshots themselves feature a lot in Bourdin's pictures. In one of the images from *Sighs and Whispers*, three (of his?) polaroids, stuck in the corner of a mirror occupying most of the frame, register the surface of illusion and the destiny of the space of illusion, occupied by the models. They are not aware/unaware of *our* presence. There is no pretence: they register the presence of the photographer. It is *his* gaze which marks the essential, erotic relation. The space occupied by the models (the bed) is not a real space of erotic encounter, but a space between images – between the wallpaper pattern and its reversal in space and between shots in time. The images become a reflection of the processes of image production and control itself. Advertising begins to reflect upon itself. Formalist devices, which in art laid claim to a higher order of perception in a suspension of the immediacy of image content, are incorporated into the economic centre of the image culture from which aesthetic perception sought to extricate its sovereign vision.

The tendency reflects a shift in consumer attitudes involving an aestheticisation of consumption, an attachment to fashion as constraint, glamour as false representation and style as repetition. In contrast to the style of representation, the clothes advertised in Bloomingdales' catalogue are remarkably old-fashioned. It is perhaps characteristic of the '70s in which media abundance and proliferation is set against the background of economic recession and industrial breakdown, that fashion photography should flourish with the decline and fragmentation of the industry to which it is attached. In the '60s, newness was the rhetoric of abundance. What seemed to become necessary in the '70s was a rhetoric which could justify a consumer attachment to the old: new images for old products. Style ceases to be a matter of what you are wearing and becomes more the way you wear it and the attitude with which you bear an image – maintaining a distance from one's self-presentation. The shift of emphasis in fashion, from the product to the product-image is undeniable. Comparison of the thickness of '60s and '70s *Vogues* reveals the new importance of the advert in the '70s. It has become an independent, semi-autonomous aspect of the fashion industry, a form of entertainment in its own right, and perhaps, an art. It is in such circumstances of media abundance that Bourdin is not only able to be accommodated, but is necessary. In such circumstances the role of the advert changes. Bourdin's subversion of consumer expectations is at least a way of catching the passing glance in the midst of super-abundance. It is not necessary simply to *affirm* the product along with other affirmations, but it is more important to short-circuit the entire mode of consumption. In the '70s it became more important to halt the restless gaze of consumption than to keep it moving. Bourdin's spatial devices operate as 'traps for the gaze'. Lacan used this phrase in relation to *The Ambassadors* painting by Holbein. He observed that, what frontally looks like a semi-abstract phallic shape hovering in the foreground of the picture might reveal itself to the passing, sideways glance of the spectator as an anamorphically distorted representation of a human skull. The appearance of the death's head in the penis is an apt metaphor for Bourdin's images. Dramatising the act of photography as an arresting process, his pictures are 'little deaths', interruptions of the (image) flow of consumer desire.

13

Fashion 'n' Passion: A Working Paper*

Kathy Myers

One of the problems with the 'content analysis' of media images is its inability to take into account image construction as an evolving process.[1] This 'freeze frame' approach, whether applied to the moving picture or the still photograph, is always faced with a fundamental dilemma. On the one hand it seeks to classify and identify the dominant regime of codes and conventions which govern image production; and on the other, it needs to struggle constantly to keep abreast of the mutations in precisely those codes. The ability of the media continually to create new meanings gives a certain instability to the image, which constantly threatens to escape the analytic categories or stereotypes within which we seek to contain it. Yet this restlessness of the image, the search for the new, is not to be confused with a democratising of the visual market place. On the contrary, the proliferation of images suggests, for example, that in the case of the representation of women, the sites of exploitation are themselves multiple and shifting. Take, for instance, the ways in which notions of the positive or career orientated woman have been adopted by advertising to promote anything from a 'liberating' range of makeup to a building society account.

At any single moment, it is possible to compare the sexual and photographic conventions which determine, for example, how a woman will be represented in a pornographic image to the codes which structure how she will appear in a family snapshot or an advertisement for nappies. A few months later, one may find evidence of the incorporation of amateur family 'snapshotness'

* This article first appeared in *Screen*, Vol. 23, No. 3/4, 1983.

into an advertisement. Equally, notions of what constitute the 'professional photograph' may affect the ways in which individuals will pose for or photograph their friends. This trade-off of conventions is not to be confused with a blurring of boundaries. The discourses of the professional and the amateur photograph are distinct. What we need to examine is the nature of the economic and ideological structures which encourage an advertisement to deploy stylistic devices familiar in the snapshot. The same questions apply to a comparison I want to offer between pornographic and fashion images, specifically those published in magazines.

While arguing that different image systems influence each other, I think it's important not to lose sight of the fact that the fashion image and the pornographic image are in the first instance produced within quite distinct sets of social and economic circumstances. Those differences affect the way in which the image is constructed as a commodity, as well as the pleasures it makes available.

A fashion advertisement in a magazine is, like any other, itself the sum of a system of commodity exchanges: printing costs, hiring of props, models' and copywriters' wages, etc. These transactions may affect the reader in terms of a higher price for the advertised product on the one hand; or a reduction in the price of the advertising medium (the magazine), on the other. However, this system of exchanges is concealed from the reader, since the advertisement never refers to the commodities involved in its own production.

One of the jobs of the advertising agency is to invent or enhance use values for the product. Within the space of the advertisement these use values will be translated into intelligible meanings. Through the creation of meaning, the advertisement works to simultaneously create identities for both the product and the reader, who will be addressed as a potential consumer. In order to engage the reader's attention, both text and image must be capable of offering certain forms of interest and pleasure. Crucially, for the image to fulfil its advertising function, it must not offer satisfaction in its own right. The advertisement works to displace satisfaction, promising fulfilment upon purchase of the commodity, at which point the reader becomes a consumer. It then articulates meaning and pleasure through a complex relationship which it establishes between reader, advertising image and commodity. This relationship is orchestrated by the overall marketing considerations, which determine not only where the advertisement will appear, but also where the commodity advertised will be distributed, retailed, etc. These marketing considerations establish the necessary conditions for consumption to take place.

Clearly, the pornographic image does not fulfil the same functions as a fashion advertisement. It is not a promotional device to increase the sales of a commodity. Where part of the pleasure offered by the advertisement depends upon the future purchase of a commodity, the pleasure of pornography is effected in the present conjunction of image and reader made possible by a past purchase. Unlike the advertising image, the pornographic image does not demand that the reader buy a specified commodity as a guarantee of pleasure. The pornographic image is itself a commodity, and it addresses the reader as an already positioned consumer – a satisfied (and satisfiable) customer.

The erotic photograph

Certain forms of pornography have historically been labelled 'aesthetic' or 'erotic'. These terms have been deployed to defend sexually provocative or arousing imagery circulated within minority markets or interest groups. The current proliferation of 'erotic' photography (e.g. David Bailey's *Trouble and Strife*,[2] Helmut Newton's *Sleepless Nights*[3] and John Hedgecoe's *Possessions*[4]) has enabled explicit allusions to sexual violence which would not be tolerated within the legal and political constraints which surround mass market 'soft' pornography.

In his acknowledgements for *Possessions*, Hedgecoe thanks: 'The owners and the occupants for the loan of their possessions', a reference to both the country house locations and the women who modelled in the photographic sessions. One of these images depicts a beautiful woman lying on the floor, her mouth gaping, like a beached goldfish, suffocating under the net of her captor. The only thing which escapes the net is fetishistic waves of golden hair. The image, like her life, is neatly truncated at the neck. The spectators are placed in a privileged sexual position above this woman. We survey her orgasmic death in the company of an anonymous man, whose shiny patent shoes peek menacingly into the top of the frame; an authoritative fetish which sexualises the dying woman's subordination. While explicit genital sexuality may be subject to censorship, explicit sexual violence it appears, is not.

One of the reasons for the exemption of so-called 'Erotica' from legal censorship is its location at the intersection of a number of different visual discourses which continually compete for the interpretation of the image. These are the visual traditions established within fine art, commercial fashion photography and hard-core pornography. The inability easily to classify the erotic photograph lends it enough ambiguity to defy censorship under a current legal system which has established an effective exemption clause for that which is thought to be 'art'.

A photograph by Tim Brown appeared in the October 1981 issue of *Camera* entitled 'Erotic Masterpieces'. Like many 'erotic masterpieces' this image takes as its starting-point the fine art tradition of the female nude established within oil painting. The woman's body is presented as aesthetic object to be surveyed and possessed, endowed with the capacity to sexually arouse. The body, as artistic prop, is also a licensed vehicle for individual artistic expression, a medium, as well as an object in its own right. What differentiates the fine art nude from the erotic photograph in Brown's eyes, is the capacity of the photograph to disrupt the tradition of nude representation by making strange the image: 'I thought the towel over her head would be disturbing, and I was right.' While fine art has developed its own tradition of representing the female form, erotic photographers such as Brown and Hedgecoe have taken their erotic inspiration from the domain of marginalised and usually heavily censored hard pornography. In the work of Hedgecoe and Brown we can trace the making safe, or the making acceptable, of many of the sensibilities of hardcore pornography. Here necrophilia, suffocation, decapitation, mutilation and sadism appear as condoned. The erotic photograph trades on a dubious tradition of sexual libertarianism which invests that which is censored with the power to disrupt and liberate. Hence the 'erotic' – whether it alludes to sadism, nihilism or whatever – is acclaimed as a sexually liberating force.

The conventions of photographic erotica however, are not exclusively derived from fine art, nor from the development of soft-core or hard-core pornography. The erotic photograph owes many of its formal devices to innovations created within the domain of commercial photography, and in particular fashion photography.

It is interesting to note, for example, that two of its most celebrated practitioners, Helmut Newton and David Bailey, made their names in fashion. Fashion work occupies the prestigious end of commercial photography. The industry's seasonal demands for 'new fashion looks' and new modes of representation require both technical and stylistic innovation. Unlike other forms of commercial photography, fashion photography is auteuristic: David Bailey confers authorial prestige upon the fashion garments he chooses to shoot. The nude has been appropriated as the showcase for the photographic auteurs' work. Whereas the soft porn image is anonymous, the erotic image is authorised.

Fashion erotica

While certain conventions drawn from the system of fashion photography have influenced the representation of the 'erotic nude' as photographic art, it can be argued equally that the codes and conventions of 'erotica' have influenced the construction of certain fashion images. Rosetta Brooks has argued that photographers like Guy Bourdin and Helmut Newton have applied the conventions of the erotic photograph in order to 'make strange' or challenge some of the 'stereotypical' notions of femininity and female sexuality which inform the dominant conventions of fashion photography. 'This emphasis upon the alien and artificial qualities of the picture make a straightforward accusation of sexism problematic . . . Newton manipulates existing stereotypes; their alienness is accentuated.'[5] In the same way as this style purports to disrupt the conventions of the art-nude, so it can be seen to make strange the fashion image. Brooks suggests that this stylistic subversion is facilitated by making the photographer's mediation of the image apparent. In so doing, she argues, the photograph distanciates spectator from image, rendering any simplistic notion of identification impossible. She continues:

> Many of his (Newton's) more successful photographs hold a distanciated engagement with the manipulative devices of fashion photography and with the process of mediation. Those alien features present in suppressed form in fashion photography and current images of women are exposed and foregrounded.

The image is presented as alien: a threat rather than an invitation. Stereotypes are presented as a falsity.[6]

One of the central problems with Brooks's argument is the equation of distanciation with subversion. Yet an analysis of advertisements aimed at an 'upmarket' female readership can demonstrate that distanciation has been created as a new norm in fashion and beauty marketing. Not all forms of stereotype are dependent upon easy audience identification with the image, and not all distanciation subverts.

The advertisement for the Revlon cosmetic range 'Formula 2' was target marketed by the Grey agency at a 'sophisticated' female readership. The notion of sophistication is juxtaposed against that of 'accessibility'. In image terms 'accessible' images rely on a straightforward notion of audience identification, supposedly inducing reactions of 'I want to be like that'. The 'accessible' image will tend to use models who look like the friendly, smiling girl next door. By comparison the sophisticated image works to secure audience recognition of image as construct – image as image – without any immediate reference to the 'real' or to personal identity. It uses the image of the woman as a vehicle to deploy other kinds of codes and conventions. Often the 'sophisticated' image foregrounds itself in a readily identifiable cultural system, for example that of fine art painting, or in the case of Helmut Newton, avant garde erotic photography. The image of woman is used as a complex signifier to associate the advertised product with other aspects of the cultural and ideological system: art, status, wealth, etc.

The 'sophisticated' appeal of the Formula 2 advertisement is constructed through a series of devices which mediate and distanciate the spectator's relation to the image: the grid over the face; the use of portrait framing and pose; the figure's serenity, her acknowledgement of her to-be-looked-at-ness without recourse to the familiarity of a direct smile at the spectator. The image is constructed as a 'classic' beauty, derived as much from oil painting (with all its economic and ideological implications of rarity, cost, status, etc.) as commercial 'packshot' photography.

This sort of *haute couture* distanciation offers us an appropriate site for the 'accentuated alienness' which Brooks notes in Newton and Bourdin's work, including the now common use of sado-

Not the girl next door: mediation and distanciation in cosmetics advertising

masochistic motifs. I would question her 'subversive' reading of such representations (a harsher look has been fairly easily incorporated into our notions of femininity via the influence of recent styles like punk). But a marketing strategy founded on reflexivity and deferred identification does problematise feminist interpretations of these images as simply and directly encouraging or condoning the activities represented.

I have suggested that notions of hard-core pornography as mediated through auteuristic eroticism affect the form and presentation of certain up-market fashion images. I want to argue that the soft-core image, familiar in magazines such as *Knave* or *Penthouse*, displays a different kind of relationship with the fashion image. What characterises the soft-core image is its amazing resistance to stylistic innovations in the fashion field. Soft-core magazines are very similar in design, format, layout and choice of model. In appearance these models tend to conform to a very particular version of what is thought to be sexually desirable: long curly hair, lightly tanned skins and a total lack of body hair – with the exception of neatly topiaried pubic growth. With their luxurious locks and toothy tanned looks, these models resemble nostalgic reappraisals of Farrah Fawcett Majors: an image which the women's fashion market abandoned in the mid-seventies. But the pleasure which this pornography offers its reader depends on this sense of sameness, identity and repetition. The soft-core magazine is itself a fetish form, resistant to change and stylistic innovation, which demands an amazing conservatism not only in the choice of model, but also in the poses and locations deemed acceptable.

Such images are neither signed by name nor identifiable photographic style. While most readers of soft porn will realise that the image is posed and constructed 'for their pleasure', it works on a principle of disavowal: 'I know it's constructed, but nevertheless . . .' To facilitate this disavowal, soft-core images tend to be made up, lit and tinted naturalistically. Readers are offered a version of the model's sexuality apparently unmediated by such devices as photographic innovation (flash light, blur, solarisation, etc.). Work on the image is denied rather than flaunted, as it might be in high fashion or erotic photography.

But the sexual codes which govern the representation of the soft-porn image may also appear in certain areas of the fashion market: for example, the advertisements which appeared in the mid-seventies for Janet Reger underwear deploy the soft-focus vulnerability of contemporary centrefolds. The position of Janet Reger at the more expensive end of the naughty nightie market is complicated by the fact that its merchandise is bought by women, and by men for their female lovers. This differentiates the lingerie market from other aspects of women's fashion, and perhaps can help to explain the persistence here of romanticised photographic imagery which has been outmoded or superseded in other aspects of the trade.

All this would suggest that different notions of the pornographic are at work in the construction of the female fashion image which can only be understood in relation to a detailed analysis of the construction of the respective markets for both. The ways in which female sexuality will be expressed are dependent not only on the context in which the image appears, but also on the intended target market for that image. While the deployment of sexual codes is continually subject to change and reorganisation, their alterations are far from arbitrary. An analysis of the representations of female sexuality could usefully attend not only to the range of codes and conventions through which they are constructed, but also to the economic and cultural rationales for their deployment.

Notes

1. This working paper is a follow-up to my article 'Towards a Feminist Erotica', *Camerawork*, March 1982, no. 24, pp. 14–19. There I argued that different contexts tend to produce identifiable sexual discourses, and by extension, specific forms of pleasure and response for the reader. The point was illustrated with a comparison of a 'soft-core' pornographic image to a fashion advertisement for swim wear.
2. David Bailey, *Trouble and Strife* (London: Thames and Hudson, 1980).
3. Helmut Newton, *Sleepless Nights* (London: Quartet Books, 1978).
4. John Hedgecoe, *Possessions* (London: Mitchell Beazley, 1978).
5. Rosetta Brooks, 'Fashion: Double Page Spread', *Camerawork*, January/February, 1980, no. 17, p. 2.
6. Ibid.

14

Don't Look Now*

Richard Dyer

'One of the things I really envy about men,' a friend once said to me, 'is the right to look.' She went on to point out how in public places, on the street, at meetings, men could look freely at women, but that women could only look back surreptitiously, against the grain of their upbringing. It is a point that has been reiterated in many of the personal-political accounts that have emerged from the consciousness-raising of the Women's Movement. And it is a fact that we see endlessly reworked in movies and on television. We have all seen, countless times, that scene of Young Love, where, in the canteen, at school, in church, the Boy and the Girl first see each other. The precise way it is done is very revealing. We have a close-up of him looking off camera, followed by one of her looking downwards (in a pose that has, from time immemorial, suggested maidenliness). Quite often, we move back and forth between these two close-ups, so that it is very definitely established that he looks at her and she is looked at. Then, she may look up and off camera, and we may go back briefly to the boy still looking – but it is only briefly, for no sooner is it established that she sees him that we must be assured that she at once averts her eyes. She has seen him, but she doesn't look at him as he looks at her – having seen him, she quickly resumes being the one who is looked at.

So utterly routine is this kind of scene that we probably don't remark on it, yet it encapsulates, and effectively reinforces, one of the fundamental ways by which power relations between the sexes are maintained. In her book *Body Politics*,[1] Nancy M. Henley examines the very many different non-verbal ways that gender roles and male power are constantly being rebuilt and re-

---

* This article was originally published in *Screen*, Vol. 23, No. 3/4, 1983.

affirmed. She does for gesture, body posture, facial expressions and so on what, most recently, Dale Spender's *Man Made Language*[2] does for verbal communication, and shows how non-verbal communication is both a register of male–female relations and one of the means by which those relations are kept the way they are. Particularly relevant here is her discussion of eye contact.

Henley argues that it is not so much a question of whether women or men look at each other, but how they do. In fact, her evidence suggests that in face-to-face interactions, women look at men more than men do at women – but then this is because women listen more to men, pay more attention to them. In other words, women do not so much look at men as watch them. On the other hand, in crowd situations, men look more at women – men stare at women, whereas women avert their eyes. In both cases, this (re-)establishes male dominance. In the first case (one-to-one), 'superior position . . . is communciated by visually ignoring the other person – *not* looking while listening, but looking into space as if the other isn't there'; whereas in the second case (crowds), 'staring is used to *assert* dominance – to establish, to maintain, and to regain it'.[3]

Images of men aimed at women – whether star portraits, pin-ups or drawings and paintings of men – are in a particularly interesting relation to these eye contact patterns. A certain instability is produced – the first of several we encounter when looking at images of men that are offered as sexual spectacle. On the one hand, this is a visual medium, these men are there to be looked at by women. On the other hand, this does violence to the codes of who looks and who is looked at (and how), and some attempt is instinctively made to counteract this violation. Much of this centres on the model or star's own 'look' – where and how he is looking in relation to the woman looking at him, in the audience or as she leafs through the fan or women's magazine (not only *Playgirl*, which has male nudes as *Playboy* has female ones, but also the new teenage magazines like *Oh Boy!* and *My Guy*, with their half-dressed pin-ups, and such features as 'Your Daily Male' in the *Sun* and 'She-Male' in *She*).

To repeat, it is not a question of whether or not the model looks at his spectator(s), but how he does or does not. In the case of not looking, where the female model typically averts her eyes, expressing modesty, patience and a lack of interest in anything else, the male model looks either off or up. In the case of the former, his look suggests an interest in something else that the viewer cannot see – it certainly doesn't suggest any interest in the viewer. Indeed, it barely acknowledges the viewer, whereas the woman's averted eyes do just that – they are averted from the viewer. In the cases where the model is looking up, this always suggests a spirituality: he might be there for his face and body to be gazed at, but his mind is on higher things, and it is this upward striving that is most supposed to please. This pose encapsulates the kind of dualism that Paul Hoch analyses in his study of masculinity, *White Hero Black Beast* – higher is better than lower, the head above is better than the genitals below.[4] At the same time, the sense of straining and striving upwards does also suggest analogies with the definition of the very sexuality supposedly relegated to an inferior place – straining and striving are the terms most often used to describe male sexuality in this society.

It may be, as is often said, that male pin-ups more often than not do not look at the viewer, but it is by no means the case that they never do. When they do, what is crucial is the kind of look it is, something very often determined by the set of the mouth that accompanies it. When the female pin-up returns the viewer's gaze, it is usually some kind of smile, inviting. The male pin-up, even at his most benign, still stares at the viewer. Even Paul Newman's frank face-on to the camera or the *Oh Boy!* coverboy's yearning gaze at us still seems to reach beyond the boundary marked, when the photo was taken, by the camera, as if he wants to reach beyond and through and establish himself. The female model's gaze stops at that boundary, the male's looks right through it.

Freud noticed a similar sort of look on Michelangelo's statue of Moses – though Moses is not looking at us but at the Jews' worship of the Golden Calf. Since Freud, it is common to describe such a look as 'castrating' or 'penetrating' – yet to use such words to describe the look of a man at a woman is revealing in ways that Freudians do not always intend. What, after all, have women to fear from the threat of castration? And why, come to that, should the possibility of penetration be *necessarily* fearful to women? It is clear that castration can only be a threat to men, and more probable that it is the taboo of male anal eroticism that causes masculine-defined men to construct penetration as frightening and the concept of male (hetero)sexuality as 'taking' a woman that

Michelangelo's Moses castrates with a glance

constructs penetration as an act of violence. In looking at and dealing with these castrating/penetrating looks, women are caught up in a system that does not so much address them as work out aspects of the construction of male sexuality in men's heads.

If the first instability of the male pin-up is the contradiction between the fact of being looked at and the attempt of the model's look to deny it, the second is the apparent address to women's sexuality and the actual working out of male sexuality (and this may be one of the reasons why male pin-ups notoriously don't 'work' for women). What is at stake is not just male and female sexuality, but male and female power. The maintenance of power underpins further instabilities in the image of men as sexual spectacle, in terms of the active/passive nexus of looking, the emphasis on muscularity and the symbolic association of male power and the phallus.

The idea of looking (staring) as power and being looked at as powerlessness overlaps with ideas of activity/passivity. Thus to look is thought of as active; whereas to be looked at is passive. In reality, this is not true. The model prepares her- or himself to be looked at, the artist or photographer constructs the image to be looked at; and, on the other hand, the image that the viewer looks at is not summoned up by his or her act of looking but in collaboration with those who have put the image there. Most of us probably experience looking and being looked at, in life as in art, somewhere among these shifting relations of activity and passivity. Yet it remains the case that images of men must disavow this element of passivity if they are to be kept in line with dominant ideas of masculinity-as-activity.

For this reason images of men are often images of men doing something. When, before the full invention of cinematography, Eadweard Muybridge took an enormous series of photographic sequences, each one in the sequence taken a few seconds after the other, one of his intentions was to study the nature of movement. Muybridge photographed sequences of naked male and female figures. In a study of these sequences, Linda Williams shows how, even in so 'scientific' an undertaking and at such a comparatively 'primitive' stage in the development of photography, Muybridge established a difference between the female subjects, who are just there to be looked at, and the male subjects, who are doing something (carrying a boulder, sawing wood, playing baseball) which we can look in on.[5] This distinction is maintained in the history of the pin-up, where time and again the image of the man is caught in the middle of an action, or associated, through images in the pictures, with activity.

Even when not actually caught in an act, the male image still promises activity by the way the body is posed. Even in an apparently relaxed, supine pose, the model tightens and tautens his body so that the muscles are emphasised, hence drawing attention to the body's potential for action. More often, the male pin-up is not supine anyhow, but standing taut ready for action.

There is an interesting divergence here in ethnic and class terms, a good example of the way that images of male power are always and necessarily inflected with other aspects of power in society. In relation to ethnicity, it is generally the case that the activity shown or implied in images of white men is clearly related to the split in Western society between leisure and work activity, whereas black men, even though they are in fact American or European, are given a physicality that is inextricably linked to notions of 'the jungle', and hence 'savagery'. This is done either by a natural setting, in which a generalised physical exertion is conflated with the energies of nature (and, doubtless, the beat of drums), or else, more recently, in the striking use of 'black power' symbolism. This might seem like an acknowledgement of ethnic politics, and perhaps for some viewers it is, but the way the media constructed black power in fact tended to reproduce the idea of a savage energy rather than a political movement – hence the stress on back-to-Africa (in the white Western imagination still an amorphous jungle), or the 'senseless' violence erupting from the jungle of the ghetto.

Such images also put black men 'outside of' class (though there has been the promotion of specifically middle-class black images, as with, especially, Sidney Poitier). White men are more likely to be class differentiated, but this does overlap with the work/leisure distinction. Work is in fact almost suppressed from dominant imagery in this society – it is mainly in socialist imagery that its images occur. In nineteenth-century socialist and trade-union art and in Soviet socialist realism the notions of the dignity and heroism of labour are expressed through dynamically muscular male bodies. As Eric Hobsbawm has pointed out, what this tradition has done, in effect, is to secure for masculinity the definition of what is finest in the proletarian and socialist traditions – women have been marginalised to the ethereal role of 'inspiration'.[6] Moreover, it is certainly no *conscious* part of this tradition that these male bodies should be a source of erotic visual pleasure, for men and women.

Sport is the area of life that is the most common contemporary source of male imagery – not only in pin-ups of sportsmen, but in the sports activities of film stars, pop stars and so on. (*She* magazine recently ran a series of pin-ups of wrestlers.) Although certain sports have very clear class associations (the Prince of Wales plays polo, not football), there is a sense in which sport is a 'leveller'. Running, swimming, ball games are pretty well open to anyone in any class, and so imagery derived from these activities does not have immediate class associations. What all imply, however, is leisure, and the strength and vitality to use it. The celebration of the body in sport is also a celebration of the relative affluence of

The naked civil servant: a muscular motorcycle cop naturalises sexual and state power

Western society, where people have time to dedicate themselves to the development of the body for its own sake.

Whether the emphasis is on work or sport or any other activity, the body quality that is promoted is muscularity. In the copy accompanying the pin-ups in *Oh Boy!*, for instance, the female readers are called on to 'getta load of his muscles' and other such invitations. Although the hyper-developed muscularity of an Arnold Schwarzeneggar is regarded by most people as excessive, and perhaps bordering on the fascist, it is still the case that muscularity is a key term in appraising men's bodies. This again probably comes from men themselves. Muscularity is the *sign* of power – natural, achieved, phallic.

At a minimum, developed muscles indicate a physical strength that women do not generally match (although recent developments in women's sport and physical conditioning suggest that differences between the sexes here may not be so fixed). The potential for muscularity in men is seen as a biological given, and is also the means of dominating both women and other men who are in the competition for the spoils of the earth – and women. The point is that muscles are biological, hence 'natural', and we persist in habits of thought, especially in the area of sexuality and gender, whereby what can be shown to be natural must be accepted as given and inevitable. The 'naturalness' of muscles legitimises male power and domination.

However, developed muscularity – muscles that *show* – is not in truth natural at all, but is rather achieved. The muscle man is the end product of his own activity of muscle-building. As always, the comparison with the female body beautiful is revealing. Rationally, we know that the beauty queen has dieted, exercised, used cleansing creams, solariums and cosmetics – but none of this really shows in her appearance, and is anyway generally construed as something that has been *done* to the woman. Conversely, a man's muscles constantly bespeak this achievement of his beauty/power.

Muscles, as well as being a sign of activity and achievement, are hard. We've already seen how even not overly developed male pin-ups harden their bodies to be looked at. This hardness may then be reinforced by aspects of setting or symbolic references, or by poses that emphasise hard lines and angular shapes (not the soft roundness of the feminine aesthetic). In her book *The Nude*

Male, Margaret Walters suggests this hardness is phallic, not in the direct sense of being like an erect penis but rather in being symbolic of all that the phallus represents of 'abstract paternal power'.[7] There is no doubt that the image of the phallus as power is widespread to the point of near-universality, all the way from tribal and early Greek fertility symbols to the language of pornography, where the penis is endlessly described as a weapon, a tool, a source of terrifying power.

There is a danger of casual thought here. The phallus is not just an arbitrarily chosen symbol of male power; it is crucial that the penis has provided the model for this symbol. Because only men have penises, phallic symbols, even if in some sense possessed by a woman (as may be the case with female rulers, for instance), are always symbols of ultimately male power. The woman who wields 'phallic' power does so in the interests of men.[8]

This leads to the greatest instability of all for the male image. For the fact is that the penis isn't a patch on the phallus. The penis can never live up to the mystique implied by the phallus. Hence the excessive, even hysterical quality of so much male imagery. The clenched fists, the bulging muscles, the hardened jaws, the proliferation of phallic symbols – they are all straining after what can hardly ever be achieved, the embodiment of the phallic mystique. This is even more the case with the male nude. The limp penis can never match up to the mystique that has kept it hidden from view for the last couple of centuries and even the erect penis often looks awkward, stuck on to the man's body as if it is not a part of him.

Like so much else about masculinity, images of men, founded on such multiple instabilities, are such a strain. Looked at but pretending not to be, still yet asserting movement, phallic but weedy – there is seldom anything easy about such imagery. And the real trap at the heart of these instabilities is that it is precisely *straining* that is held to be the great good, what makes a man a man. Whether head held high reaching up for an impossible transcendence or penis jerking up in a hopeless assertion of phallic mastery, men and women alike are asked to value the very things that make masculinity such an unsatisfactory definition of being human.

Notes

1. Nancy M. Henley, *Body Politics*, Prentice-Hall, 1977.
2. Dale Spender, *Man Made Language*, Routlege & Kegan Paul, 1980.
3. Henley, *Body Politics*, p. 166.
4. Paul Hoch, *White Hero Black Beast*, Pluto Press, 1979.
5. Linda Williams, 'Film Body, an Implantation of Perversions', *Cinétracts*, vol. 3, no. 4, Winter 1981, pp. 19–35.
6. Eric Hobsbawm, 'Man and Woman in Socialist Iconography', *History Workshop Journal*, no. 6, 1978, pp. 121–38.
7. Margaret Walters, *The Nude Male*, Paddington Press, 1978.
8. See, for example, Alison Heisch, 'Queen Elizabeth I and the Persistence of Patriarchy', *Feminist Review*, no. 4, 1978, pp. 45–56.

15

The Business of Couture

Juliet Ash

Most decades, since the 1890s when Worth travelled across the Channel to Paris to set up the first fashion house, have seen major design houses indicating the potential of cut, fabric, texture and colour to less-inspired mortals with padded wallets. Time (as Roland Barthes acknowledges[1]) in the fashion business was signified by a mainly coherent 'look', a look to the future, a look to the past (revivals and nostalgia), a blinkered look, or a subliminal look. What was actually *seen* by the majority were one or two images blurrily photographed in tabloids, women's magazines or *Tatler* in the dentist's waiting-room. But whether it was the 'look' of a decade, as Dior's New Look in the late 1940s was presented, or the look of the year – as was the case with Courrèges' space look in 1964, there was one overriding image towards which the followers could aspire. Fashion journalism, though not the trade journals, still attempts to do this with one or two images frozen in time. But the 1980s, in espousing pluralism, creates inherited contradictions. The statements of decades and years have emerged into a miasma each season of reinterpretations of moments, capturing at their best neoteric images, at their worst merely nostalgia.

Fashion is a confusing business. Take the Paris, London, New York and Milan collections. The traditional line from many writers and particularly feminists, used to be that Haute Couture was emblematic of sexist frippery and exorbitant wealth. Not so punks, revivalist mods, teds and rastas; they were pure. Their roots and music legitimised their obsession with appearance. Their fashion consciousness gauged their class consciousness, or so went the argument.

This view often persists when Paris comes under scrutiny. When gay designer Jean Paul Gaultier provided a glimpse of female flesh via a bra parody he was awarded the ritualistic sexist denunciation. Yet when, in his 1984 collection, he featured a futuristic exposure of male midriffs the reaction ranged between sideways glances and sighs of relief. Now men would recognise the discomfort women had experienced by being turned into 'sex objects'.

In fashion design terms, it was a signal that pleasure and desire can be aroused from the exposure of men's erogenous area between chest and phallus, and between folds of silk and taffeta. It wasn't 'sexual objectification', but an appreciation of human form, interacting with the sensuousness of fabric. Jean-Paul Gaultier took up the banner for men in our image-conscious female world. Most fashion journalists ignored his continuing male theme in 1985. His romantic menswear in autumn of that year consisted of white chiffon skirts, lace and leather combined, ribbons in the hair and trousers cut at the back exposing a bum decolletage, pirate-high at the front with braces. Instead journalists concentrated on his extravaganzas for women. This allowed them to self-righteously proclaim that body-consciousness equals straightforward sexism without having witnessed his revolutionary menswear collection.

It isn't enough for feminists and others to eulogise the rediscovery of clothes after their 1970s' entombment in dungarees. The 1980s have also brought us the myth of 'post feminism', with one of its implications being that everything that the women's movement in the 1960s and 1970s fought for has been achieved. For the majority of people the argument is nonsense. But the evidence is plentiful in the fashion world. Couture clothes allowing more freedom are interpreted in media coverage by the likes of Sally Brampton and other fashion writers and sold to the wealthy; interesting discoveries in cut are buried by the nostalgia for bustles; conservative high street chains deny purchasers the passion of Paris until it can be toned down two or three years after its eruption.

* * *

To go to Paris is to enquire into the reality of a cultural re-enactment conjured up frequently but flimsily by fashion journalists. How do the collections feel? What do they mean? The world of appearance has, for more than a century, resided defiantly in Paris, more specifically in the Tuilerie Gardens. The atmosphere of Manet's painting *Music in the Tuileries* of 1862 could well inform the muted silence outside the tents 'Pérrault' and 'Sully' in Paris sewn to the sand with ropes. The fashionable international set look out of the picture at the audience watching them. They totter on pinched high-heels and drip with foxes; BCBGs (Bon Chic, Bon Genres!) – prisoners of style. The conformists clash with purple loafers and red-mixed yellow print-on-mohicans. 'La Faune' (the fauna) of young men, clean-shaven, hands deep in wide trousers, float in the expectant hush before the first spring/summer fashions shows wrap them up in the canvas Christo had finished unwrapping from the Pont Neuf the previous evening. But the music of 1862 is suddenly disrupted by the sound of 1985. A collection rehearsal is underway and the sound of the Specials AKA's 'Free Nelson Mandela' blares out from the tents, drowning the ineffectual whispering of the fashionable elite. The street informs Paris fashion as it did Paris at the turn of the century.

The fashion collections in Paris are a visual experience in which fragments of lost cultures intermingle with rip-offs and are assimilated into subversive rituals; where accessories of officialdom oscillate with sensuous cuts and fabrics; where gender becomes irrelevant in splendour that drapes the human form; where music is a back-drop and feet dance up the runway to take off in performance art. The buyers and sellers in the audience are reduced to passive admirers of 'les créatures' and money no longer counts. Photographers lean against the catwalks, waiting to select and reselect their angles to communicate with the world one 'look' out of many. But what the eye beholds is a welter of images to arouse the sensations.

The body is wrapped by Issey Miyake's fabric, the hugging citrus brights from Montana, or the simplicity of component pieces composed by Comme Des Garçons. There is a fullness and movement in skirts, slash-hemmed tunics, handkerchief points as skirt-backs; layers move round the figure continuing the previous year's themes, in flat boots and white knee-socks for baby-dressed-hooped nostalgia by Vivienne Westwood. Fantasy flirts with reality and bold prints for swimwear counter the demure eccentricities of nun's-garb bustiness. The proud sparing silhouettes of Azzadine Alaïa contrast with the elaborately alarming cuts of Jean-Paul Gaultier. Shape is hard-soft and has no limitation, checks in blue and black are surrounded by stripe and mismatched with circular patterning, or long black waistcoats flare over straight suppleness. Contrasts and contradictions are all in this flamboyant world.

From catalogue hand-out titled Milanorendemoda 36 (1987)

The content of what is presented jars constantly within its own framework; clothes of rebellion, subverted religion, careerist women, and professionals at leisure, stiff-peaked turban hats and monks' robes camouflaging the largest brief-case ever seen. There are crinolines jostling with simple perfect cuts, the most difficult to technically achieve, easy and comfortable to wear and exciting to mass-produce.

Collections of staid designer houses like Chanel, Miyake, and Yamomoto nudge with those of street-influenced Westwood and Jean-Paul Gaultier and lesser knowns such as Natalie Girbaud, Chantale Thomas and Junka Shamada, the last three being women. There are exotic shapes, men's shirts for women made of simple component pieces, exposed midriffs; full skirts cut-away in the front and dropping at the back. Shape plays around with proportions, mismatches and asymmetry. Body-consciousness means feeling around the body with draped fabrics and hoops more than the exposure of flesh. There are 1950s restrained clothes and layers from the 1920s, witty Edwardian fairground clothes from Vivienne Westwood and camp menswear/womenswear moving together in waistcoats for women and bows for men. Gendered persons melt into an androgynous image, stomping, dancing up the cat-walks. Cultures and history are plundered for inspiration. Out of it all something new emerges. This is the avant-garde of fashion, some of it functional, transformable into high street garb some time in the future; most of it dramatic, skilful in the making and imaginative, looking forward to creating a world without restraints, where life would be more pleasurable with the wearing of beautiful clothes, just as life could be enhanced by more easy access to paintings, sculpture and music, not merely squandered by those with enough money.

Each season, fashion stops for a few weeks to watch itself after the passion and traumas of making deadlines. To most of us it is inconsequential or at most worthy of a quick glance in the press, because High Fashion is made inaccessable – particularly in Britain – a marginal art-form priced too high, just like painting, music and opera. The articulation of dress represents here the personalised visions of designers who see future possibilities in their art and the stage is theirs. There are no imposed boundaries and I came away from the collection that year with Monet's edict to Clémenceau irreverently reverberating in my mind: here, as in Monet's paintings, 'by situating a-perception into sensation' designers had allowed the observer a glimpse of an enhanced 'knowledge of self and the universe'. It happens in London's Olympia collections, but in Britain the designer is restricted by cultural conservatism and financial restraint.

London fashion shows are subsidised by a pittance from the government, the fabric industry is in decline and fabrics are difficult to obtain. Production falters, and Fashion Schools are considered the poor relations of computer graphics.

In Paris they opened two new Fashion Schools in January 1986 to add to the already existing schools, particularly La Chambre Syndical from where many new fashion designers graduate. To us in Britain, even retaining fashion schools in the 1980s is a hard job. What contributes to the excitement of the Paris Collections is the knowledge that throughout the year art and fashion go hand-in-hand. The description for the MA programme at the newly opened Institut Français De La Mode (IFM) proclaims its intentions as the 'studying of textile conception, creation, marketing, manufacturing and modern technology in order to examine, analyse and consider the major fashion industries throughout the world'.

Fashion in France, and most of all in Paris, is as much about creativity as about production. Both are recognised culturally by the French people (machinists are still proud of their vocation) and by the Ministry of Culture – as important to their country as is their pride in food and wine. It could be argued that this national focus has, at times, been dangerously close to political compromise. During the Second World War, many Paris fashion designers and houses collaborated with the Germans to 'sustain the industry for post-war re-emergence' so they said. Yet under a socialist government, the pay-offs are visible and stimulating throughout Paris, and in the end financially tangible.

Paris fashion is informed not just by the seasonal collections but by an integrated cultural policy which respects the art of both fashion design and the textile productive process. It recognises that retailing is not merely a matter of statistics and profitability but also expanding new areas of retail creativity. Thus the 'Morais' – the area traditionally associated with artists now housing the Picasso Museum – has become a 'new clothing retail area for young designers'. One fashion magazine proclaims, 'Place des Victoires is too expensive for people just starting out, Les Halles is too schizophrenic, St Germain happened twenty years ago.'[2] And this is where Azzadine Alaïa – Paris's most noteworthy designer of 1985–6 – has his concealed shop.

Art and Fashion are inextricably linked in Paris when it's seen that Boussac (France's Textile Giant) employed nine young artists to design original prints, produced them in its Alsace factories for its Summer '86 line, and presented them at 'Prémier Vision' in March 1985. And 'Prémier Vision' itself has become the world's leading fabric fair, just outside Paris in conjunction with the collections. This is no wonder when France's newer textile (bar traditional silk and the newer cotton and linen) manufacturing industry employs in all 327 000 employees in expanding centres such as Lyons. This, compared with 231 000 employed in Britain in 1985 and still in decline. And textile production in France is not just manufacturing. 1985 also saw the Textile Centre of Lyons and Unitex of Lyons promote an International Silk Conference which sponsored a Fashion Show featuring twenty Paris designers, among them Yves St Laurent and Jean-Paul Gaultier, combined with 26 of the most innovative silk fabric producers in Lyons. Added to this, Oscars are presented to top fashion designers and

20 or more fashion houses, 1000 ready-to-wear manufacturers and a 50 billion franc garment industry all situated in Paris, feed into and off the seasonal shows.

Clothes have fascinated all societies. Today, France (and Italy) recognise this cultural compulsion with their economic support. But, in Britain, Mrs Thatcher could be accused, as Clémenceau was by Monet, of 'reducing the world to your [her] measure'. The talent of our designers, many of them women, may be given a hand-shake at Number Ten, but there is little back-up industry to make the images in fashion come alive – even if we may agree with the photographer William Klein, who said in his film *Mode in France*: 'You go to a collection, you see those people parading down the catwalk, everything is ideal – music, beautiful people, the lights. So you buy a dress and then what happens? You go out and get run over by a car. Just to have a dress doesn't mean your problems are solved.'[3] Most of us will never buy those clothes, just as we can't buy the Monet painting. But even the multifarious images are concealed – for the most part – from popular visual consumption, secreted behind a journalist's individualised selection of one part of many.

Notes

1. Roland Barthes, *The Fashion System*, Farrar Strauss & Giroux, 1983.
2. R. Voight, 'Textiles and the Cloth Becomes Clothing', *Passion*, Nov. 1985.
3. Stephen O'Shea, 'Defying Convention', *Passion*, Nov. 1985.

16
From the Inside: An Interview with Three Women Fashion Designers

Janet Lee

Fashion: in the making

Fashion remains one of the most visible signs of consumer culture. It is no longer only to be found in the pages of *Vogue*, or in girls' and women's magazines. As women's interests are taken more seriously, fashion features are given much more extensive coverage in the popular press, in the Sundays, as well as in the 'quality' dailies. And the more media there is, the more spaces there are to be filled. Men, too, have decisively got in on the act. Football fans and inner-city casuals dodge the eyes of the police by masquerading as well-heeled, well-dressed city brokers. The less power people feel they can exert over their environment, the more they attempt to do over their own bodies. Fashion, after pop music, has always been the darling of the youth media, and as pop music and video become predictable, the focus has shifted increasingly to personal image, furniture – lifestyles.

Although women and girls have found jobs in the fashion-media world, it has been men who seem to have hit the highlights. To find out what its like being a woman designer in the business, and to get some idea of the behind-the-scenes process, I talked to three young women who have all made names for themselves in the last few years. Alison Lloyd of Ally Capellino was joined in the interview with her partner – and boyfriend – Jono Platt. Claire Angel of English Eccentrics works in a team of three, and at the time of the interview Pam Hogg had just found herself a business manager.

Alison Lloyd and Jono Platt established Ally Capellino in 1979. Ally had just left a full time job at Courtaulds with 'no prospects'.

Ally Capellino wearing her own clothes

Since then she and Jono have transformed their initially small business into a hugely successful company with a £1m turnover. How then did Ally and her partner go about setting up in business?

Ally: I started making hats and jewellery which took off reasonably well – we were selling to Miss Selfridge, and then within six months we were producing clothes. The Individual Clothes Show was instrumental to it all really. We

	thought of doing jewellery, bags and hats. In the end we had T-shirts, trousers, shorts, swimsuits, hats and scarfs.
Jono:	It was a very big thing for us that first show. Just to be part of it cost us £150, that was without the cost of producing the clothes, which at the time was an unbelievable amount of money.
Janet:	Where did you get the money from?
Ally:	We had this innocent theory that if you committed yourself to something then you'd get the money. We did sample machining and Jono's wages as a pattern-cutter for Betty Jackson kept us going. We earned £100 for three days' work, which we saved. The show cost us £650, we got £400 worth of orders and then Whistles put in an order for £650 so we were all right. Having Lucie from Whistles buy from us was a great help; she roots out new designers, people realise this and go and see what she's got in her shops.

Claire Angel's experiences have been quite different. She joined English Eccentrics three years ago. The company had already been established by Helen Lipman with the help of a financial backer. Helen first set up business with a stall in Kensington Market. She then joined forces with her sister Judy and then Claire Angel. Officially Judy and Claire are still employees, but they play a central role in running the company.

Janet:	How did English Eccentrics organise their first collection?
Claire:	We were in a pokey little studio, our roles weren't really defined, we were all sort of mugging in with ideas and things, unlike now where Helen designs the fabric, Judy looks after the knitwear and I create the shapes and do the fashion side of it. It works well now but at that time we didn't have any idea of suppliers or printing places or anything. We dragged our first collection round in the back of a car just going to different shops and trying to sell it. Eventually we took it to a Burton's subsidiary, quite a big high street shop and secured a huge order, something like £5000. We were so excited.

Pam Hogg was even less well prepared for the business side of

English Eccentrics

fashion. She trained originally as a painter at the Glasgow School of Art, and then went on to specialise in printed textiles. Moving into fashion grew out of a feeling of disappointment about what other designers went on to do with her fabrics. She realised that in fact she had been working all along with some kind of end product in mind. Even so, the move into production created all sorts of unimagined problems:

Pam: When I produced my first collection I knew nothing about the fashion business and did everything myself including the actual printing of the fabric and making of samples. I showed at the Paris Prêt where I was approached by Mode Avant Garde to show alongside celebrated designers such as Jean-Paul Gaultier in a travelling fashion show. I also took several orders but unfortunately, due to my being so unprepared, I was only able to concentrate on one outlet, Chatters of South Molton Street. This in itself was problematic as I had no capital to finance the production and therefore found myself in a catch-22 situation. I needed the capital to get the fabric and to pay the outworkers, but I wasn't getting paid until well after the clothes were made. It wasn't until three years later in 1984 that I showed again properly at Olympia with the 'Psychedelic' collection. The press loved it but the buyers were scared and although it was in every magazine I only took a few orders.

Janet: How did you manage financially from then?

Pam: I extended the 'Psychedelic' into the 'Hippie' collection for the following winter season using similar but heavier fabrics, and by then all the buyers were clued into velvets and desperate to buy, having missed out the first time round. I was inundated with orders and had to close my books. I moved from £5000 to £55 000 worth of orders in one season and paid off my bank loan in two months.

None the less it seems that production, marketing and distribution still prove enormously difficult for young designers educated into a fine art way of thinking.

Ally: We didn't know anything about production, finance or selling. We had learnt nothing in college about when you were supposed to deliver or how payments are made. After our first show we didn't even think about getting the clothes made up for orders until about four months later. We'd bought all our original fabric for the samples from a department store at retail prices so we still had to

Pam Hogg (left) in 'Dalice in Wonderland' Collection

hunt round for new fabric. We didn't even know much about buying wholesale. Now we are a lot more professional. We've got a staff of ten including ourselves. This includes a sales marketing executive, a book-keeper, a secretary, two machinists, a full-time pattern cutter and a part-timer. Jono used to do a lot of pattern-cutting but his time is now mostly taken up being the Managing Director, which means looking after the finance and making sure we get the loans we need. Not having capital held us up a lot at the beginning. Now our turnover is about £700 000.

English Eccentrics have also managed to expand by taking on staff on both the production side and for sales and distribution.

Claire: We couldn't have done all this without a backer. The banks don't take you seriously unless you've got a man behind you, and at the same time you have to borrow money because you're always three steps behind. You have to pay the people who are making up for you and you can't do that without a massive security.

Pam Hogg, however, has tried hard to go it alone with a minimum of back-up help.

Pam: I have one outdoor machinist who does the bulk of the sewing, and an assistant who finishes. There are production teams around London that, depending on availability, can be used when necessary. However, I try to rely on them as little as possible as I have experienced the horrors of late arrivals and hundreds of wrongly made garments.
Janet: What is the process from design to production?
Pam: I work in a very unorthodox way. I cut straight into the fabric as soon as the ideas have formulated. I find that drawing beforehand stunts the natural direction. I follow any interesting mistakes, which sometimes determines the whole of the collection. After having adjusted and readjusted the garment I then make the pattern by taking the first rough sample apart. It is then recut and passed on to my machinist to finalise the small finishing details.

After the garments have been shown to the buyers the production team will make a satisfactory copy, and when the fabric arrives they start production.

Ally: We work one year in advance to the clothes coming into the shops. As I'm finishing one collection I'm already thinking about the next, so I start looking out for fabric and slip back to the drawing board when I've got the time. Our fabrics are all woven printed or dyed for us. You've got four or five months to get the collection together but two or three of these can be spent waiting for the fabric. Of course you get better service once you're a bit better known. Once I've got the fabrics I finalise the drawing and give them to the pattern-cutter who makes up approximations. We either scrap them or do more work to get them right. The more you get behind you, in a way, the more difficult it is. You've got to give people what you're known for and yet you want to give people something new. We then make our own samples to sell at the exhibitions or the fashion shows, and we take orders from them and put them into production through various factories who then deliver the final garments to us.

Jono: Then we have to sort it out, pack them into boxes and send them out. We now sell to Jones and the Beauchamp Place Shop, The Changing Room. Then there are the big stores like Harrods and Harvey Nicholls. They place big orders and pay on time.

Janet: What about prices? Do designer clothes have to be expensive?

Claire: For a start it's more expensive to make here than it is in Spain or Portugal, so we're supporting British industry by making in England, and anyway we don't have the numbers to make it really worthwhile going abroad. We use natural fibres, wool, silk and cotton, so that adds up. Our dresses are about £100, jackets £200. We'd like to get our prices down but there isn't a feasible way of doing it at the moment.

Ally: I don't think we're expensive considering the amount of effort that goes into producing the clothes and the limited editions they're made up in. They don't fall apart and you can wear them for years. People are prepared to pay £120

	on a linen dress – I don't think I have to justify it – we couldn't sell them for less.
Pam:	My clothes are relatively cheap but obviously it depends on the fabrics I use. I try to keep my costs as low as possible. Garments generally range from £25 to £150; however, I would also love to use fabrics I like regardless of the cost, but it will probably mean producing two ranges.
Janet:	What sort of women buy your clothes?
Ally:	Professional and mostly over 25. Often they're worn with other clothes, even jumble-sale stuff. I like it when I see people put them together differently; it's inspiring and refreshing.
Pam:	The range is amazing. I see girls in the nightclubs wearing them and lots of celebrities are now regular customers.
Janet:	Finally, does the fashion industry offer equal opportunities in terms of class race or gender?
Ally:	It shouldn't make any difference in this industry. What you need is energy and enthusiasm and a certain amount of talent. The most successful designers, I suppose, are pretty middle class, but even that's a generalisation because the term 'middle class' covers such a huge category. Buyers are very definitely prejudiced though. They expect people to have all the middle-class values, you know. When we started off we were hopeless at dealing with them.
Pam:	I have never encountered any discrimination. But I've never been scared to follow my own path. At art school I had all these battles with my tutors. I gave them one hell of a time but I walked off with every award that was going, even though I wasn't doing what they wanted me to. If you believe in what you are doing you just get on with it.

All three designers felt, as Pam Hogg put it, that they should just get on with it. And although many of the big names in fashion are still male, women are increasingly bringing in a new, less cut-throat dimension to the business. They have all had to learn as they go along, including learning how to become employers. None are overwhelmed by the desire to make a fortune; they seem more keen on working for themselves and enjoying what they are doing.

In this sense they are not so different from other self-employed people working in the new media. All three are working not just for the customers but also for the magazines whose coverage and copy is crucial. Today, more than ever, young designers have to furnish the media with the images they need before they clothe the public.

17

Heavy Duty Denim: 'Quality Never Dates'*

Dirk Scheuring**

They presented 'The Thing' at the press conference of the Cologne Inter-Jeans Fair. I was not prepared for it at all, although afterwards it became clear to me that I could have worked it out. Had not the secretary of the Work, Sport and Leisure Clothing Trade Association already predicted, in München-Gladbach, a 'trend to classic blue denim' and talked about a 'blue miracle'? Had not the Jeans Wear Fashion Circle threatened new developments like the austere and rustic 'New Frontier Romantic', or the carefree urban 'Paris in the Forties' look, or even a monstrosity called 'Hippy Corsair'? Had it not been made clear right from the start that the hard-wearing blue fabric – 'Indigo – eternally young and attractive' – would be unleashed on the youthful and would-be youthful jeans-buyers of the following year 'in many varieties'?

'Many varieties' – that still left everything in the balance. But then at the press conference fashion show, a young male model sauntered down the cat-walk in time to a subdued disco beat, and he had 'The Thing' on. A double-breasted blazer.

We've all seen double-breasted blazers; they are nothing new, and quite modern this summer. But this one here was made of coarse, firm, hard-wearing, indigo-blue denim! What did it mean?

Herbert L. Piedboeuf, the general secretary of the German Institute for Men's Fashion, put me on the right track. At first I paid hardly any attention to him; a middle-aged man of average height in a moderately splendid grey suit, who, while holding forth on the new fashions passing in front of him, kept his left hand

* This article was originally published in *Spex*, 1985.
** Translated by Martin Chalmers.

sunk casually in his jacket pocket and gestured confidently with his right, all the time bouncing dynamically on the tips of his Italian slippers. But then he talked about the tendency to 'produce themselves' which 'young people' had, and which was such an advantage to the fashion industry, and smiling understandingly, he admitted, 'We did the same ourselves, after all, when we were that age . . . '

Then I realised that the man was right. He was perhaps in his mid-forties, so he must have been a teenager in the second half of the 1950s. In those days he wasn't bald yet, and he had smeared pomade onto his hair and had conjured a sculpture out of it with his comb, and his parents had hated it. He had practised rock-'n'-roll dancing, dreamt of a moped and, of course, worn jeans. He had made a production of himself, and naturally had hated suits. Suits were for the old and established, jeans for the young and rebellious. Konrad Adenauer, symbol of the former, always wore double-breasted; rock 'n' rollers, symbol of the latter, wore jeans, cowboy pants. The exaggerated V-shape silhouette, the puffed-up manliness of respectable suit-wearers, contrasted with the stove-pipe silhouette of youth. Barely thirty years later we have the synthesis in the shape of a blue denim double-breasted jacket.

Phase 1: the birth of a myth

It all began in 1850 with those primitive jeans which an immigrant of German origin called Levi Strauss had produced as work trousers for the Californian gold-diggers. They had the same simple, straight cut as the ordinary grey woollen work-trousers of the time, but the firm blue cotton cloth proved to be more resilient, and the new trousers established themselves and made Strauss a rich man.

One can still buy the primitive Levi's today, practically unaltered. It's the 501 model, with fly buttons instead of a zip, which doesn't taper from the knee and is therefore of medium width at the ankle, and which has to be washed five times and then put on wet to fit properly: the classic 'shrink to fit' method.

During the Second World War, the American government declared these jeans a 'vital commodity' which could only be sold to those working in or for the US army. The first jeans came to

Europe and Germany with the American soldiers, but they did not become important as a symbol of youth rebellion until ten years after the end of the war.

Bill Haley, whose 'Rock around the Clock' came out in 1955, didn't wear them yet; neither did the black rhythm-and-blues men and – later – rock 'n' rollers like Little Richard and Chuck Berry. The blacks would have raised hell to avoid wearing work trousers that made them look as poor as they really were. They wore the finest cloth they could afford. But the second wave of rockers, the hard, wild young white men, most of whom came from a southern farm, or at least village – like Elvis Presley, Gene Vincent, Eddie Cochran – they wore jeans. Not always, but often enough to serve as a model.

Two films were also important in laying the foundation for the myth of jeans and youth rebellion – *The Wild Ones* with Marlon Brando, and *Rebel Without a Cause* with James Dean. Both actors wore jeans, and both wore them in the same, soon-to-become-classic, youth-rebel way: the profane Levi's with the straight legs, turned up on the outside for the farm-boy-at-high-water look.

So men like Herbert L. Piedboeuf, whose generation built the idea of generation conflict on such models, do know what they're talking about, when they lecture on the tendency of young people to 'produce themselves.' It was probably then that the present general secretary of the German Institute for Men's Fashion began to be interested in all the little trifles and details which constitute youth fashion. With jeans it was always the little things that counted: for example, how wide the turn-up at the foot had to be – two inches was the right width. That gave the wearer the desired tough, rugged, youth-rebel appearance. Youth did not yet have any representatives in the media, who could have summed it all up with a catchy slogan – 'The blue flag of liberation' perhaps – but, ultimately, that's what everyone thought.

In fact, the first alterations to the primitive jeans came from their wearers. It was a matter of details. Towards the end of the 1950s, the young urban blacks of America discovered jeans and began to remodel them slightly, and at the beginning of the 1960s the British mods, who adopted their fashion along with their music, continued the development. A process of refinement and urbanisation began. First the turn-ups at the foot disappeared and the jeans were turned up or sewn up on the inside so that, when standing straight, they precisely met the instep of the foot, no more, no less. Apart from that, they were taken in at the bottoms, so that they tapered and clung to the calf; that produced a sharper silhouette and didn't look so rustic and clumsy. To achieve an even smoother and undecorated line on Levi's, the two characteristic double-arched stitched patterns on the back pockets, the leather company trademark at the belt and the little red flag, were all removed with nail scissors.

Meanwhile other American jean brands had also established themselves in the European market, although only minute deviations in cut distinguished them from the Levi's originals. Wrangler's, for example, were cut more loosely around the bottom, so that they were a better fit on more broadly built figures. But these differences were and are trivial and only important within an intact youth culture and an intact jeans myth. For the rest of humanity, for suit-wearing adults and the other uninitiated, even for the manufacturers, one pair of jeans was like any other pair of jeans.

Phase 2: the invention of flapping

It all changed in 1966. In that year a young London tailor called Colin Wild invented trousers with a flare. Trousers, that is, which, like jeans and the other tight trousers young people favoured, clung to the leg as far as the knee, but from there spread out like the sides of a trapeze. Previously this had only been seen in seamen's trousers. The idea was that Swinging London could not really begin to swing until the clothes of its protagonists did so too. Admittedly, Colin Wild's trousers were made of traditional suit cloth, but they were so successful and were copied so often, that now the jeans manufacturers for the first time took up this suggestion from the subcultural market. After more than 100 years, the shape of jeans was radically altered for the first time. The things grew wider and wider at the foot; the collars of the denim jackets which went with them, and which till then had also remained unaltered, simultaneously grew longer and longer. The hippies had arrived.

While youth culture officially awarded itself a consciousness for the first time, slowly made increasingly better use of the media, and everywhere, publicly, thought about getting rid of capitalism –

or at least pretended to do so – capitalism itself responded. The relationship between youth buying-power and pop music had been well known for a long time. But with the introduction of flared jeans the clothing industry for the first time reacted to the youth market on a large scale. Previously there had simply been jeans; now there were different jeans. The manufacturers discovered that there was a relationship between the expansion of consciousness and of the trouser leg: at last youth fashions would behave like every other fashion. It wouldn't simply change without an outsider getting wind of it. Now changes could be calculated and influenced.

At first things just kept on going. At the beginning of the 1970s, men's shoe sizes 41 or 42 could be hidden under the flare of the jeans; when the high point was reached in the 1973–4 season, size 46 also disappeared effortlessly. Some models were of such an extreme cut that the legs already began to widen half way down the thigh, so that they practically only sat tight on the skin around the backside, but puffed out into enormous bells at ground level.

At ground level, because meanwhile, everything had got much longer. After all, it was fashionable for everything – hair, skirts and trousers, too – to hang down longer and longer, more and more loosely, because everything that hung down and, naturally, also flapped, fitted very well with the current themes like, for example, personality expansion, free love, I-don't-give-a-shit-you-fucking-capitalists, and so on. It was best of all if the enormous flare of the jeans trailed along the street so that one stood on it and the hem frayed, which meant that one cared even less about everything. When shoes with platform soles were invented, another five to eight centimetres had to be added, which once more greatly pleased the jeans manufacturers.

Phase 3: youth gets its way

The diversification process escalated, since the youthful subculturalists didn't let the constant efforts of the industry to meet their wishes stop them from again and again altering the jeans on their own account. The flare, for example, could be enlarged even further with carefully inserted wedges of materials, and the length could be varied with coloured cloth borders. Other brightly patterned cloth remnants had to be found to decoratively patch the various holes in the trousers. Holes had to be there, as a beacon of resistance to the addictive extravagance of capitalism. The idea was to make a brand-new and fashionable pair of jeans look as if one had already been wearing them for five years without a break. Experts swore by the method of burying the just-purchased trousers for a couple of weeks and letting them rot.

There had to be decorations of other kinds as well. The period of the clear line and the sharply contoured silhouette was long past. Patches, for example, with peace symbols were much loved for a while. Some preferred countless stars, hearts or knots, which usually adorned the material covering the lower leg; further up they pressed uncomfortably on the skin because of the tight fit. Drawings also appeared frequently, and it was possible to tell whether someone was consciously plumbing an artistic talent or whether it was just a bored grammar-school pupil who had doodled on his or her thighs during the physics class. In the latter case, because of the seated position, the resulting figures and band names were upside down.

Phase 4: the conquest of the upper class

The no-longer-young went further and further in their hopeless search for something that they had lost ten or twenty years before. In the mid-1970s one encountered the pathetic phenomenon of the middle-aged 'swinger' everywhere; would-be Absaloms whose heads were as smooth as a fish-bowl on top, but whose still remaining wreath of hair had been cultivated to fall from just above the ears down to the shoulders. The pressure of surplus layers of fat tugged at the button-holes of skin-tight fitted shirts, and the bell-bottoms flapped at every step, suggesting youthful elasticity, while at the top the trousers sat like a corset which tried to compress bum and protruding stomach.

Now that the traditional jeans manufacturers produced their trousers in several widths, in every possible colour, as well as in elephant and needle cord, other companies, attracted by the older and better-earning customers, broke into the business. Designer jeans were invented to conquer the fashionable upper middle classes. Since the double or triple price of these pieces of clothing could hardly be justified by the highly visible trademarks of Calvin

Klein, Pierre Cardin or Gloria Vanderbilt alone, these models had to stand out from the profane competition. This was achieved by omitting the back pockets, by quadruple seams and similar nonsense. By now the youth and leisure fashion system was so flexible and running so smoothly that each of these changes immediately filtered through to the lower price ranges. As soon as a new idea had appeared, an Italian company could be found to copy it cheaply.

This constant individualisation had become necessary because in the 1970s the older generation – including parents – had also discovered jeans as clothing. The concept of 'leisure fashion' had arisen, which meant that in this disguise every father or mother could slip into a youth role after work. The idea of youth as the only worthwhile time in life had gradually spread further and further since the 1968 revolt. The enthusiasm which had been possible at that time was a consequence of the coincidence of a political, as well as a general mood of dissent, with a feeling of security, which even for those fighting against it, had its basis in the functioning of the capitalist system. At first this directly infected only a couple of university professors and other intellectuals. In the following years, however, its effects took hold of ever larger parts of the population. Youth became popular because it 'could get things moving'. The only disturbing thing about it were the young people themselves. Jeans as a signal of youth were increasingly uncoupled from their former significance as a signal of revolt. For the youth themselves it was no longer enough to wear jeans: one had to wear jeans that the no-longer-young would not wear.

Phase 5: the subculture is overtaken

The jeans, leisure fashion and sportswear industry – there was now no longer any kind of distinction between them – was now so alert that any suggestion of a new trend within subcultural youth could be processed in a flash.

With one blow, the flared trouser leg was gone. In 1977 the media disseminated pictures of British punks with their preference for tight trousers, by 1978 hardly any flared trousers were sold, and by 1979 even the most hard-boiled old hippy no longer mentioned the once so decisive alteration in jeans.

From then on, the only thing not immediately available to try on, mass-produced, was the Ramones-like tear in the jeans just below the knee. All the other alterations which some fashion-conscious individualist undertook were immediately available to the general public. Leopard spot, striped or tartan patterns, zips attached to every possible or impossible place on the trousers – what difference did it make if one bought them today from a specialist shop in London's Kings Road or some sub-cultural semi-professional in a corner of Kensington Market, two months later at Fiorucci, or six months later at C&A or in the Ganja Head Shop.

By 1980, at the latest, the mainstream then overtook the subculture. Up to this point, the opinion that the adherents of developments in pop music considered to be avant-garde, were at the same time the avant-garde in clothes, had still predominated. But then, when jeans in carrot shapes came onto the market, their avant-garde were the Poppers[1] – a counter-figure to the punks, a youth type blueprinted by *Zeit* magazine, who obeyed the laws of capitalism instead of rebelling against them. The whole world then immediately accepted the new shape, except the music avant-garde, who needed another two or three years to get used to it.

The carrot-shaped jeans – jeans which are cut wide at the backside and the thighs, but narrow at the feet – first appeared around 1880 as a modification which had allowed more freedom of movement during work, but had long been forgotten. More important is that in 1980 they pointed to a decisive change in silhouette – for the first time the slim stove-pipe shape which had always signalled 'youth' had been abandoned. The cut of the jeans began to resemble those of the suit trousers of the 1940s and '50s. The fashion industry followed up with denim jackets which were substantially fuller at chest and shoulders than the traditional ones; some had padded shoulders like suit jackets. During the last five years, the youth fashion silhouette has become increasingly puffier; it corresponds ever more closely to the idealised male V-shape characteristic of the 'classic' suits of the 1940s and '50s.

This suit shape with its exaggerated shoulders, and trousers into which an elephant leg would fit, was introduced at the end of the 1930s by a London tailor – isn't it always London tailors? – called Scholten. Inspired by the uniform tunics of the royal guards officers, he invented a cut which, by using quantities of superfluous cloth in the shoulder area, and by a dart from the chest to the middle of the body, simulated an enormous super-manly chest. The corresponding trousers indicated leg muscles as thick as treetrunks. American films – aren't they always American films? – then propagated this type, inflated with textile muscles, as an ideal, almost like the Cinemascope format. Everything American was always projected more than life-size anyway. This masculine form established itself as a symbol for the power and solidity achieved with increasing age and maturity, and it was exactly that against which the jeans myth was set up in the 1950s.

Phase 6: the abolition of youth fashion

When capitalism was still prospering it was hip to be young, or at least to have the image of youth, because what were seen as the failings of youth (for example, their idea of abolishing capitalism) were easy to digest. In pre-war America, from which the image of the textile superman comes, it was less hip to be young. Youth meant the absence of power and money. The 'zoot suit', the enormous suit so beloved of ghetto youth, represented the high point of efforts to achieve a powerful silhouette through the tailor's skill.

It was precisely this silhouette that returned in the 1980s. As a result of world-wide recession, youth is once more synonymous with impotence. Today, no one any longer feels the need to live fast and die young; everyone is waiting to become more powerful and wealthy with increasing age, and hoping for one of the remaining places under capital's sun.

At the Cologne Inter-Jeans Fair, Joro Hertwig, general secretary of the Association of German Textile Retailers, was able to announce that, 'Young customers are increasingly turning to sporty-formal, casual-comfortable fashions.' 'Sporty-formal', that's the word! It's 'sporty-formal', for example, to wear baggy jeans and an outsize blazer made of coarse, hairy horse-blanket material with a shirt and tie, but with the shirt hanging out of the trousers. And one can hardly imagine anything which corresponds more closely to the 'sporty-formal' ideal than a blue denim doublebreasted jacket.

501 advertising by kind permission of Levi Strauss & Co.

'Everything that looks scruffy is passé', according to the German Institute for Men's Fashion. In an article in the trade paper *Sportswear International*, under the headline, 'What on earth is happening in the jeans market', Heiner Sefranek, another fashion industrialist in his 40s, and deputy boss of the Mustang plant, confirmed that 'the *zeitgeist* has burst the sound barrier of age difference'. 'Real boundaries between youth, sport and conventional fashion no longer exist,' he states. In other words, there is no longer any fashionable symbol for youth. It has become unwearable.

It reminds one of the wise words of Herbert L. Piedboeuf, who has followed all the developments of the last thirty years: 'Youth has, as you know, a tendency to produce itself – after all, we did the same when we were that age.' The man knows what he's talking about; and he and his colleagues have also noticed that youth wants to present itself in a completely different role from their day. During the fashion show he observed with considerable acuteness that, 'At a time of economic restrictions it seems as if fashion is the only area in which one can display something.' And what is to be displayed is 'sporty-formal'; which is why double-breasted jackets are being made from jeans materials.

A Levi's advertising spot running in British television and cinemas at the moment shows the last possibility for using the jeans myth for advertising purposes. A young citizen of the Soviet Union – presumably a sportsman or a chess-player – has been allowed to travel to the West, and on his return his case is searched by petty, grey-faced Soviet border officials in say grey uniforms. They discover a copy of *The Face*, and confiscate the decadent thing. They continue the search but don't find anything else and finally pass the case on with grim-faced fuss. At home the boy unpacks it, and heaving a sigh of relief pulls out a pair of jeans which were hidden right at the bottom.

Only in Communism, goes the message, is the jeans myth still in power. Here the blue trousers can still appear as a symbol of the freedom which capitalism brings. Advertising can still be carried out with it at this level. Of course the smuggled jeans were the classic 501 model. 'Quality never goes out of style!'

Note

1. Poppers: A German youth style in the early 1980s prefiguring the shift towards expensive Italian casual fashion.

Part IV

Music Now

18

Women and Pop: A Series of Lost Encounters*

Gina Rumsey and Hilary Little

Only 28 per cent of the readership of the *NME* are women; few of our female friends would buy it. Most of us have other experiences of pop's infiltration of our environment. When the press recommend a dance track to the record collection for its exhilarating and innovatory new beat, for example, they may not have in mind that common dancefloor scenario, the man who asks you to dance and then, when you inexplicably refuse, grabs you in his manly arms, drags you to the seating arrangements and fails to hear you telling him to let you go over the deafening roar of the music. A friend of ours was ejaculated over after a prolonged electro-smooch in a disco. Very effective for background music, you might say; but the major consequence of pop's presence in a situation like this is to surround us with aural sexism: we can't dance alone for the sake of dancing and *enjoy* it when the soundtrack goes 'Push, push, in the bush'. Such continual pressure doesn't leave much time or energy to concentrate on the theoretical: we know only too well that pop's environment has, for most of us, a lot more to do with sexual diplomacy than it does with the music itself.

Bearing this in mind, it is almost irrelevant to point out that there are now more women actually engaged in the process of making rock and pop than ever before; and not just the traditionally 'glamorous' singers like Sade and Annie Lennox, but instrumentalists like Tina Weymouth, Gillian Gilbert and Kim Gordon of Sonic Youth. Perhaps few women know, or care. And we usually come across their records in the collections of the people who can

* This article first appeared in *Monitor*, No. 4, 1985.

Charlotte Bill of 'The Fates' in rehearsal

mentally afford to stand back and take a long, 'objective' look at the broad spectrum of pop and its more marginal exponents – men. It's cool to like the arcane, and it adds to your image – unless you're the female rock fanatic whose friends all think she's funny for taking this trivial pursuit so seriously. Most women don't, they use music as a social glue, and if this is its primary function, theory becomes irrelevant. The story of one woman who wished she had more friends: when she found a crowd, they were all bikers, mainly men into some kind of 'ironic' machismo, Heavy Metal fans. Now, as one of the gang, she wears denims and an Iron Maiden T-shirt – the trappings of a male sub-culture, although she is a woman. Or, the girl whose parents worshipped Mozart and who, aged eight, had never heard of the pop charts; who thought that being 'no. 3' meant that you only had three points, out of a possible thirty – and found herself a perfect target for the school bully-boys: 'Who done Metal Guru, then?' Within a few weeks, she could recite everything backwards, and they had to make up the titles before they could catch her out. There are social advantages attached to musical knowledge.

Women know, then, that where a knowledge of pop is necessary in order to gain social acceptability, they must acquire pop. So we dance to it, show appreciation when boyfriends play us records, buy a few for ourselves so that our rooms can have the right atmosphere. But most of us aren't interested in probing pop. If we were, we might discover that Iron Maiden have a song called 'Charlotte the Harlot' and that they compose war-mongering epics about 'raping the women and wasting the men'. The implications are not pleasant; the commonest response to criticism is to say that this sort of thing is not meant seriously, that it's 'only a laugh'. If you want a real laugh, go to the Donnington 'Monsters Of Rock' festival and sell hamburgers. 'Do you like to fuck? We like to fuck! Let's all have a fucking good time!' bawls the man at the mike. At the hamburger counter an endless stream of pasty-faced young men in black and denim press up all at once like some surrealist horror-painting. Some return four or five times, clutching twenty-pound notes. Their supportive girlfriends look bored and tired, stilettos sinking into the mud. The event's climax is a loud fireworks display. Fun for all the family.

If you think Heavy Metal is a joke, you may not feel the same about Punk. Punk was going to renew music for everybody – male and female – and you could point to the fairly large number of women performers. The problems for women in attendance – in the audience – remain, however. A girl being taken by her boyfriend to see The Clash can fall asleep with her head in a puddle of beer, no problem (you have it first-hand). This hardly has the ring of rock myth, but it's difficult not to feel that such inattention had less to do with apathy in the face of the much-touted conflagration than with the simple perception by this woman that what was going on was irrelevant to her: nobody ignores what's important to them, even if they've never heard of the band before. But, had they not been under escort by their boyfriends, it is unlikely that the minority of women who did go to see The Clash would have been there at all: Punk's legacy of music dealing with 'real life', 'combat rock', late-night encounters on urban streets, the pain and pride of solitary contemplation of the human condition, has the added peril for women of rape. This fear tends to detract from our feelings of excitement and exhilaration as we go to gigs wondering whether our friends will still be around at the end of the evening to get us home safely. Not only does this circumscribe our sense of being young, free and single – we do not have freedom of movement – but rape, unlike street-fighting, has no glamour attached to it – is is hardly spoken of, although it is a large component in the mental furniture of *female* solitude. It's no accident that what most of us find we lack is *street* credibility. We lack both the emotional investment in male experiences of unsupervised adventure, and the first-hand opportunity for acquiring them on the same terms as men – at the same time, rock's vocabulary lacks the record of our experiences which would invite us in. Vicious circle.

Some female fans, however, do defy the common assumption that 'real music' – post-punk guitar rock, marginal experimentalism – 'is for men'. When the concerts of a rock band whose audience is mainly male begin to attract more than a certain minority proportion of women, the original audience tends to desert: the group's got bland, they've 'sold out', they're producing 'cocktail music' (a field of performance associated with women – Sade is the latest example). So male-identified women move on too (the 28 per cent perhaps), taking it as read that when, for example, Ian McCulloch tells the *NME* readership that 'Ocean Rain' is 'kissing music', he is addressing a feminine audience, and hence damaging himself in the rock credibility stakes (and the *NME* panned the record). It is possible for women to align themselves with the mainstream of 'alternative music' because this 'real music' is often less blatant (because more idiosyncratic) in its hidden assumption that everybody (everybody who counts) can identify with the important/interesting issues spoken for by men. Once again, women as an audience are subsumed into this invisible 'everybody' and our particular social/political/existential experiences of the world, where they are not forgotten or ignored (as they must be by women who 'identify' when Ian Curtis sings 'Here are the young men / A weight on their shoulders') have to be diverted into other cultural areas – into feminist politics, for example. So that women who feel little inclination to identify with male spokesmen may fall by the wayside altogether as far as rock is concerned – they will not hear or be heard.

Which doesn't mean they don't want to play. But being musically inventive alone will *not* get you an audience. Wearing team colours – a form of performance in itself – is a surer route to acceptance, and being in the right place at the right time does after all carry the possibility of later graduating to performance. Doing it alone – without gang identity – you can end up a raving hippie, albeit dextrous. This does not mean, contrary to what boyfriends may think, that you have no ideas worth hearing; you *can* find contemporary content in outmoded styles (think of Billy Bragg). Another point: a lot of feminist music is folk – the cheapest way to make music, as well as the only way of circumventing the need to hire a PA system, with all the connotations of electronics, machismo, weightlifting. But a loud noise makes a lot of waves, and signals the wish to do so. Those with no encouragement in sight need an extra dose of arrogance to dare to call themselves performers.

So why isn't there more feminist music? Feminists aren't the only women afraid of performing. The truth of course is that there is, but that it is relatively unknown. We could point to the precedents – the Raincoats, Toxic Shock, Delta 5 – and many women would say 'Who?' Still most typical, and widely known, are variations on the stereotypical glamour/animality of Tina Turner, or Cyndi Lauper telling us that 'Girls just wanna have fun', or Grace Jones walking down the street in disguise, 'Feeling like a woman/Looking like a man'. You might think Grace Jones's 'androgyny' was disturbing, but this is a watered-down disturbance – like the 28 per cent, one woman in every crowd, always certain of being an individual exception, marking herself out from other women. We once dreamed of feminism being a mass movement, not another excuse to put on a suit.

Rock, not feminism, suffers from our absence. Feminism exposes rock. Tracey Thorn complained, in *Spare Rib*, that the music press never printed her feminist views, despite the fact that she always explains them to her interviewers. Feminism does not sell records; at the moment it has no mass audience. Rock's vocabulary dictates that being a feminist is not the way to be cool, to be socially acceptable, or to have a good time at the disco: willing participation in these rituals means lacking an interest in what questions or excludes them. Pop's role as social wallpaper makes this thoughtlessness easy to achieve. As 'entertainment', it is by definition not to be seen as harassment. It trades in myth and nostalgia, promises a better world or (the other side of the same coin) rearranges old stereotypes of decadence and squalor. Pop's Rambo is 'the Rebel', a touchstone which still sells long after the fact (Billy Idol!). Feminists know that if rock/pop was really revolutionary, they would be embraced as the greatest rebels of all – real rebels, the genuine article, not just another piece in the jigsaw of popular ephemera. However, Frankie T-shirts sold, feminism doesn't.

Does this put feminism and pop in opposing camps? Some of us *enjoy* this music. What about the 28 per cent, some of whom must be feminists? When they're fourteen, girl fans attract a lot of study and analysis – they are a definable group/market, they have numbers on their side. But what happens when we grow up and become a minority in the audience for 'serious' music? How can we find each other? This needs to be done; we need to hear from you.

19
Against Health and Efficiency: Independent Music in the 1980s*

Simon Reynolds

Once, rock drew its transgressive power from flaunting the body, celebrating the 'raw truth' of desire. The directness, dirt and insistence of r'n'b was the dangerous energy in pop. Even as recently as 1982 the notion of 'sexmusic' was touted in hip circles as a hot shock, a subversion. A confused rhetoric, drawn directly or indirectly from sources like Marcuse, D. H. Lawrence, the Situationists, Semiotexte and the post-structuralist debates about desire, it provided a new turn on the old rock idea of the sexual as *misbehaviour*. But now, today, this 'sexmusic' seeps from every pore of the chart, saturates every media, but shorn of New Pop's incendiary rhetoric ('Sex and Sweat Is Best', 'Sex, Sweat and Blood'). The delinquent animalism of r'n'b and funk has occupied the entertainment mainstream, but as an acceptable form of healthy vitality. Bodymusic is the norm, oppressively.

Our culture has long since ceased to demand deferment of gratification or sublimation of energy: it *insists* on enjoyment, incites us to develop our capacity for pleasure. 'Youth' – because coterminous with sex, style, hedonism, fitness – has become the supreme value in society, almost the definition of health. Our economy demands an intense and versatile desire on the part of consumers: growth depends on a high turnover not just of commodities and fashions, but increasingly a gamut of off-the-peg self-expression (therapies, self-improvements, cultural experiences).

---

* This essay is an enlarged and revised version of an article that originally appeared in *Melody Maker*.

Pop has always been bodymusic, but the body is now the prime locus of power's operation, where power solicits us. Being a *success in life* involves a maximisation of your body's potential for health and pleasure (aerobics, sexology, nutrition, massage, touch therapy, TM, etc.). Today's athletic humanism echoes nineteenth-century muscular Christianity in its adherence to the 'work hard, play hard' ethic.

The alternative scene, home of oppositional meanings, has always defined itself as pop's other. So in today's independent label music, diverse as it is, we can find a common impulse to rise above the body. For instance, chartpop is based around the primacy of the dance beat, but what's striking about the indiepop of the last four years is its undanceability – how it has abandoned the New Funk Dreams of 1980–82 (the hope of combing seriousness or radicalism with an accessible dance music), abandoned even r'n'b, for strictly albino roots like the Velvet Underground, Television, Byrds, psychedelia, folk, country. What's happened is that 'serious rock' is once again a 'head' culture like it was in the late 1960s/early 1970s. (Given the cerebral, anti-sensual cast of punk, maybe New Pop was a hiccough in the broad sweep of progressive work from 1967 to today.) In this head culture, the correct, 'higher' response to pop is a bodily passive contemplation, and the prime scene of consumption is the bedroom. Indiepop *is* danced to, but strictly demands physical responses that contravene the norms of dance and sexual attraction, that involve a *sacrifice* of cool. Jangly-pop ought to be danced to with fey, above-it-all gestures like Morrissey, while the Beefheart/Fall-derived thrash of bands like A Witness or the Shrubs provokes a kind of delirium. Increasingly, what's most appropriate is *immobility* before a bombardment or irradiation of noise: the music of Jesus and Mary Chain, Husker Du, Sonic Youth, A. R. Kane, incites us to flip our wigs, or be frozen in noise, blissed out. This is a new psychedelia.

Pop's body culture, on the other hand, is all about dance and spectacle, not meaning; about fascination, not interpretation. Pop hasn't been this divided since the early 1970s; there's been a revival of that progressive rock snobbery over 'that disco shit', with the Smiths' 'Panic' hit polarising hipsterland. For some, the song's intolerance for black culture ('burn down the disco/hang the blessed D.J.') was racist, for others the song became an anti-pop anthem.

What's disliked about the black pop and its white imitators that fill the charts is its notion of sophistication (a flashy lifestyle, reflected in a *class*-y sound) and its 'vulgarity' (a hypersexuality foreign to most indie fans' experience). Indiepop and chartpop have totally different approaches to the love song. Chartpop foregrounds sexual passion, specific body need. The guarantor of true love is physical ecstasy, sexual success, when relationships and bodies *work*. The soul voice is ubiquitous – in its hoarse, husky texture and r'n'b earthiness you can practically hear arousal and dilation of blood. The r'n'b voice makes manifest the physicality of the body. But indiepop love is a cerebral affair, and so the voice is a more transparent, colourless medium for the words (the main influences are the *pure* voices of Syd Barrett, Roger McGuinn, Arthur Lee, Lou Reed, the folk and country idioms), rather than drawing attention to itself, to the materiality of the body, its spasms of exertion or lack. For indie love is constituted/consummated not in the flesh and its throes, but in intense exchanges of *language* – the *unique* details of courtship, confidences, the scene. 'If I can't talk to her/I wanna talk about her' – 'Lover and Confidante', The Blue Aeroplanes.

The actual experience of being-in-love is represented differently – not as wracked passion, but as an almost out-of-body experience, a dreaminess or even neurasthenia. 'I'm enchanted ... I'm entranced' – 'Crystal Crescent', Primal Scream; 'I'm hypnotised/You trip me and I fall' – The Mighty Lemon Drops. This is a rapture not of the senses but of perception; there's an absence of tactile imagery; a distance seems to intervene between lover and loved one; the girl is an enigma or vision, far off, 'like an angel'. For some, love is a psychedelic trip; for others it's represented in quaint, almost Mills and Boon terms of devotion and idealisation. Groups like The Weather Prophets have talked of the attraction of Biblical language, of the absolute obsession/abjection, the 'forever', to be found in country music. Overt sexiness is emphatically *not* sexy, what's striking is the absence of the pelvis, friction, juice, even of heat from this music. And love is vested in difficulty as much as success – there are far more unrequited or tragic songs than in chartpop.

This return to romance is oppositional. Chartpop has grown

ever more 'adult' in its treatment of relationships – either more explicit and suggestive or more mature and 'progressive'. The idea of a redemptive/devastating love has come to seem a superstition in this age of yuppie self-management and self-sufficiency. Counselling and the media inculcate a new ideal of the relationship as a balanced, negotiated partnership between autonomous agents – an *exchange*. The indie scene is interested in precisely the jeopardising or loss of self through terror or awe, precisely the absolute investment of the self, that is forbidden in this secular economy of self. A belief in a transfiguring love can only stem from a notion of the self as irretrievably weak or lacking – such ideas are outlawed by progressive humanism, which proposes a perpetual shoring-up of the self. (The ultimate obscenity in this demystification of experience is the notion of *death education* – the delusion that it's possible to prepare people to cope with this, the last unmanageable thing in our world.) So against the health and efficiency of chartluv we have the stricken awe of The Bodines: 'it scares the health out of me!'

* * *

By a strange process we've reached the point where 'purity' seems more radical than libertinism, more transgressive than sin. The indie scene is obsessed by a dream of purity – of 'pure love', of a 'pure' or 'perfect pop' that evades the taint of the Eighties (overdeterminism by criticism, mongrelisation due to eclecticism, hi-tech sound). And where all these ideas converge is in two (very much linked) periods – childhood and the Sixties. The Sixties are like pop's childhood, when the idea of youth was still young.

An idea of innocence pervades and possesses the scene. You can see it in the names – Soup Dragons, The Woodentops ('we should be climbing trees'), the Mighty Lemon Drops, the Pastels (their logo is the name childishly scrawled in crayon), BMX Bandits, Talulah Gosh, The Hobgoblins. A huge proportion of indie groups have pictures of children or childish things on their record sleeves. Many of their love songs seem to have the air of furtive first love, gazing across schoolyards, waiting by the gates. You can see this innocence in the way fanzines privilege naivete and enthusiasm and mess (and use graphics from old annuals and children's books). A multitude of desires crystallise in the fantasy

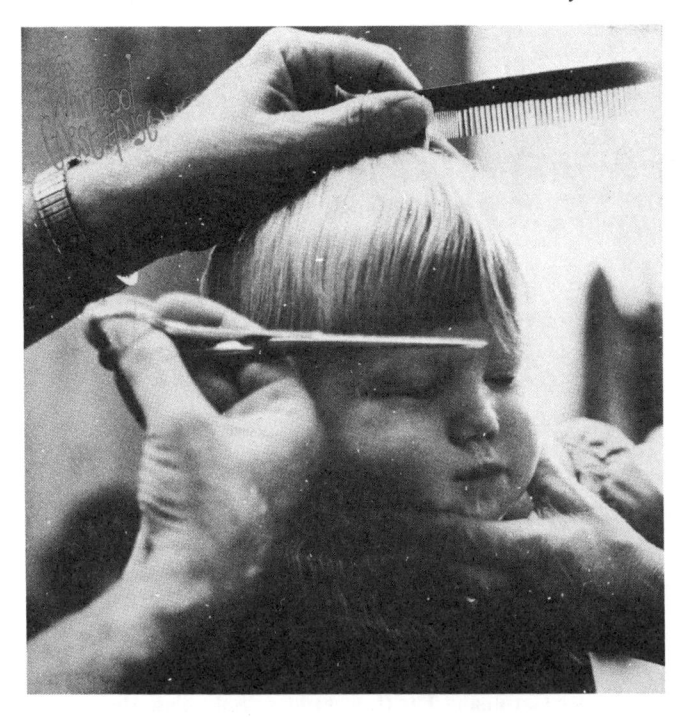

Whirlpool Guest House, 'The Changing Face'

of being like a child again – grief for a lost spontaneity, impulsiveness and unselfconsciousness (including a simple response to pop, unmediated by critical thought); the desire to recover the ability to dream, to have a magical wide-eyed relation to the world; a hope of remaining unsullied ('worldliness must keep apart from me', as Edwyn Collins from Orange Juice sang it over six years ago).

This is a romantic conception of childhood that could only be held by literary types (i.e. your typical music press reader/indie fan). Ordinary people would find this idealisation and nostalgia absurd. *Real* kids want to grow up as fast as possible, to be glamorous like Madonna or George Michael, to leave behind their toys for make-up, complicated hair-do's, sophistication and sex.

The Sixties apply because then was the last time ideas of childhood as a utopian state of being held sway. The Yippies,

Jesse Garon and The Desperadoes, 'Splashing Along'

Situationists and radical psychoanalysis saw play as the crucial component in cultural revolution. The music of Pink Floyd, The Byrds, Love et al., abounded with imagery of childhood, Edenic gardens, fairy tales, reflecting a belief that to grow up was to be brutalised and dis-enchanted. Our indie scene's espousal of the sexual politics of the wimp recalls the Sixties interest in androgyny. But today it's less a question of liberation into a world of free-flowing, polymorphous desire, as liberation *from* sexuality: The Smiths' refusal of maturity is as much a rejection of the strictures of adult sexuality as of work. Both realms are ruled by competitivity, roleplay, the performance principle.

Style is where the Sixties and childhood converge. Many indie fans adopt the kemptness and austerity of an 'ordinary person' of the Fifties or Sixties: there's a taste for pre-permissive clothes – cardigans, overcoats, slacks, short jackets, caps, headscarves, quaint jewellery, short-back-and-sides (absolutely *no* long hair or perms). But mixed in with these items are overtly childish things – dufflecoats, birthday-boy shirts with the top button done up, outsize pullovers; for girls – bows and ribbons and ponytails, plimsolls and dainty white ankle socks, floral or polka-dot frocks, hardly any make-up and no high heels; for boys – beardlessness and bare ears and tousled fringes. One garment above all has come to represent the scene – the anorak – the kind of short anorak, in bright optimistic patterns that remind you of curtain material, that a child might have worn in the Fifties or early Sixties. Some hardcore activisits on the scene will go all the way and sport a satchel or duffle-bag and then they'll *really* look like a Start-Rite kid. But to add to this confusion of pre-youth culture, sensible adult and sensible children's clothing, stray psychedelic/Sixties beat elements and the odd punk/Goth hangover, intrude – although the effect of these primary colours and garish patterns is also infantile, because childhood is the only time such bright colours are appropriate.

What's remarkable about the style is that it doesn't accentuate the figure: it conceals the signs of physical-maturity/sexual difference. Indeed, to look cool in this indie style it helps to be small as well as thin. Against the mainstream image of a desirable body – vigorous, healthy, suntanned, muscled for men, curvaceous for women – the indie ideal is slender, slight, pale of skin, childishly androgynous. The possibility of a high incidence of anorexia amongst indie boys and girls is intriguing, because anorexia is regarded as a subconscious rejection of sexual maturity. Both style and physical ideal seem to indicate a desire to distance oneself from adult responsibility, to opt out of the material and sexual rat-race. For women, dressing within the terms of conventional sexiness – tight clothing, make-up, high heels – runs the risk of 'responsibility' for unwanted sexual attention. So there's a feminist impulse behind this style – lesbian feminists have been dressing like this for years. It's a fair compromise between the desire to dress up and evading conventional glamour.

* * *

Pop is about fantasies. Pop isn't about a narrow reflection of the 'reality' of where an individual is already at, but about where or who you'd *rather* be. The fantasies in mainstream black/white pop are of 'the good life', 'good times' – which usually corresponds to a conventional and naive notion of 'sophistication'. Indie-pop's fantasy of 'innocence' or 'naivete' actually constitutes a more sophisticated response to our cultural present and to pop history. In the face of the 'complexification' (Lyotard) of the modern world/Eighties pop culture, indiepop is about a stylised 'authenticity', an elaborately constructed virginity. An hallucination (a flashback) of a simpler, more genuine time (the Sixties/childhood).

But these elements of artifice are rarely, if ever, consciously acknowledged by indie-poppers, perhaps for fear of breaking the spell. There's been a silent renunciation of criticism and analysis, a shrugging-off of the yoke of rhetoric, a retreat to an unbudgeable, sedimental 'what really counts' – Good Songs, 'quality', integrity, the immediate pleasure. These groups are innocent even of an idea why Good Songs might matter. Practically all writing on the new indiepop takes after the style of the fanzines that service the scene – excessively focused on the writer's own excitement, full of surface agitation, low on insight. Praise or condemnation is hysterical but blunt, conveying little of what's specific about any group. Talking about the 'movement' as a whole, Simon Frith wrote in *Village Voice*: '[there's] none of the loose avant-garde interests of the early Eighties. This has been, unusually, a British pop movement without a proselytising theory.'

But behind this apparent simplicity, this 'purity'/'purism', lies an eclecticism – a weaving together of different musics and different vocabularies of dissidence. So innocence or a camp Englishness can get matched with American beatnikism of the Dylan/Velvet Underground kind; the imagery of the North (drawn from Sixties films like *A Taste of Honey* or *Saturday Night, Sunday Morning*) gets combined with folk-rock or country; Ramones or Buzzcocks thrash gets married to Spector/Shangri-la's pure pop. What these American traditional/bohemian musics provide is a kind of anti-Americanism from within the USA, which can be used in the struggle against contemporary Americanisation. America represents the supreme incarnation of the modern, of the coming health-and-efficiency culture: a hyper-technical, superabundant society whose underside is the loss of community. In pop terms we're talking about MTV and video, stadiums and nightclubs and wine bars, growing links between Hollywood and rock and between advertising and rock, in the service of global behaviour control (rock helping to make certain lifestyles and their accompanying commodities attractive). Against these the indie scene defend lo-fi, the pub, conviviality. There's a vision of a 'real' working class, a lost Britishness that existed in the Sixties: this is set against the Thatcherite vision of classless, 'popular capitalism', of a Britain that would be more like America. Those modern figures – the yuppie, the soul boy, the B-boy – are all infatuated with the American vision of the future. So we get the following paradox: what's most British today is the aspiration to be like the Americans: what's marginal, dissident, practically *unpatriotic*, is the indie scene's defensive Englishness – a patriotism located in the past, a nostalgia for a never-never Britain, compounded from Sixties 'social realist' films and the golden age of British pop.

What's condensing is a new folk tradition, based around mourning the loss of the 'real' and the 'natural', the lack of the norms and bonds that tie but also console. This 'folk' isn't ethnically organised, but a rootless communality without geography, that's articulated through the media. It lives in the interstices of possibility, those gaps in the social fabric where it's possible to convince yourself for a while that you've not grown up, not given in. Remember the double meaning of 'innocence' – not just unworldly, but *prior* to blame, not yet responsible *in* or *for* the system. Sixth-formers, students, art-schools, the new 'dole cultures', alternative career structures (e.g. local government work in Left-controlled areas), the media – wherever it's possible to subsist outside the pressures of adjustment and adaption, the pressure to make your mind up. For many this exile/asylum will only be temporary . . . and so the music is saddened by dreams, torn between fatalism and the imprecise desire for something more. 'There are brighter sides to life. And I should know because I've seen them/But not often.' (The Smiths, 'Still ill'.) These are the people who only know what they do not want. All that's left is a stubborn will to misfit, to cling to one's dissatisfaction, even in the face of an ever more accommodating leisure capitalism.

What tantalises these people is the memory that music was once *meant* to change reality, rather than just provide a hiding-place or consolation. Pop is the largest thing that looms in these people's lives, but as something that has slipped out of 'our' hands and become a system that excludes our experience. Hence the defensive vision of 'perfect pop'. Indiepop is like a parallel system, unacknowledged by 'Pop', but bound in reaction: it deals with all the matter written out of pop's script – squalor, antagonism, frustration, difficulty, doubt.

'Youth' has been co-opted, in a sanitised, censored version, as a key component of the burgeoning culture of health and self-improvement. Desire is no longer antagonistic to materialism, as it was circa the Stones' 'Satisfaction'. So the most radical project possible in pop today is that attempted by The Smiths – a rewriting of youth in terms of maladjustment, awkwardness, introversion misery. Morrissey represents those who *fail* to live as the young are now expected, fail to have sex/fun/style. The Smiths incendiary forays into the domain of pop TV (where Morrissey's dancing, an astonishing alchemy of gracelessness into cool, mystifies the public and usually results in their singles plummeting *down* the charts) constitute what David Stubbs once called 'ostentatious absenteeism' (like those gauche adolescents who insist on attending parties, only to parade a chaste disdain).

Late in 1986 the Smiths finally decided to move from right-on indie label Rough Trade to massive and massively square major EMI – a belated bid to make good what should always have been their destiny, to be The Rolling Stones of their time, i.e., the most appropriate gesture of defiance *to* the times. A number of kindred indies were also plighting their troth to major labels like WEA and Chrysalis. This is a gallant step, for the obvious risk is that 'innocence' may not survive success. But the alternative for the scene is to allow itself to disappear in an inward, downward spiral of referentiality (commentary on mainstream pop) and inter-referentiality (attempts to take the piss out of indie insularity, like Pop Will Eat Itself's 'What's So Good About Candy?', and Age of Chance's cover of Prince's 'Kiss', are very *small* jokes). David Stubbs again: 'all this twang, twang, this dull two-step of circuit powerchords and jejeune jangles, will react the same fossilised, Pebble Mill stage as Trad Jazz . . . if they carry on like this, time will force them to forfeit their significance.' The celebration of a unity of alienation becomes a ritual of exile, the music a craft to be passed down. Would this alter the *meaning* of the subculture? Or is ambition and the evangelistic impulse inseparable from pop?

What I've analysed above is something that has been coalescing since 1979, something that's *settled firmer* with each reversal the rock avant-garde has received in its attempts to radicalise the mainstream. This is a white-middle-class bohemianism that's cleansed of the fast-living and self-destruction of earlier forms of rebellion: musics have been separated from the delinquent lifestyles that originally gave birth to them and have been *remotivated*, coupled with ascetism and romance. This lore of romance is perhaps one of the 'forbidden popular knowledges' which Foucault urged us to occupy and defend against those experts of the soul who seek to demystify and plan our lives. With its resistance to progress/com-plexifi-cation/technicism, with its return to tradition, this coalescence is perhaps the first anti-modernist revolt in pop history. A quiet withdrawal, as much from the old youth culture as from straight society. Backs turned defiantly to the future, back to 'the things that really count'?

20
After Subversion: Pop Culture and Power

Paul Oldfield

Popular culture has long been held up to us, by participants and critics, as a carrier of resistance, a potentially subversive practice. Perhaps now, reviewing the intellectual or academic theories that have sustained this claim, the language and orthodoxies of 'subversion', of 'power' and 'desire', can be traced and then put in doubt, volatilised more than a little.

The Situationist International were the first to demand and imagine the 'revolution of everyday life'. Where, before, the individual had been alienated and oppressed in the domain of work, there was now a consumer, leisure culture, and with it 'government by seduction'. Guy Debord's 'Spectacular commodity society' depended on consumption and non-participation. The Situationists anticipated an extra- or transpolitical revolution. Theirs was a cultural struggle in which passivity and non-communication would disappear with the creation of 'situations', the rediscovery of *play*, and spontaneity. Subversion, which the Situationists derived from Lautreamont, Ernst and Dada, was a privileged term, and creativity 'the ultimate weapon'. *Détournement* was the appropriation of culture, its recycling in collage: 'Every element of past culture must be either re-invested or scrapped.' It was the 're-insertion of things into play' and re-united 'beings and things'. Even more than creativity, love, because it was clandestine, not co-opted into the circuit of spectacular pleasures, would enrich experience. Finally, the disappearance of power is guaranteed by the 'subjective will' and an 'insatiable desire'. Already the satellite concepts of resistance have been introduced: subversion, play, desire.

Situationism, or the tendencies it drew on, has been a persistent presence in youth culture (and its study). The counter-culture of the late 1960s, described in Richard Neville's *Playpower*, and its music from psychedelia to progressive, was indebted to the 'beach beneath the pavement'. Subcultural studies also emphasise that youth cultures throughout the 60s were developed through *détournement*, a resistance through ritual by appropriating consumer items and endowing them with new values. But the most programmatic 'Situationist' interventions suggest best what Raoul Vaneigem foresaw: not just the ease of recuperation but the always-already-recuperated character of any contents of the spectacle. Malcolm McLaren's Sex Pistols, with their contrivance of situations (the EMI episode), subversion (collage graphics), undoing of the spectacle (TV appearances), diatribes against passivity, are now interpreted, even by the most orthodox commentators, as a renewal for the industry. McLaren's Bow Wow Wow, too, had as their main contribution the recognition of the fact that the spectacle can be turned inside out, with hype, manipulation and contrivance on display, and still function as normal. McLaren has been reviled as 'that faeces of culture'; Jamie Reid's private view was picketed by '80s Situationists. Raoul Vaneigem had already understood that for the spectacle, flirtation with non-conformism and the shocking, is a lease of life. And that in the 'happenings' and sociodramas of his period, spectators are induced to participate in the 'organisation of their own passivity'. The incoherence of the spectacle is articulated as the 'spectacle of incoherence'.

Situationist subversion always fails because it *does* 'demand the impossible'. Even in the '80s, McLaren's avatars believe, to quote pop group Scarlet Fantastic, that we can 'gatecrash paradise'. These utopians imagine unlimited licence, unbridled individualism, the end of *all* repression. But simply to become an individual, speaking being is to introduce discipline *within* yourself, to enter the conduits of language and society. Without this repression and structuring, you can't take up any place in the world at all.

What *is* possible is just a lapse in order. Malcolm McLaren himself, rewriting history with his *Great Rock 'n' Roll Swindle* text, compares the chaos he contrived to a historical interlude like the Gordon Riots. Such ludic intervals are already familiar in many cultures as a Saturnalia, the world turned upside down. But this riot and disorder depends for its meaning on the very order it inverts. The prevailing order sanctions its negative: no doubt neither can exist without the other. Situationism is always a play area within order.

Post-structuralism's project is the un-doing of the founding concepts of Western philosophy. Instead of a 'revolution of everyday life', it is more a subverting activity confined to the text. It challenges the notions of a 'meaning' as the ultimate destination of texts, of a *signified* that puts an end to the substitution of different *signifiers*, of the 'author', or boundaries to the text. The centring or privileging of terms that structuralism allows is replaced by a *play* of signs, an indeterminacy of meaning. This sliding of signification, in which meaning is never reached or never finished, is accorded a libidinal value, it is the *pleasure* of the text, or *jouissance* (enjoyment, orgasm). Although its play, its introduction of desire to the text, its confrontation with 'author-ity', the individual self, and its critique of bourgeois institutions made it, with Situationism, a joint contributor to the counter-culture, it has had a particular significance for radicalism and pop in the '80s. To understand this, we need to know a little more about its appearance in the English-speaking world in the '70s, and the influence of its language and strategy. (Perhaps it was partly introduced to pop by Dick Hebdige's assimilation of punk, which perhaps will sponsor every theory of resistance, to the concepts of *bricolage* and the emptiness – 'blank generation' – that inhabits and undoes meaning.) Post-structuralist writing has naturalised and enforced strategy and indirection, as well as the imminence of failure. What seems to happen now is that in any article there is the moment of closure, the signifying process is seized up, there is a lurch into meaning – 'logocentrism' – and a succeeding article will develop from it. Or the text simply calls out for a supplementary text; there is no border. To sustain the subversion of the possibility of mastery, we have: glossolalia, fantastic and impossible accumulation of billions of words and papers, a canker of projects and institutions.

But subversion can be more rarefied than this. The strategy that Post-structuralism has been identified with most clearly is 'deconstruction'. The word has been so far deflected and misappropriated, suffered such attrition, that it is almost an embarrassment. But it is the practice that accompanies *the end of theory*. 'Theory' is renounced: it is to become 'simply a genre again' and to lose its primacy (Lyotard). Theory is not to 'express, translate, or serve to apply practice', it must collapse back into practice, be 'local' rather than 'totalising' in its 'struggle against power' (Foucault). Deconstruction is *the* practice. It is not possible to do more than 'shake' or unsettle the system we oppose, and it is necessary to 'slip into the logic', to be implied in what we subvert. 'Concepts are indispensable for unsettling the heritage to which they belong' (Derrida, *Of Grammatology*).

Deconstruction was conceived as a difficult and very specific set of practices or operations within written texts. But it is a shadowy presence in the pop of the '80s. What has mainly been assimilated is no more than a distrust of theory and an emphasis on strategy. It is still orthodox practice for bands to discourse interminably, but with a shapeless opacity, to fight shy of any accusations of a theory. And for PIL, Heaven 17, BEF, ABC, a grand *strategy* of planned success was their subject matter. For Heaven 17, the industry itself, and for ABC the conventions of 'love' in that industry, were their medium. But such *self*-consciousness and visible re-production of pop's workings is very far from deconstruction's subject-less, intricate work on much more intractable concepts. The band that alone attempts deconstruction is Scritti Politti. Scritti's departure from the independent business and their change of styles has been interpreted as part of the New Pop's entry-ism, its sanctioning of the mainstream as the place in which to put across ideas. But more than that, it was an abandonment of *both* the ideology of independence/alternatives *and* that of entry, the grafting of new aims onto the charts, 'working from within'. Scritti work with pop, in its closure, not against it, nor do they co-opt it for our enlightenment. Scritti understand that order isn't so monolithic that only utopian demands or provocations are possible. There's subversive work to be done on the powers we exercise over ourselves. Nor is this an *oppositional* practice. Their music exploits the breaches and deficiencies that are already there in the prevailing discourse. For Scritti's Green Garsted, pop music can *always* be a subversion of the imperatives of meaning. He attempts to elude the closure or reclamation of pop's pleasure. Instead of any fulfilment or resolution, Scritti's music delivers the bliss of a lover's discourse in all its ellipses, contradiction and repetition, its endless pursuit of an unattainable object. The disembodied, depthless, non-linear effects, and the borrowings of pop's language of love try to undo desire's usual articulation in coherent drives and stable identity *while reinscribing or repeating the very 'soul' language that's used to heal and complete the self in today's pop*: the sweet *nothings* heard beside, within the sexual healing. But such an immaculate pop and so delicate a deconstruction, which hardly seems to touch on institutions, may be hard for consumers to experience as a shaking or subversive effect.

Post-structuralism's engagement with the suppressed discourses of 'madness' and 'desire' has more generally reverberated through pop and pop writing until *Blitz* magazine could appear with that single iconic word 'Desire' on its front cover in 1985. It was Barthes, in *The Grain of the Voice*, who brought the language of the 'pleasure of the text' to music criticism. Writing on music, he observes, is always an accretion of adjectives: the predicate is 'always the bulwark with which the subject's imaginary protects itself from the loss that threatens it'. Where music has served to constitute a listening subject, Barthes wants to re-instate it as 'an access to jouissance, to loss'. He appeals to the 'grain' of music, the *friction* between music and language, where *plaisir* is possible. This is the materiality of music, it is not *expressive*, it comes directly from the body. Henceforth the evaluation of music will be the 'account of an individual thrill', of an 'erotic relation' with the performer, but it will not be *subjective*: the pleasure will be in the loss of the subject. Thus appears the demand, heard among academics and pop journalists now, for attention to the materiality, the surface, of music, and an admission of unfounded fascination, the subversion of endless desiring: within pop itself, the privileged performers being the Cocteau Twins, This Mortal Coil, or composers of ambient musics. Or even such disparate genres as hip hop and house, which have in common only the supersession of communication by the surface effects, the obliteration of any text. But isn't sound always recuperated or invested with meanings by *music*?

Where Barthes imagines music deriving from 'a body without a civil identity', J-F. Lyotard isn't so prepared to attribute a subversive value to the materiality of music/the body. For him, sounds, like phonemes, derive value from the network of their possible relations. The body is the site where sounds become music, it is desensitised to noise: Lyotard almost seems to say that the body composes and is composed in music. Music is the device that invests libido, it is policed and policing. Lyotard's account of musical history relates it to the political. Western classical music depends on dissonance and resolution, an anticipation across time, an expectation that something will be restored – it is compared with the rise of perspective, which constructs depth, in Lyotard's argument about the development of theatre scenery and the space of modern politics in the Renaissance. It is the distribution of music in silence, the policing by silence, where the argument encounters power and resistance. Lyotard denies the silence of authority (of the spectator, or the psychoanalyst) and says, with John Cage, that there is no silence, no Other that has dominion over sound. We make music *all the time*. This could issue in an aesthetic that would simply abandon the boundaries of music and music-making. In pop, what else but a pathological noise aesthetic? But at least the saturation of the media with body-as-subversion could be challenged by the presentation of 'music' as a founding and organising machine for authority.

More recent theories of power and resistance, developed by Foucault, Guattari and Baudrillard, are only now beginning to be inscribed in pop and pop aesthetics. Foucault, after several historical studies in the growth of disciplines and institutions (prisons, clinics, asylums) that practised seclusion, surveillance and therapy, presented a more advanced account of power in his 'History of Sexuality'. 'Interdiction, refusal, prohibition, far from being the essential forms of power, are its . . . worn, extreme forms. Above all, relations of power are *productive*.' Power works, not by repression, but by engendering discourse, (e.g. psychoanalysis), by encouraging participation and self-analysis. From diffuse 'pleasures', our sexuality and our very selves are constituted and administered, by our self-management, and all in the name of liberation. For Foucault, resistance is possible wherever there are relations of power, resistance is 'coextensive and contemporaneous' with power. The intellectual should be able to locate 'the inertias and constraints of the present, the weak points, the openings'. It falls to Guattari, whose writings on power are not dissimilar, to imagine, now that power is dispersed and control has become atomised, cellular, that a micro-terrorism or 'molecular revolution' is possible. This *micro-politics* will not represent people, nor interpret desire: it will be a multiplicity of desires, a loosely, *transversally* aggregated set of fringe groups that dissent from established capitalist and familial structures. The 'events' of May '68 are still a model for Guattari (as is the free Radio episode in Italy in '72), but there is the reservation: no doubt many marginal groups will be incorporated as an acceptable form of protest.

What influence has this had in attitudes to pop? Foucault's theory of power is adopted as a model for Simon Reynolds's article 'Against Health and Efficiency' (see p. 245 in this volume). Resistance to the youth culture of managed pleasure, self-gratification and the 'science of relationships' is attributed to 'a forgetting of the body in pop' (abandonment or subversion of dance by Birthday Party, Smiths, Husker Du, Jesus and Mary Chain); to an investment in love, tragic, unrequited and problematic (Smiths); and to obsession, an imbalance in desire, failure and withdrawal (Birthday Party, Smiths again). While the Smiths and the Jesus and Mary Chain may have caused surprise, a shudder in the body pop, it is more difficult to claim them as dissenters in our culture.

In the article, there is a conflation of the concept of dispersed and productive power and the managerialism, the bureaucracy, that Situationism had in its sights. Management, efficiency and planning are not coterminous with the new micro-powers. The discourse of failure, un-control, the problematic, although regarded as grounds for therapy, is massive and is not *opposed* to the productivity of power: no doubt the sciences or disciplines that are being instituted have made possible and articulated this very discourse.

My further doubt concerns the 'serenity of pure noise' and the withdrawal that is 'otherworldly'. These are described as 'the beginnings of a new head culture, a psyche-delia'. In *Monitor* (issue no. 4) there had been an encomium on this new psychedelia, this unearthly grace and demand for the impossible. This re-opening of the doors of perception, this development of an inner abundance, is also far from resistance to self-gratification and 'personal productivity': consider, too, in a later article in the same series, the reference to a 'music that can enlarge the *vocabulary* of our desires'.

The new psychedelia that has transpired in the '80s imagines not deconstruction, deficiency or destabilisation, but an utter dissolution of the boundaries of our selves. The music of AR

Kane, Loop, Hugo Largo, etc. has been approached by the music press (myself included) in terms derived less from Foucault's micro-resistances than from Kristeva or new French feminists. This music doesn't so much free the play of signification as suggest a reversion to a pre-linguistic condition, a pre-history of the individual, a nirvana that precedes entry into the world. Music for the womb-dweller. Unlike the pop strategists discussed earlier, these bands don't conceive their nirvana as a public convulsion against power, just a secession from selfhood. Much as I've celebrated them, it has to be said that they leave no chance of leverage on or within the networks of power, which reassert themselves after the 'trip', and even determine the very availability and meanings of this experience. Brilliant secession, yes. Subversion, no.

But retreat into abstention or apartness could, after all, be the nemesis of the social order itself, if we give any credence to Jean Baudrillard's theories of power and mass culture.

The call to abstention and refusal would, if not invested with glamour and other-worldly properties, answer to the resistance imagined by another theorist, Jean Baudrillard. Baudrillard's theory differs from those already discussed, in that power is now a retreating, evanescent phenomenon, which surrounds itself with discourses, crises, and above all *resistance* as its guarantees. To understand how this vertiginous and difficult position can be reached, we need to have recourse to his differentiation between *representation* in its philosophical and political senses, and *simulation*. As in the account of post-structuralism earlier, what is at issue is that meaning or the 'real' has absconded: without the ideal, the absolute, with only signs that refer to each other, there can be no representation, no mediation of the real. Instead of reflecting, or misrepresenting, reality, the image, signifiers, conceal the fact that there is nothing beyond them: this is *simulation*. Baudrillard's writing of social history, which occupies much the same ground as Foucault's, depends on and illustrates his contention that representation is everywhere affirmed, and simulation denied or absorbed by the ideology of representation.

'Social history' is the advance of socialisation, the rise of institutions and discourses that incorporate and take as their object more and more groups. In an earlier period than ours, as Foucault showed in his studies, socialisation was by surveillance, by being under a central gaze (the 'Panopticon' of the prisons). As the social order has developed, practically everybody has been included in its domain, but the focus of power, the central model, has disappeared. Today there are 'The Masses' and the machine that creates meanings for and represents them, 'The Media'. But we are no longer in the society of the spectacle that the Situationists described. It is not passivity or non-communication that is expected from the masses, there is no alienation by the mass media: rather (and here again there is the ghost, misleading though it is, of Foucault) participation is demanded. Yet it is not that power is dispersed as operative, productive micro-powers. Power is disappearing. For Baudrillard, the masses are inert, passive, their opacity is unrepresentable. What stands in for representation or knowledge of the masses is the survey, the poll, the questionnaire, which can only yield statistical averages, an unstemmable tide of unreliable figures. Opinion polls start influencing opinions; what was 'politics' is reduced to a spectacle; meaning and communication are replaced by *fascination* . . . The media are an instrument for soliciting the participation of the people, for eliciting responses, for ensuring and showing that they *are* represented, their opinions heard. More and more, as Baudrillard says 'it's *your* programme, it's *your* event'; there are phone-ins, undirected discussions, all to urge the masses *not* to opt for the spectacle and passivity, to re-invest issues and affairs with seriousness. But it is this very process that is bringing nearer the catastrophe of *simulation*, for in the place of the gaze of authority, what Baudrillard also calls 'the central model', of the panopticon, there is only . . . the listener or watcher him/herself. The alienation that made political and other representation possible, that called forth an *exchange* of views, the relations of power, is supplanted by a circular trajectory of information. Where does authority derive from? The answer is *You*. The answer to your demand . . . from *You*. This commutativity, this vanishing of power, is covered: my own examples would be the radio phone-in, where there is the 5-second delay, the censor button that *might just* be pushed, to assure us of censorship, to maintain a veil behind which *authority* is lurking; or the selective publication of opinions that is conveniently made possible by soliciting them in an impossible volume.

Power, in its retreat, has to re-invent, to *simulate* relations of power. The accepted method of power, dissimulation, by which it conceals its exercise, must be displaced by simulation, the concealment of the absence of power. Its strategy is to insist on the reality of social and economic issues, to risk the discourse of crisis, to propogate resistance. From the default of power and meaning, there are theorists who will rediscover meaning in the micro-politics of desire, who will call up the 'desire' of the masses and re-create the relations of power. Power and resistance can co-exist in a mutual support that has not yet had to acknowledge the irretrievable loss of meaning. Baudrillard recommends, in place of the practices of revolt, emancipation, and subjectivity, the renunciation of subject-hood and meaning: resistance-as-object (the very condition that the advocates of desire, unhappy collaborators, denounce as 'passivity') is more appropriate a response to power's last manoeuvre.

Perhaps the evanescence of power, the surfacing of simulation, is most nearly and dangerously approached in the Sigue Sigue Sputnik affair. Not only were Sigue Sigue Sputnik a recycling, like a faded xerox, of several depreciated past moments of disturbance or resistance (the scandal of the film *A Clockwork Orange*, Ziggy Stardust, *The Diamond Dogs*, the Pistols), but they were only fraudulent in that no fraud had been perpetrated. Both the industry and the group need the simulation of power and subversion, a swindle, or a hype, or both . . . but little more than £30000 had changed hands, not £3 million, and the only dishonesty was in the idea of swindle or controversy, those ever-more depleted means of re-instilling the belief that there is manipulation and/or subversiveness. A moment's hesitation and we see it as a power-and-subversion *effect*, with nothing behind it, no clear intention (read the almost wilfully uninteresting interviews): but nor should we let this simulation reassure us that there is anything to be fathomed, any production or power-relations, anywhere else. Power operates near to its danger-zone, but still pulls it off – either the disappearance of our social order *or* a Top Five record: Sputnik made it to Number Two.

The subversion that pop culture has often imagined, the subversion of activity, infiltration, revolution, eruption of repressed desires, can be forgotten. All that's possible today is the renunciation of *agency*, varieties of refusal to recreate power, to be yourself: simply *disappearance* from or discrediting of the places where power and resistance keep propagating each other.

Notes

Roland Barthes, *Image–Music–Text*, Fontana, 1977.
Michel Foucault, *History Of Sexuality*, Vol. 1, Penguin, 1980.
Toril Moi, *The Kristeva Reader*, Basil Blackwell, 1986.
Jean Baudrillard, *Simulations*, Semiotext(e), 1983.

21
Fear of the Future

David Stubbs

1956: Presley, Haley, kids, ripped up cinema seats.
1966: The Velvet Underground, 'Revolver', monochrome to colour.
1976: Punk. Ripped-up photographs.
1986: The new Bob Geldof LP? Sigue Sigue Sputnik's resprayed version of a happening?

There's currently a dissatisfaction with the apparent smallness and impotence of pop and rock, their seeming inability to offer any sort of crucial blow. When is the Big Thing due? Who's going to Drop The Bomb? Now secretly, now openly, everyone's got their ears cocked for this single happening, a future shock in rock, a sign that it's tomorrow at last. Networks have been constructed nationally to ensure that anyone who wants to can have a pop. Local schemes, a proliferation of examples and icons have tempted a glut of self-expression. And with all the consequent, claustrophobic bustle, all this running-out, the near-blackening of the screen with honest effort, it's impossible to make out the note of absolute difference, the note that will bring down the walls of Jericho. In spite of a *sandstorm* of pluralism, all the hard-won resources at our disposal, new space in the media, historical legacy, it seems rather a long while since anything actually 'happened', as seemed to be promised. Early-warning systems are primed and alert, but a watched kettle has failed to boil. Or has all the water merely vaporised, into a fog of steam?

The time of the signs

These are complicated times, the time of the signs, troubled by the staggered existence of a dozen or so pop phases, flirted with, never fully abandoned, all eventually unmoored from time (today, someone will decide that the Smiths are all dried up; tomorrow, someone else will hear Little Richard for the first time). Scenes fall into abeyance, old props surface mysteriously, new ideas are sent back in their wrapping yesterday, obsolete notions are plundered from the attic tomorrow. Signifier barges toppling signifier as a huge, reluctant traffic jam of old vehicles forms down the road to the future. You'll find everything in those boots. Erich Von Stroheim, gender, African, tupperware – and that's just the terrible LP by Orchestral Manoeuvres In The Dark!

After punk, which made a free-for-all of post-modernism, the British music scene in particular (punk's cramped birthplace) has been bogged down in a monsoon of spiky initiatives. Punk exhorted a mass mobilisation of subjectivity. Trouble was, that eventually came to mean that the only people within earshot were those already participating. The result? A vast underlay of meta-music, symbiotic relationships, music about writing, about each other, so that, far from being poisonous, nobody in the world gives a hoot about, let alone understands, what 'we' do but 'us'! Is *anybody* watching?

Unity

Punk engendered a spirit of 'fairness' which made for pluralism. Hence, fragmentation. Punk came spiked with irony. With irony came a loss of faith. Hence again, fragmentation. Rock is no longer a matter of giant ombudsmen, big figures who explain us, behind whom we assemble *en masse*. It's not just the rock monolith which has exploded, but the audience which sustains it, the chimeras and rhetorical sweeps that propel it. Underconfidence in the scene has been prompted by the welcome and devastating introduction of jazz, African, folk and avant-garde giants onto the periphery of things, most of which have caught the corner of rock's eye and withered its glance. Some choose to look the other way, an increasing plethora of *utter* rock bands, from The Jack Rubies to The Mighty Lemon Drops, thrashing through thickets of guitar in search of the perfect powerchord. In this situation, it's really just a little small-minded to find accountability or definition in a

Costello, let alone a Dylan. The vestigial notion of 'allegiance' to such figures smacks, these days, of a totalitarianism of sorts, a hankering for the choric roar of Punk, a need for 'togetherness'. There's so much to absorb!

Moreover, none of this diversity amounts to a solution. There's a hundred things to get hooked on, everyone of them a question mark, none of them quite 'it', that desired totality. That was always the problem of punk – ostensibly inclusive, structurally *exclusive* – or, back to basics.

None of us are standing in the same spot. The days of One Vision are gone forever – the 'we' of rock journalism is no more than a convenience, a derelict construction. 'Opposition', the gathering-together of us to resist a various 'they' is now situated in non-musical areas and issues. So, around Ian Botham, a 'we' is constructed that feels that cannabis ought to be legalised; around 'Spitting Image', a 'we' that derides Thatcher and a whole host of media gargoyles; around Bob Geldof a 'we' that demands that They Feed The World (with the added bonus of Paul Weller and Freddie Mercury linking arms!). These new third-person plurals could include anyone from age 16 to 35, anyone into anything from Dire Straits to the Jesus And Mary Chain, even people with no interest in music whatsoever.

Strategies and resources

The itch to tear the masses from their complacent transfixion remains, in spite of our impotence and their absorption! But tolerance levels have risen beyond our reach. Today, intolerance does not take the form of public indignation. The likes of Chakk and Einsturzende Neubauten are *routinely* ignored. And with the likes of Conflict consigned to a dustbin category of delinquency, the likes of The Mission and The Furs whacking up a leather noise that's ultimately as sentimental as a Slade reunion, the possibilities of some unreconstructed 'rebellion' damaging forever the formica surface of bourgeois culture have been neatly contained, the voice of youth commandeered to sell jeans, or Bruce Springsteen albums.

Of course, some say that pop is stale because fresh blood isn't being allowed to pump through – vital, struggling bands are being systematically denied access. The truth is, however, that even the *little* access granted to rock and pop have proved to be too much for its own good, too illuminating. Think of the reasonably material denizens of the left-field that have already burst-onto-our-screens-but-only-rhetorically. Cabaret Voltaire, Test Dept, The Jesus And Mary Chain, The Exploited have all 'collided' with the cathode rays, only to evaporate, effectively, in a fog of blank blinks.

It was only with Punk that the urge ripened to *penetrate*. Entryism was never high on the agenda of, say, Led Zeppelin. That band made such a point of indifference to the prospect of mainstream 'infiltration' that they didn't even bother releasing singles, were a complete mystery to straightforward pop fans. Punk craved demystification, scrawled certain demands on paving slabs and, as three-minute crossover gradually occurred, these demands were gradually met. But punk worked too well. It was exposed. 'The Tube'! Here, you can thrill to Big Audio Dynamite while munching fish-fingers and crinkle-cut chips, lap up Echo and The Bunnymen followed by Honeywell computer adverts and the 7 o'clock news. These bands have not just appeared on television – they've *become* television. The media lights have been turned on these people.

The problem is, then, that the audience has become blasé about pop. A surfeit of media coverage, from Janice Long to the Video Show, has eroded the capacity to be alarmed, or frustrated. Now we have armchair, or pub hipsters, the sort that haven't bought an LP in two years, or been to a gig for a while, but still keep their hand just far enough in to preserve their sense of themselves as discerning creatures. They buy *The Face*. They realise that Cameo are streets ahead of Nick Kamen, The Cure manifestly a cut above Wang Chung. Quite adequately equipped to make the best of pop in the media environment, they don't need to bother catching a cold out on the street in search of the groundswell of the new. All you need is a good aerial and a tick-sheet! Hence, sales of the music press plummet by more than half in the 1980s, fewer people than ever bother wading through Peel. These are no longer the Dark Ages as regards media access to pop. The consequences of that for post-punk are that it loses its crucial sense of *otherness* and dark difference.

And so, heightened media access has created conditions that make it paradoxically difficult for the likes of The Bodines or Bogshed to get TV exposure, or even a small place in the public's ken: firstly because that sort of thing has suffered a diminishing of its curiosity value, and, therefore, ceased to be quite so fascinating; secondly because the Bunnymens, Banshees, Cures, etc., have consolidated their hard-won position as Faces. And around these greased fossils, these spiked dinosaurs have coalesced a new breed of sedentary, post-punk semi-yuppies, quite as reactionary as any Genesis fan. It's they, not a 'hostile' media haplessly attempting a stab at pop difference, that must be held to blame for any supposed stagnation in pop.

1987, then: with pop and rock apparently *drifting ahead*, over-determined by Punk, stripped of surprise, unable to offer a crucial blow, in effect as lowly and amiable as the Spinners in a packed boozer, while entry into chartpop has more or less seized up altogether. Make no mistake, however – there are a thousand brilliant things worthy of attention, more than you could ever hope to hear. A thousand little Phillip Boas, AR Kanes, Band of Holy Joys, Arthur Russells and Tashans lie in glorious fragments, too infrequently mentioned in the same breath, waiting to be swept up by a gust of disgust. Till then, they're unable to count. Moreover, they're scarce and peripheral. Meanwhile, the careful adequacy of the mainstream continues apace – dinosaurs 'develop' and 'mature', confuse celebrity with biography. But pop and rock can't simply continue ignominiously, without disruption or total regeneration and hope to retain volatile buzz. Sooner or later, the incandescent sub-text implied by monikers such as The Age Of Chance or Erasure will no longer be sustainable; their wilted spike will mark them out as trad jazz, taking a genre to its logical pension; Mitse Mizell Trios, Johnny Swing and his Guitarmen playing Darby and Joan rock.

Re-invent the conditions of oppression!

'Fascination' is now as scarce a resource as pop once was. With more pop available, and easier access, a primal impulse that yearns for *exclusion* of the common herd has been frustrated. With practically everybody conscripted to the ranks of pop youth, a sensitive elite, under the pretext of 'rescuing' culture, seek hip refuge in whatever nooks remain unlit by the media – hence, the soulboy, who's got the trick perfected to a fine art of being a well-known figure about town, whilst leaving everybody guessing as to what pop fix he's ravishing himself on. The funk 12" import has a high currency value – black, American, difficult to obtain.

Soul-cialists coalesce in clubs where rigorously exclusive door policies operate. Illegal 'warehouse' functions abound in which the most primitive of pop music is used to pass on information as to time and place – word of mouth. No media environment here – to be in on this, you'd have to be out on the lost 'street'. This subculture is not principally concerned with articulating demands, or cherishing musical values. No missionary zeal here to spread the word. They want to be noticed, and left alone. The whole stance is an inversion of the parish status of the old Black, celebrating his exclusion, rather than lamenting it.

Or, there's the grubby end of Indie culture, another pretence that demands are not being met. Once again, the charge is laid that a conspiracy is at large – inspired by terror – to overlook the scurry of grassroots activity, with the praises sung of ever more hopeless and generic bands (Stoke's finest!). This notion that local noise deserves a fair hearing, mistakes pop for a council-house waiting list, free milk, part of a socialist scheme!

These hardcores are proof of an innate need in youth culture for opposition, its fundamental resistance to the integration it pretends to yearn for.

Ignorance: authenticity

For those with an inkling of the futility, or even the fatigue of the scene, its tinny, tacky assault, there's a growing chorus of despair. Where's the spirit, the spontaneity, the unfettered *ignorance*?

Once, these people were convinced that Elvis Costello was as deep and as hard as you could get. Then they read an interview in which the great man reverently listed his sources – his C&W heroes, for instance. And his fans would duly whizz round to Virgin Megastore and flick through the appropriate, indigenous sections – to discover something even *more* 'real'. George Jones, perhaps! Wearing, to boot, a pair of trousers so godawful as to indicate for sure that he'd never read a copy of *The Face* in his life. Clean! Likewise, as post-modern pop seemed to splutter into a breakdown of confidence, Billie Holiday, Hank Williams, Charly,

Curtis Mayfield, Miles Davis and Lightnin' Hopkins among others were re-discovered and celebrated for having set the pop planet in motion, for hailing from some Homeric age that pre-dated pop and philosophy – the days when songs were songs, proceeding directly from their physical or spiritual source, lacerated by the anguish of oppression but unburdened by referentiality: introspective.

What are the 'disillusioned' looking for in these grainy, budget re-issues? The reminding presence of body and soul, perhaps, that has somehow dissolved from a pop increasingly under siege from irony and diversity? But there never ought to have been any such flesh in the pan. Pop is not a folk culture and is even known to bite the hand that tries to pass down. Rather, it's a confused sum of identities and gifts from abroad. Perhaps what's sorely missed is a certain, gritty feel beneath the feet – ground. The real thing. Roots. But in this day and age, you'd have to extend your leg a long way down to touch whatever lump of terrain is buried beneath the rusty syntheses and variegated clutter of our gregarious culture. This, of course, is the time of the signs. Every gesture groans under the weight of its several precedents. We're too well sussed, disgusted at our learnedness, our inability to make direct emotional responses. Spontaneity, wood, grit, soul – they're all components of a pestering, irretrievable folk-memory that makes us feel *small*. Bessie Smith, Leadbelly, George Jones, all undermine confidence in the present and, of course, the future. For some people, pop has lost its footing. The future looks bleak. It's a nostalgia of sorts, a hankering that exists on several levels, from the crass to the clever and wistful.

Another option to finding authenticity in other and earlier musical forms is to find solace in pop's own past, when some kind of harmony and straightforwardness appeared to prevail.

1962! The year when technology ought to have ground to a prudent halt, with the development of the Morris Minor and the asesthetically pleasing transistor radio. The year when we all swung in time, all heading in the same direction (the 1970s). The year when 'we' didn't smirk at what 'we' were doing. The year long before a chaotic surfeit of options set in, scattering all and sundry to the four corners of the pop planet. The year before sex became a thudding imperative, when there was a bouffant consensus on style, and, most importantly, when *we* were probably all children, bathed in soft focus, prepostmodern and, therefore, preproblematic. Bitter authenticity and sweet pseudo-ignorance are both a retreat from the future, both are subtly dispersed and immersed in contemporary pop, both are twice-told tales rapidly losing their sting.

Final pop

Among the Futurists, an air of finality looms. In the contemporary climate, with just about everybody with a spike crowding for attention, what counts is *definitiveness* – higher and harder than the rest. With the proliferation of pop, attention spans shorten and half the battle is against easy boredom and alternative distractions. No one wants to spend all their time listening to a single singer/songwriter reflecting wryly. So in the last two years or so, there's been the spectacle of Sigue Sigue Sputnik as 'final pop group', attempting to commandeer the twenty-first century and the colour purple by sheer front. There's been The Jesus And Mary Chain, almost absolutely black, 'the final rock group', almost blacked out in their heads, almost lost in their own black hole of noise.

The *crunch* has come – seize, or be seized. Every production job seems to reverberate with a prophesy of the Bang To Come. Both global and pop economics are throwing up ever more ultimate characters. Prince, who's pulling out all the stops, trying to invoke God's approval with the echoing clap-trap on 'Mountains'. Pile it all on as never before and never again! Everybody is *up*! Pop is currently brimming over the tumbler with uppers and upper-uppers. Cameo's 'Word Up', Big Audio Dynamite's 'Upping Street', to say nothing of Janet Jackson's tight 'Control'. What's more, hip-hop is busy boiling all its sugar *down* to crack, Schooly D has edited hip-hop *down* to a vicious, supercilious scratch. Hip-Hop is the ultimate distillation of rock's naked bravado, its endless put-downs, counter-blasts and competition results in a breathless, vowel-less series of better and better 12-inches, each topping the last. They've got it down to a t-bone – any residual flesh is ruthlessly cut away with flick-knives.

At the other end of rock, there's the Swans, who have masochistically edited their sound down to a series of hope-less, catatonic thuds. Neither the rappers nor the Swans give an inch.

None of this 'shocks' or 'subverts', of course – rather, it supplies a select breed of addicts with purer and purer shots of narcotic bliss. It's difficult to imagine any of the above *exceeding* this shrinking space they're now in, and they seem to know it.

Fear of the future

Speculation has all but dried up in pop. Speculation shrivelled with the 'demise' of Simple Minds. Very popular indeed, for one suspended moment they achieved the poise of a cat on the fence. Caught between action and reflection, Abba and Lou Reed, Herbie Hancock and Jim Morrison. The tip of Xanadu was visible over the rooftops! Charts and dirt-box, boys and girls, all abandoned their traditional enmity briefly to link up and form a high arch. There they were, 'anything is possible', ready to take a quantum, speculative leap from a never-never point in a past of their own making into a future clouded with 'vague, wistful, inordinate hope'.

Of course, they tumbled into the U2 rockery. Xanadu melted and collapsed a generation after have-a-pop generation took turns to clamber up and slide down its shiny surfaces. And now, a third generation – Westworld, Curiosity Killed The Cat, Swing Out Sister – squat liberally among its ruins, brewing a weak soup from coloured bits of rubble.

Punk is responsible for our future-less impotence, the pernicious adequacy of things. Its have-a-go dynamic, its invitations and incitements, somehow only seem to have rendered pop small and common, in an age when what people secretly want is a large rarity. Ten years or more – this final throb of the rock narrative has shattered and de-mystified the monolith, long since outlived its usefulness. Its notion of 'threat' is in tatters – rhetorically, it's only succeeded in spouting excuses to clutch at the kerb.

Today, what must be rekindled are mystery and fascination – in essence, the un-punked 'ghost' of rock. A music that occupies larger premises, such as the pretentious psychedelia (from now on, high praise) of The Legendary Pink Dots, the fluent but indigestible bliss of AR Kane, the thing-in-itself-ness of Skinny Puppy. Sexless, beerless, function-less, far-out noise – a new 'purity', perhaps.

22
We Are the World?*

Greil Marcus

What follows is a reading of a text – in this case, the 'We Are the World' record – and then some thoughts on why it seems to me inadequate, not only as a reading, but as a locating of the text.

The reading

The late Lester Bangs on the 1976 Second Annual Rock Music Awards telecast, hosted by Alice Cooper and Diana Ross:

'The highlight of the evening was the Public Service Award. Alice complained that: rock music personalities are foremost and basically people – contrary to rumour. People with the same dreams, desires and feelings as everyone else. They're ambitious but they're not selfish or self-involved – but caring! . . . and I can't read this card. Their careers are time-consuming, but they still invest whatever time they have in . . . Diana: " . . . what we in this industry are most proud of – the Public Servce Award".

They gave Public Service Awards to Harry Chapin for contributing to World Hunger Year, and to Dylan for helping get Rubin "Hurricane" Carter out of jail. . . . Then Diana delivered the *coupe de grâce*: But seriously, folks, there's an incredible movement growing in the United States, concerned citizens who believe that whales have the right to life. And through words and through music the team of David Crosby and Graham Nash express their own concern, by giving a special concert so that the whales

---

*A composite of an article published in *Artforum*, May 1985, and a talk given at a conference of the International Association for the Study of Popular Music in Montreal, July 1985.

are still alive. I think that is absolutely incredible and we honour them with our fifth Public Service Award. Well, once again, I don't think they're here, but we'll accept it for them. Alice made a crack about Flo and Eddie being there, speaking of whales, and Diana continued: "No, seriously, I do know that a lot of my friends are concerned about this area and it's something that I personally would very much like to be interested in."'

Things haven't changed much since then. Rock stars still invest whatever time they have in what they are most proud of. The only difference is that the Rock Music Awards have been replaced by the American Music Awards, and whales have been exchanged for Ethiopians.

Following the AMA telecast last January, more than forty performers gathered to make a record to raise funds for Ethiopian famine relief. AMA host and big winner Lionel Richie had already written the song with Michael Jackson; Quincy Jones produced. Diana Ross, Bob Dylan, Bruce Springsteen, Dionne Warwick, Tina Turner, Willie Nelson, Steve Perry, James Ingram, Kenny Rogers, Paul Simon and the rest 'checked their egos at the door' and, under the name of 'USA for Africa', cut 'We Are The World'. As Oscar Wilde might have said, it takes a strong man to listen without laughing. Or throwing up.

As I was cleaning the floor, I had to admit that as a tune 'We Are The World' isn't at all bad – but a more vague composition about specific suffering could not be imagined. Small print on the sleeve claims 'USA for Africa . . . has pledged to use . . . all profits realized by CBS Records from the sales of "We Are The World" . . . to address immediate emergency needs in the USA and Africa, including food and medicine', but there isn't a word in the song about how, or why this might be necessary. In the first verse one is told that 'There are people dying'; in the last verse, that 'When you're down and out' (the Ethiopians are 'down and out'?) 'if you just believe, there's no way we can fall.' Literally, that means if Ethiopians believe in 'USA for Africa' the stars will realise their own hopes. That's it for Ethiopia.

While grammar is no help, contextualisation comes to the rescue: certainly the superstars of 'USA for Africa' knew their efforts would receive such overwhelming media coverage that their proximate inspiration would be clear to all. Thus, once past 'There are people dying', the rest of the song can fairly be about not the question but its answer – a celebration of the rock music personalities who are singing it.

'There's a choice we're making / We're saving our own lives' – those are the key lines of 'We Are The World', repeated again and again. Dylan sings them, Steve Perry sings them, Springsteen sings them, Ray Charles sings them, Stevie Wonder sings them. Within the confines of desperately MOR music, Charles is magnificent, Wonder superb, Springsteen sounds like Joe Cocker, and Dylan – well, if a comedian attempted a Dylan parody this broad he'd be laughed off the stage. But that's irrelevant. Within the context of contextualisation, recognition is all: objective parody is more recognisable, more saleable, than subjective performance. The point is voracious aggrandisement in the face of starvation – a collective aggrandisement, what those in the industry are most proud of. Melanie Klein posited the infant's projection of itself on the world, and its instinctive attempt to devour the world; beneath perfectly decent, thoughtless intentions, that's what's to be heard on 'We Are The World'. Forget the show-biz heaven of 'We are the world, we are the children / We are the ones who make a brighter day'; listen to the way that, projecting themselves on the world, the 'USA for Africa' singers eat it. Ethiopians may not have anything to eat, but at least these people get to eat Ethiopians.

Obviously, I think the subliminal message of 'We Are The World' is destructive. The message is, ye have the poor always with you; that there is a 'We' – you and I – who should help a 'Them', who are not like us; that as we help them we gain points for admission to heaven ('We're saving our own lives'); that hunger, whether in the USA or Africa, is a natural disaster, in God's hands, His testing, perhaps, of those Americans who are, as their president has put it, homeless and starving 'by choice', and if they aren't, how in God's name did they reach such a fate? And if they are, aren't the Ethiopians? For that matter – small print and small 'USA for Africa' contributions to American hunger relief (10 per cent) aside – doesn't the spectacularisation of Ethiopian suffering trivialise suffering at home, and hide its political causes in a blaze of goodwill? Bad politics, which can be based in real desires, can produce good art; bad art, which can only be based in faked or compromised desires, can only produce bad politics. Such carping is as vague as 'We Are The World' –

but there is a message hidden in the song that is more specific than anyone could have intended.

As with Michael Jackson in 1984, the highlight of the 1985 Grammy telecast was the unveiling of the new Pepsi commercial. Lionel Richie, earning $8.5 million as a Pepsi spokesman, strolled through a three-minute spot, advertised as the longest non-political TV advertisement in the history of the medium. The theme was pressed hard. 'You know, we're all a new new generation', Richie said, 'and we've made our choice' – most notably, he was saying without saying it, the choice of Pepsi over Coke.

Pepsi first tried this theme in the 1960s, when it pushed 'The Pepsi Generation' as a slogan. In the time of the generation gap, of seemingly autonomous youth, the line didn't work. As based in abundance as the '60s were, the catchiest ideology of the era was anti-materialist; the corporate co-optation rubbed raw. But the new generation of Richie's commercial really was new – the post-'60s generation, which is indeed all-inclusive, which does have room for anyone from that passed time: a new generation whose members, according to media wisdom, have traded utopianism for selfhood, but nevertheless look hard for quality time to spend on family, friends, and areas they personally would very much like to be interested in, so long as those areas are sufficiently distant – say, eight thousand miles distant.

Actually, the 1985 Pepsi commercial was a lousy commercial: a stiff combination of a Lionel Richie video and an insurance company ad. Compared to the 1984 Mountain Dew break-dancing commercial it was merely long. But 'We Are The World' is a great commercial. It sounds like a Pepsi jingle – and the constant repetition of 'There's a choice we're making' conflates with Pepsi's trademarked 'The Choice of a New Generation' in a way that, on the part of Pepsi-contracted songwriters Michael Jackson and Lionel Richie, is certainly not purposeful, and even more certainly beyond the realm of serendipity. In the realm of contextualisation, 'We Are The World' says less about Ethiopia than it does about Pepsi – and the true result will likely be less that certain Ethiopian individuals will live, or anyway live a bit longer than they otherwise would have, than that Pepsi will get the catch-phrase of its advertising campaign sung for free by Ray Charles, Stevie Wonder, Bruce Springsteen, and all the rest. But that is only the short-term, subliminal way of looking at it. In the long-view, real-world

280   We Are the World?

way of looking at it, within the realm of contextualised geopolitical economics, those Ethiopians who survive may end up not merely alive, but drinking Pepsi instead of Coke.

As American singers came together for the 'USA for Africa' sessions, Canadian performers gathered to make their own Ethiopia record. Among the contributors was Neil Young. 'You can't always support the weak', he said in October 1984. 'You have to make the weak stand up on one leg, or half a leg, whatever they've got.' But the Ethiopia benefit session? It was something he personally very much wanted to be interested in.

Autocritique

Now, this is not just 'a reading of the text' – it's also an attempt to say 'Stop'. But what *is* the text here? Is it, as I've argued, to be found in a hidden subtext, itself located less in Hollywood or Ethiopia than in the offices of the advertising agency that handles the Pepsi account? Or is that merely perverse? I thought my claim that while 'Ethiopians may not have anything to eat, at least these people get to eat Ethiopians' was perverse – until a few minutes ago, when Stan Ryven pointed out the logo of the preceding Ethiopia record, Band-Aid's 'Do They Know It's Christmas?', which featured the Eastern Hemisphere as a plate, a fork on the left, a knife and spoon on the right.

Let's return to the record – perhaps the text is there. If it is, is the text then in the music, solo spots framed, really justified, by gospel chorale, which suggests the individual affirmation of universalist humanism. As my daughter put it, 'The music washes over you and makes you feel good – and it's a game, too, trying to identify each singer, and then checking against the video.'

Is the text in the lyrics – in, say, the demagogic touch 'It's true' ('We make a brighter day'), which turns the avant-garde notion of a work of art which contains its own critique into a work which denies the possibility of critique?

Is the text in the singing – in the grace of Dionne Warwick's moment, which for a few seconds can lift the listener *out* of the song (it may be the only moment of pure music in 'We Are The World'), or in the return-to-bullshit of Willie Nelson's cracker-barrel-philosopher shtik?

Is the text off the record? Is it suffering in Ethiopia, and the real lives that might actually be saved? Is the text not the artifact but the event – in the way the session was organised, in the selection of what sort of performers were to be included and what sort were to be excluded? In the exercise of the ideology of universalist humanism, which brings everyone together, mainstream commercial success became the sole principle of aesthetic legitimacy, which meant, in practice, that non-millionaires were judged to have no legitimate reason to speak to the audience. As they were excluded, rock was redefined; non-millionaires were excluded from rock. Is the text a certain argument in acts about the shape of pop music? Perhaps this *is* the real text – the way the ideology of universalist humanism, which seeks to transcend all differences, destroys the possibility of apprehending the diversity in which all conversation, all real communication, and all real culture, is based.

Just as in the USA today there is only one person – Ronald Reagan, whose genius is his ability to appropriate every appealing cultural manifestation (the Olympics, Dirty Harry, Rambo, random acts of everyday heroism, the saving of random children dying of cancer) – only one American, Ronald Reagan, whose genius is his ability to be the super-celebrity whose celebrity is used to legitimise the reality of the cultural manifestations he appropriates, to, finally, legitimise or deny the reality of everyone else; just as in the USA today there is only one person, the universalist humanism of 'USA for Africa' proposes that in the world today there is only one cause: Ethiopian starvation. It's a transcendent cause which transcends all causes. All local affairs are not just trivialised, they're made invisible, suspect, shoddy – like the performers excluded from the 'USA for Africa' sessions. They become excluded from discourse as such – hard to talk about, impossible to talk about.

To me, this text, perhaps any text, is a field of complexities, ironies compounding ironies. I leave you with one image, one more subtext. When the first shipment of 'USA for Africa' aid to Ethiopia was covered on television, one could see that the air carrier chosen was Flying Tiger. Flying Tiger was established in Southeast Asia in the 1950s by the CIA as a commercial front; in the '60s it functioned as a primary conduit for the heroin trade; today it is merely a minor commercial airline. I wonder if this small irony, this small symbolic pseudo-fact, has any meaning – or if, within the monolithic discourse of universalist humanism, the very possibility of irony is smothered. I wonder if the megalithic nature of that discourse, which I think is anti-cultural, and anti-popular, and anti-rock & roll, is not the true text of 'We Are The World'.

Index

ABC 171–2, 179, 259
Abba 79, 80, 94
Abrams, M. 122
Absolute Beginners (MacInnes) 134
accents 80–1, 108–11
Acton, Harold 125
addressees of lyrics 94–100
Adenauer, Konrad 226
advertising 183–4, 187–8, 190–1, 194–5, 235
Adverts, The 75
aestheticisation of culture 28
Age of Chance, The 254, 271
Ahearn, John 162
Aladdin Sane (David Bowie) 137, 178
Alaïa, Azzadine 210, 213
Ali 156, 160
Album Cover Albums 172
All Aboard With The Roogalator 173–4
'All the Madmen' (David Bowie) 138
'All Of My Heart' (ABC) 171, 179
'All The Young Dudes' (Mott the Hoople) 137
Ally Capellino 215–16
Alternative TV 76, 85
Always Now (Section 25) 179
Amazulu 42
Ambassadors, The (Holbein) 188
American International Pictures 63

American Music Awards 277
American Werewolf in London, An 58
'Anarchy In The UK' (Sex Pistols) 75, 81, 84, 97–8, 99
androgyny 42–5, 70–1
Angel, Claire 217, 221, 222
Angelic Upstarts 95
'Angels With Dirty Faces' (Sham 69) 97, 98
Annie Hall 43
anoraks 251
anorexia 251
AR Kane 246, 262–3, 271, 275
'Armagideon Time' (Clash) 174, 176
art, graffiti and 162–5
art graduates 38–9
Astaire, Fred 67
Au Pairs 140
authenticity 272–4

'Back Home' (England World Cup Football Team) 97
'Bad Moon Rising' (Creedence Clearwater Revival) 58
Bailey, David 191, 193
Bananarama 42
Band-Aid 280
Band of Holy Joy 271
Bangs, Lester 276
Barrett, Syd 247
Barron, Steve 53

Index

Barthes, Roland xv, xviii, 208, 260
  bourgeois art of song 89
  'Face of Garbo' 70
  geno-song 76–7
  grain 51, 71, 260
  ideolect 91
bass playing 86
Baudrillard, Jean 261, 263, 264, 265
Bauhaus 177–8
beat culture 34
'Beat it' (Michael Jackson) 53, 70
Beatles, The 25–6, 75, 84, 123, 169
  plundered 175–6
Beefheart, Captain 139, 246
Bell, Edward 178
Berlin, Irving 79
Berry, Chuck 84, 227
Biba 36
Big Audio Dynamite 274
'big dipper' style 77–8
Bill, Charlotte 240
'Billy Jean' (Michael Jackson) 53, 70
Birthday Party, The 140, 262
'Bits And Pieces' (Dave Clark Five) 85
black men
  images of 202–3
  sexuality 70–1
Black Panthers 45–6
Black Sabbath 105
Black Widows 13, 14, 15
Blade 160
Blake, Peter 25
blazer, denim 225
Blitz xiv, 38, 260
Blondie 158, 162
Bloomingdale's 183
Blow Up 40
'Blowin' In The Wind' (Bob Dylan) 97
Blue Aeroplanes, The 247
'Blue Moon' (Frankie Lymon and the Teenagers) 58
Blue Rondo A La Turk 178

BMX Bandits 248
Boa, Phillip 271
Bodines, The 248, 270
body, the xx, 260
  heroin, politics and 150–4
bodymusic 245–6
Bogshed 270
Bolan, Marc 105
Boomtown Rats 80
Borofski, Jonathon 163
Botham, Ian 269
Bourdieu, Pierre 27
Bourdin, Guy 183–8, 193, 194
Boussac 213
Bow Wow Wow 257
Bowie, David 54, 80, 105, 129, 132–40
  androgyny 70, 135
  as hero 107, 136–8
  plundered 178
  Thin White Duke 132–3
  Ziggy Stardust 88, 106, 139, 265
Bowie-boys 137–8
Boy George 70, 138
Bragg, Billy 243
Braithwaite, Fred, *see* Fab Five Freddy
Brampton, Sally 209
Brando, Marlon 227
Branson, Richard 35
Brick Lane market 30
Brideshead Revisited 125, 170
British Electric Foundation (BEF) 259
British Movement 143, 146, 148
Brooke, Rupert 124
Brooks, Rosetta 193–4
Brooks, Shirley 52
Brophy, Philip 58–9
Brown, James 51
Brown, Tim 192
Brown, Willy 148, 149
Burchill, Julie xiv
Burton, James 83
Buzzcocks, The 174
buzzsaw drone 86
Byrds, The 246, 250

Cabaret 141
Cabaret Voltaire 270
Cage, John 261
Camden Lock market 32–3
Cameo 270, 274
Camera 192
'Can You Feel It' (Jacksons) 53
capitalism 228–9
Cardin, Pierre 231
'Career Opportunities' (Clash) 97, 99
Carpenter, John 58
carrot-shaped jeans 232
Carson, Tom 82
Carter, Angela 26, 27, 46, 47, 66
Carter, Erica 25
Carter, Rubin 'Hurricane' 276
Carter Family 79
Chakk 269
Chambers, Iain 56
Chambre Syndical, La 212
Chanel 211
Chaney, Lon 67
Chapel Market, Islington 31
Chapin, Harry 276
Chaplin, Charles 70
Chariots Of Fire 170
Charles, Ray 278
Charles, Tina 94
'Charlotte the Harlot' (Iron Maiden) 241
Charly 272
Chatterton, Thomas 124
Chavez, Cesar 5
Chicago 79
childhood 248–51
Chiswick 173
chorus singing 81–2
Christgau, Robert 83, 85, 86
Chrysalis 254
cities, heroin and 154
Clash, The 81, 84, 162, 173, 177
 lyrics 95, 97–8, 99
class and poverty dressing 26–7, 46–7
classicism 148–9
Clémenceau, Georges 212, 214

Clockwork Orange, A 136, 144, 265
Cochran, Eddie 227
Cockerel Chorus 82
cocktail music 242
Cocteau Twins 260
Cohen, Phil 30
Collins, Edwyn 249
Cologne Inter-Jeans Fair 225, 233
'Combine Harvester' (Wurzels) 79
comincs 160
Comme Des Garçons 210
community of deviance 154
Compact 170
Company of Wolves 66
Conflict 269
Conran, Jasper 28
'Control' (Janet Jackson) 274
Cooper, Alice 71, 82, 276, 277
Costello, Elvis 136, 272
country music 246, 247
Courrèges, P. 208
couture 208–14
Crane, Les 76
Creedence Clearwater Revival 58
Creole, Kid 20
criminality, graffiti and 166–7
 see also delinquency
Crisis 5, 17–18
Crosby, David 276
cross-burning 144–5
'Crystal Crescent' (Primal Scream) 247
culture
 aestheticisation of 28
 as commodity 171
'Cum On Feel The Noize' (Slade) 96
Cure, The 270
Curiosity Killed The Cat 275
Curtis, Ian 147, 242
Curtis, King 84

Dali, Salvador 178
Dalston Junction, Hackney 31
Dalton, David 123

Damned, The 80, 84, 95
dance 56, 67–8, 246
'Dance Little Lady Dance' (Tina Charles) 94–5
Dave Clark Five 85
Davis, Miles 273
Days in Europa (Skids) 143
'Dead Cities' (Exploited) 78
Dean, James 124, 227
death education 248
'Deck of Cards' (Wink Martindale) 76
Debord, Guy 256
deconstruction 258–60
delinquency 8, 14
  see also criminality
Delta 5 243
denim 225–35
Derrida, Jacques 103, 259
'Desiderata' (Les Crane) 76
designer jeans 230–1
designers 28, 38–9, 215–24
  see also couture; fashion
Desperate Bicycles, The 83
détournement 256, 257
Detroit 15, 21
'Detroit Red' (Malcolm X) 5
Diamond Dogs, The (David Bowie) 265
Diana, Princess of Wales 27, 44, 46, 47
Dior, Christian 208
distanciation 194–5
'Do The Strand' (Roxy Music) 115–17
'Do They Know It's Christmas?' (Band-Aid) 280
Dondi 160
Donnington 241
Dr Hook 79
drone, buzzsaw 86
drugs
  pachucos 14
  graffiti and 161
  see also heroin
drumming 86
Duncan, Clyde 5, 6
Duras, Marguerite 23

Dylan, Bob 79, 276, 277, 278
  hobo look 38
  lyrics 95, 97, 99

eclecticism 252
Einsturzende Neubauten 269
Eliot, George 23
Elle xiv
Ellison, Ralph 3, 19–20
Elm, Robert 148
EMI 254
England World Cup Football Team 97
English, Lewis D. 12
English Eccentrics 217, 221
Eno, Brian 104, 105, 139
Enterprise Allowance Schemes (EAS) 28, 38, 39
entrepreneurs, subcultural 34–9
Entwistle, John 86
Erasure 271
erotica 191–6
Esquire 9
Ethiopia, see 'We Are The World'
'Everything's Gone Green' (New Order) 179
Exploited, The 78, 270

Fab Five Freddy 156, 158–9, 162, 163, 168
Face, The xiv, 38, 235, 270
Factory Records 148, 178, 179
Factory Sample, The 179
Falklands War 170
Fall, The 139, 246
fanzines (fan magazines) 37, 248, 252
Fascism 142–9
fashion
  couture 208–14
  photography 183–8, 192–6
  punk 37–8, 40, 42–3, 231
  second-hand 24–48
  shift in attitudes 187–8
  sixties and childhood 250–1
  women designers 215–24
fashion graduates 38–9
'Fashion Moda' 162

female gangs 13–15
feminism 243–4
'Fernando' (Abba) 79, 94
Ferry, Bryan 103–17, 132
Fife, Fay 40, 80
fifth-columnists 16–17
final pop 274–5
Final Solution 148
flared jeans 228–9, 231
Flaxman, John 178
Flett, John 48
Flying Tiger 281
folk music 90, 243, 246, 247, 253
For Your Pleasure (Roxy Music) 107, 111, 112–14
forced rhythm 86
Formula 2 advert 194, 195
Foucault, Michel 110, 255, 259, 261, 262, 263
France 213, 214
  see also couture
Frankie Lymon and the Teenagers 58
Freeman, Robert 172, 174
Freud, Sigmund 72, 200
Frith, Simon 80, 252
Futura 156, 159, 160, 162, 168
  subway cars 164–5

Galliano, John 48
Gang of Four 140
Garbo, Greta 70
Garrett, Malcolm 174
Garsted, Green 259
'Gary Gilmore's Eyes' (Adverts) 75
Gaultier, Jean Paul 208–9, 210, 211, 213
Geldof, Bob 269
geno-song 76–7, 78
German Institute for Men's Fashion 233, 235
German Sisters, The 153
Gilbert, Gillian 239
Gilroy, Darlajane 38
Giraldi, Bob 53
Girbaud, Natalie 211

girls
  punk, feminism and 137
  subcultures and 35–6
  see also female gangs; women
'Give Peace a Chance' (Plastic Ono Band) 81
glam-rock 105, 135, 137, 178
Gleason, Ralph J. 95
Glier, Mike 163
Glitter, Gary 82, 105
Glucksmann, André 150
'God Save The Queen' (Sex Pistols) 77
Goldsmith, Harvey 35
Good Time Music Of The Sex Pistols 174
Gordon, Kim 239
graffiti 156–68
graffiti kings 166
grain 51, 56, 71
Green, Al 51
Grey agency 194
Guattari, Felix 261–2
guitars 83, 86
Guthrie, Woody 79

Hackett, J. 123
Haircut 100 176
Haley, Bill 79, 83, 85, 227
Hall, Stuart 26
Halloween 58
hard-core pornography 192
Haring, Keith 163
Harry, Debbie 40, 158–9
'Have You Seen Your Mother, Baby, Standing in the Shadow?' (Rolling Stones) 128
Hawkins, Screamin' Jay 71
health 245–6
Heartfield, John 94
Heaven 17 259
Heavy Metal 241
Hebdige, Dick xv, 36, 258
Hedgecoe, John 191, 192
Hendrix, Jimi 39–40, 83, 107
Henley, Nancy M. 198–9
Hepburn, Katharine 70

Heroes (David Bowie) 139
heroin 150–4
Heron, Gil Scott 167
Hertwig, Joro 233
Himes, Chester 19
hip-hop 157, 274
hippy culture 26, 34–7, 228, 229–30
Hitler, Adolf 145
HMV 174–5
Hobgoblins, The 248
Hobsbawm, Eric 203
Hoch, Paul 200
Hogg, Pam 38, 217–19, 220, 221–2, 223
Hoggart, Richard 77–8
Holbein, Hans 188
'Holidays In The Sun' (Sex Pistols) 85, 91–2, 93, 174
Holliday, Billie 272
Holly, Buddy 83
Holzer, Jenny 162, 163
'Hong Kong Garden' (Siouxsie and the Banshees) 99
Hopkins, Lightnin' 273
horror films 58–9, 63–4, 65–7
Howard, Brian 125
Human League, The 38
humanism, universalist 281–2
Husker Du 246, 262
'Hymn' (Ultravox) 179

'I Put a Spell on You' (Screamin' Jay Hawkins) 71
I Was a Teenage Werewolf 63
iD 24, 38
ideolect 91
Idol, Billy 244
'If The Kids Are United' (Sham 69) 98
'If You Leave Me Now' (Chicago) 79
ignorance 272
'I'm Talkin' About Freedom' (Syl Johnson) 99
'I'm Waiting For The Man' (Velvet Underground) 86
'Imagine' (John Lennon) 97

independent music 245–55, 272
Ingram, James 277
innocence 248–9, 251, 253
Institut Français De La Mode (IFM) 212
Iron Maiden 241
It's Only Rock 'n' Roll: 1957–62 175

Jack Rubies, The 268
jackets 43
Jackson, Janet 274
Jackson, Michael 50–2, 277, 279
  see also 'Thriller'
Jackson Five 50
Jacksons, The 53
Jagger, Mick 70, 80, 105, 124, 129, 134
  lyrics 88, 89
Jameson, F. 40, 48
Janet Reger 196
'Janie Jones' (Clash) 95
'Jazzin' for Blue Jean' (David Bowie) 54
'Jean Genie, The' (David Bowie) 137
jeans 226–35
Jeans Wear Fashion circle 225
Jesus and mary Chain 246, 262, 270, 274
Johnson, Syl 99
Jones, Brian 39, 107, 123–30 *passim*
Jones, David 133–4
  see also Bowie
Jones, George 272, 273
Jones, Grace 243
Jones, Quincy 277
Jordan, Neil 66
Jourdan, Charles 183
Joy Division 147
  see also New Order
'Jungle Rock' (Hank Mizell) 79

Kamen, Nick 270
Kane, Arthur 86
Keaton, Diane 43
Kennedy, Jackie 27

Index

Kenny, Robert 16
Kind of Loving, A 170
King Bees 132–3
Kinks, The 83, 173
'Kiss' (Age of Chance) 254
Klein, Calvin 230–1
Klein, Melanie 278
Klein, William 214
Knave 195
Koch, Mayor 159
Kraftwerk 260

Lacan, Jacques 188
Ladda, Justen 162
Laing, Dave 54
Landis, John 57–8
Lauder, Harry 77
Lauper, Cyndi 243
Laura Ashley 35, 41
Leadbelly 273
Led Zeppelin 105, 270
Lee, Arthur 247
Lee 156, 158, 164, 168
  art world and 162, 163
  criminality 166, 167
  official work 159
  style 160
Legendary Pink Dots, The 275
leggings 44–5
Leisure fashion 231
Lennon, John 26, 79, 81, 97, 132
Lennox, Annie 239
Lester, E. W. 17
'Let's Dance' (David Bowie) 138
Levi's 226, 227, 228, 234, 235
Lewis, Jerry Lee 79, 83, 87
'Liar' (Sex Pistols) 95
Lipman, Helen 217
'Little Bit More, A' (Dr Hook) 79
Little Richard 71, 79, 227
live albums 74
Lloyd, Alison 215–17, 219, 221, 222–3
Lodger (David Bowie) 139
Logic, Laura 84
London
  fashion shows 212
  markets 29–31, 32–3

'London Calling' (Clash) 174
looking 198–202
Loop 263
Los Angeles, riots in 9–15, 17, 18
Los Angeles Times 10, 11–12, 15, 17
Love 250
Love Affair 74
love songs 247–8
'Lover and Confidante' (Blue Aeroplanes) 247
Low (David Bowie) 139
Lowry, Ray 174, 176, 177
lycanthropy 66
Lyons 213
Lyotard J.–F. 252, 258–9, 260–1
lyrics, punk 87–100

machismo 13–14
MacInnes, Colin 134
Madonna 42, 249
Mailer, Norman 165
Majors, Farrah Fawcett 195
Making of Michael Jackson's Thriller, The 68
Manet, Edouard 209
Mannish Boys 134
Manpower Services Commission (MSC) 47
Manzanera, Phil 105
Mapplethorpe, Robert 42
Marcus, Greil 125
markets 29–33
Martindale, Wink 76
Marx, Karl 52
MaxMara 38
Mayfield, Curtis 273
McCartney, Paul 53, 79
McCulloch, Ian 242
MC5 83
McGowan, Cathy 40
McGuinn, Roger 247
McKay, Andy 105
McLaren, Malcolm 25, 173, 257
McRobbie, Angela 23
media 264, 269–71
Meinhof, Ulrike 153
Mekons, The 83

men, images of 199–206
men's clothes, women and 43–5
Mercury, Freddie 80, 269
Mexican-American youths, *see* pachucos
Mexico 15–16
Michael, George 249
Michelangelo 200, 201
Mighty Lemon Drops, The 247, 248, 268
Ministry of Culture (France) 213
Miranda, Billy 19
Mission, The 269
'Mississippi Goddam' (Nina Simone) 99
'Mittagerzen (Metal)' (Siouxsie and the Banshees) 93–4
Miyake, Issey 210, 211
Mizell, Hank 79
Monet, Claude 212, 214
Monitor 262
Monk, Thelonious 20
monologues 76
'Monsters of Rock' festival 241
Montana, Yves 210
'Moondance' (Van Morrison) 58
Moore, Joan W. 13
Moore, Scotty 83, 84
Morgan, Betty 13
Morley, Paul xiv, 174
Morrison, Jim 107
Morrison, Van 58, 132
Morrissey 246, 254
Mosely, Bill 165–6
Mott The Hoople 137, 173
'Mountains' (Prince) 274
'Movement' (New Order) 179
'Mr Jones' (Bob Dylan) 95
'Mr President (Have Pity On The Working Man)' (Randy Newman) 87
MTV 53
Mud 105
muscularity 205
musical knowledge 240–1
Muybridge, Eadweard 202
'My Generation' (Who) 86
My Guy 199

Nash, Graham 276
National Front 143, 145–6
Nazism 141, 143–4, 145, 146
Neal, Larry 20
needle, the 150–1, 153
Negro Quarterly 5
Nelson, Norris 18
Nelson, Willie 277, 280
'Never Been In A Riot' (Mekons) 83
Neville, Richard 257
New Musical Express (NME) xii, 239, 242
New Order 147–8, 179
New Romantics 138
'New Rose' (The Damned) 84
New York
  graffiti 156, 157, 159–60, 162
  Transit Authority 156, 159, 165–6
'New York' (Sex Pistols) 95
New York Dolls 83
New York Times 5
Newman, Paul 200
Newman, Randy 87, 88, 89
Newton, Helmut 112
  erotica 186, 191, 193, 194
  fashion 183, 184, 193
'Nice One Cyril' (Cockerel Chorus) 82
Night of the Living Dead 58
Nolan, Jerry 86
nostalgia 40–1, 272–3
  see also plunder
'Number One Enemy' (Slits) 97–8

Ocean Rain (Echo and the Bunnymen) 242
Off The Wall (Michael Jackson) 50
'Off the Wall'' (Michael Jackson) 55
'Oh Bondage Up Yours' (X-Ray Spex) 75, 80, 84–5, 93
Oh Boy! 199, 200, 205
Ondaatje, Michael 150

Orgasm Addict (Buzzcocks) 174, 175
Osbourne, Ozzy 71
Osmond, Donny 52
'Out of Time' (Rolling Stones) 88, 89
overcoats 43–4
overwriting 161
Owen, Malcolm 80

P., Mark 80
pachucos 5–7, 8, 18
 zoot-suit riots 9–15, 19
pachuquismo 13–14
painting, graffiti 156–68
'Panic' (Smiths) 246–7
'Panic in Detroit' (David Bowie) 138
Paris fashion 208–14
parody 64–5
Parsons, Tony xiv
Pastels, The 248
Pauline of Penetration 40
Paz, Octavio 5–7, 9
penis, the 206
Penman, Ian xiv
Penthouse 195
Pepsi Cola 279–80
Perry, Mark 76
Perry, Steve 277
Peters, Michael 67
phallus, the 206
Phantom of the Opera, The 67
pheno-song 76, 77, 78
photography 183–8, 189–90, 191–6
Picasso, Pablo 178
picto-graphic style 159–60, 164
Piedboeuf, Herbert L. 225–6, 227, 235
Pink Floyd 250
Pipes of Pan At Jajouka (Brian Jones) 124
Plastic Ono Band 81–2
Platt, Jono 215–16, 217, 221, 222
'Play With Fire' (Rolling Stones) 88
Playgirl 199

plunder 169–80
 see also nostalgia
pluralism 267, 268
Poitier, Sidney 203
Pop, Iggy 135
Pop Will Eat Itself 254
Poppers 232, 236
pornography 191–6
post-structuralism 258–9
poverty dressing 26–7, 45–7
power
 images of male 202–3, 205–6
 looking and 198–9, 201–2
 pop culture and 246, 256–65
Prawn Cocktails 170
'Prémier Vision' 213
Presley, Elvis 174, 177, 227
Pretty Things, The 174
Price, Vincent 57, 59, 60, 67
Primal Scream 247
Prince 53, 274
'Problem' (Sex Pistols) 95
Promotions 35
protest songs 97
psychedelia 246, 262–3, 275
Psychedelic Furs, The 269
Public Image Ltd (PIL) 140, 259
Public Service Awards 276–7
punk
 analysis 74–100; lyrics 87–100; music 82–7; voices 75–82
 Bowie's influence 137–8
 exposed 270
 fashion 37–8, 40, 42–3, 231
 impotence following 275
 plunder 172–4
 selling 25, 37
 unity 268–9
 women and 241–2
'Pyjamarama' (Roxy Music) 105

Quartet (Ultravox) 179
Quintanilla, Reverend Francisco 16–17

radical chic 45–6
Ragdon, Rebecca 150
ragmarkets 29–33

292 Index

Raincoats, The 37, 243
Ramones, The 81, 82, 86
Ranking Anne 259
rap 156–7, 158–9, 167–8
rape 242
'Rapture' (Blondie) 158–9
Ray, Ola 59
Ready Steady Go 123
Reagan, President Ronald 167, 281
'real music' 242
'Rebel Rebel' (David Bowie) 137
Rebel Without a Cause 227
record sleeves 172–9
Red Army Faction 153
Red Riding Hood fairy tale 66
Reed, Lou 135, 247
Reid, Jamie 174, 257
representation 263
Residents, The 176, 260
resistance 261–3
Revlon 194
rhythm 85–7
Richard, Keith 129
Richie, Lionel 53, 277, 279
Ridley Road market 32
riots, zoot-suit 7, 8–18
rip-offs 159
'Rock Around The Clock' (Bill Haley) 227
rock 'n' rollers 226, 227
Rogers, Kenny 277
Rolling Stone xii
Rolling Stones 54, 105, 123, 129, 130, 173,
  fusing worlds 125
  lyrics 88–9, 95
  nihilistic chaos 128
Romero, George 58
Ronson, Mick 135, 137
Roogalator 173
Ross, Diana 51, 276–7
Rotten, Johnny 75, 76
  vocal style 77, 78, 80, 81, 100
Rough Trade 254
Roxy Music 104–8
Roxy Music 106, 107, 111
Royal Albert Hall 128

Rubber Soul (Beatles) 176
Russell, Arthur 271
Ryven, Stan 280

Sade 239, 242
'Satellite' (Sex Pistols) 174
'Satisfaction' (Rolling Stones) 254
Savage, Jon 40
Saville, Peter 178–9
'Say, Say, Say' (Michael Jackson and Paul McCartney) 53
Scary Monsters (David Bowie) 178
Schnabel, Julien 163
Scholten, H. 232–3
Schwarzenegger, Arnold 205
Scott Heron, Gil 167
Scritti Politti 259–60
second-hand dressing 23–48
Section 25 179
Sedgwick, Edie 123–30 *passim*
Seen 160
Sefranek, Heiner 235
Sergeant Pepper's Lonely Hearts Club Band (Beatles) 25–6
servicemen 8, 9–12
'17' (Sex Pistols) 95
Sex Pistols 76, 81, 85, 257, 265
  lyrics 91, 95, 97–8
  plunder 173, 174
  see also Rotten, Johnny
sexism 90–2, 239
sexmusic 245
sexuality
  glam-rock 135
  horror films 65–8
  model's look 200–1
  photography and 186–7
  soul music 56–7
  see also pornography
Sham 69 74, 90, 97, 98, 99
Shamada, Junka 211
She 199
Shelley, Peter 80
'She's Bringing You Down' (Vibrators) 95
shirts 44

shopping 24–5
Shrubs, The 246
Sighs and Whispers 183–8
Sigue Sigue Sputnik 265, 274
Silverman, Kaja 42
Simon, Paul 277
Simone, Nina 99
Simonon, Paul 86
Simple Minds 275
simulation 263, 264–5
Siouxsie and the Banshees 93, 99
Situationists 250, 256–8
sixties 121–30, 249–51
Skids, The 143
skill, musical 83–4
skinheads 144
Skinny Puppy 275
Slade 82, 96, 105, 135
slashing 161
Sleepy Lagoon murder 22
Slick Chicks 13, 15
Slits, The 37, 97–8
Sloane Ranger Handbook, The 171
Small Faces 173
Smash Hits xiv
Smith, Bessie 273
Smith, Graham 178
Smith, Patti 42–3, 128, 129
Smiths, The 246–7, 250, 253, 262
Sniffin' Glue 80
soccer teams 82
soft-core pornography 195–6
Solanas, Valerie 129
solos, instrumental 84–5
'Something' (Beatles) 84
Sonic Youth 246
Sonnenkinder 125
Sontag, Susan 71
soul music 99, 271–2
Soup Dragons 248
space, graffiti and 160–1
Spandau Ballet 148, 178
speculation 275
Spender, Dale 199
Spitting Image 268
sport 203, 205
sporty-formal fashion 233, 235

Springsteen, Bruce 277, 278
St Laurent, Yves 213
'Stab Yor Back' (Damned) 95
'Stand By Your Man' (Tammy Wynette) 96
stardom, rock 134–5, 136–7
'Starman' (David Bowie) 135
Starr, Ringo 86
Station to Station (David Bowie) 135
Stein, Jean 123
Stella, Frank 163
Stewart, Andy 77
Stewart, Rod 132
Sticky Fingers (Rolling Stones) 129
'Stiff Little Fingers' (Vibrators) 95
Stiff Records 173
'Still ill' (Smiths) 253
'Stranded' (Roxy Music) 114
Stranglers, The 77, 82, 84, 89–90, 98
Strauss, Levi 226
street markets 29–33
structuralism xviii
Strummer, Joe 80–1
Stubbs, David 254
style, *see* fashion
Styrene, Poly 27, 37, 75, 80, 85
subcultural entrepreneurs 34–9
subcultural songs 78–9
'Suffragette City' (David Bowie) 137
Sullivan, Chris 178
Sun 199
Swans, The 274–5
swastika 146–7
Sweet 135
Swing Out Sister 275

Tagg, Philip 76, 79
TAKI 183 166
Talulah Gosh 248
Tartanry singing 77
Tashan 271
Tatler, The 171
tattoos 151–2

Television 246
Tell Us The Truth (Sham 69) 74
Tellez, Frank H. 12, 13
Temperton, Rod 55
Temple, Julien 54
tempo 86–7
Tenney, Jack B. 16
Test Dept 270
Textile Centre of Lyons 213
Thatcher, Margaret 179, 214, 253
This Mortal Coil 260
Thomas, Chantale 211
Thorn, Tracey 243
Thriller 50, 51, 54–6, 67, 72
'Thriller' video 54–71
'Tommy Gun' (Clash) 95
Top of the Pops 135, 178
Top Shop 31
Tottenham Hotspur 82
Townshend, Pete 86, 136
Toxic Shock 243
trains, graffiti on 159–60, 164, 165–6
treated sound 89
Tschichold, Jan 178–9
Tube, The 270
Tucker, Maureen 86
Turbeville, Deborah 183
Turner, Tina 243, 277

Ultravox 178, 179
'Under My Thumb' (Rolling Stones) 88
'Undercover of the Night' (Rolling Stones) 54
unification 90–4
United Kingdom fashion industry 212, 213, 214
United States of America
   effects of war 7–8
   independent music 252–3
   zoot-suit riots 8–18
Unitex of Lyons 213
unity 268–9
universalist humanism 281–2
'Upping Street' (Big Audio Dynamite) 274
USA for Africa 277–82

Valdez, Luis 19, 22
Vanderbilt, Gloria 231
Vaneigem, Raoul 257
Velvet Underground 246
Venegas, Amelia 13
Verdusco, Luis ('The Chief') 12
Vibrators, The 80, 95
Vicious, Sid 86, 124
videos 53–4
Viking Youth 145
Village Voice 160
Vincent, Gene 227
Virgin Records 35
'Virginia Plain' (Roxy Music) 105
vocal stance 79–80
voices, punk 75–82

Walker, Junior 85
Walters, Margaret 205–6
Wang Chung 270
'Wanna Be Startin' Somethin'' (Michael Jackson) 70
War Production Board (US) 9, 18
Warhol, Andy 121, 123, 124, 125, 129, 130
Warren, Governor 16
Warwick, Dionne 277, 280
Washington Post 9–10
'We Are The World' (USA for Africa) 277–82
WEA 254
Weather Prophets, The 247
Weller, Paul 40, 269
werewolf mythology 66
Westwood, Vivienne 25, 51, 173, 210, 211
Westworld 275
Weymouth, Tina 239
'What's So Good About Candy?' (Pop Will Eat Itself) 254
'White Riot' (Clash) 80–1, 84
Whitehead, Peter 128
Who, The 83, 173
'Whole Lotta Shakin' Goin' On' (Jerry Lee Lewis) 86–7
Wild, Colin 228
Wild Ones, The 227

wild-style 157, 160
Williams, Hank 272
Williams, Linda 202
Willis, Paul 153
Wilson, Harold 123
Wilson, Jackie 51
Wilson, Mari 170
With The Beatles 172, 174, 175
Witness, A 246
Wiz, The 55
Wolf Man, The 72
Wolfe, Tom xii–xiii, 26–7, 45–6
women
   Bryan Ferry and 112–15
   pop and 239–44
   representations of 189–96
   see also female gangs, girls
Wonder, Stevie 278
Woodentops, The 248
'Word Up' (Cameo) 274
Work, Sport and Leisure Clothing Trade Association 225
Worth, Charles F. 208
Wrangler's 228
Wright, Richard 19
writing, graffiti 157, 161, 164–5

Wurzels, The 79
Wynette, Tammy 96

X, Malcolm 5
X-Ray Spex 83, 93
   see also Styrene, Poly

Yamomoto, Y. 211
Yates, Paula 42
Yippies 249
York, Peter xv
'You Bastard' (Alternative TV) 85
Young, Neil 280
Young Americans (David Bowie) 135
youth as social problem 122–3
'Youth Leader' (Angelic Upstarts) 95

Zeit 232
Ziggy Stardust, *see* Bowie, David
'Ziggy Stardust' (Bauhaus) 177–8
Zoot Suit 22
zoot suits 3–7, 19–20, 233
   riots 7, 8–10

Advertisement

More youth questions — and some answers

Whether you're a teacher, youth worker, social worker, employer or parent, you'll know that young people and their needs have never been more important.

YOUTH IN SOCIETY, the National Youth Bureau's interprofessional magazine for everyone concerned with and about young people, puts issues like juvenile crime, leisure and community involvement into perspective.

Every month, experienced practitioners offer insights into their own approach to work with young people and suggest ways in which you can apply their techniques and learn from their successes and mistakes.

And the Bureau's information team provides details of the latest books and resources, courses and conferences — essential information for everyone responding to the needs of youth in society.

YOUTH SERVICE SCENE, the Bureau's monthly newspaper, contains the latest news, information and resources for youth workers and others concerned with youth affairs and social education.

Whether you work full-time or part-time, in the statutory or the voluntary sector, *Scene* keeps you in touch with what's happening nationally and in other areas, and up to date with the latest theory and practice.

We'll gladly send you sample copies and subscription order forms if you contact us at

NYB

National Youth Bureau, 17-23 Albion Street, Leicester LE1 6GD. Telephone 0533.471200.

Advertisement

YOUTH AND POLICY
the journal of critical analysis

a journal devoted to the serious, critical study of policy in youth affairs and the analysis of issues surrounding youth in modern society

IF YOU ARE CONCERNED WITH YOUTH, CAN YOU AFFORD NOT TO SUBSCRIBE?

Four issues per year, by subscription

ISSN 0262 9798

UK subscription rate £14.00 p.a.
special rates available on request

Order from:
13 Hunstanton Court
Ravenswood Estate
Low Fell, Gateshead
NE9 6LA

ARTFORUM
INTERNATIONAL

65 BLEECKER STREET NYC 10012 212·475·4000